Commodities

FOR

DUMMIES®

2ND EDITION

Commodities
FOR
DUMMIES®
2ND EDITION

by Amine Bouchentouf

WILEY

Wiley Publishing, Inc.

Commodities For Dummies®, 2nd Edition

Published by
Wiley Publishing, Inc.
111 River St.
Hoboken, NJ 07030-5774
www.wiley.com

WILEY

About the Author

Amine Bouchentouf is a Partner at Commodities Investors, LLC (CI), an international financial advisory firm headquartered in New York City that provides long-term strategic advice to individuals, institutions, and governments around the world. CI also invests directly on behalf of clients in a wide range of industries relating to natural resources, from crude oil and gold to natural gas and steel.

Amine is a world-renowned market commentator and has appeared in media in the United States, Great Britain, France, the United Arab Emirates, and Brazil. He is a member of the National Association of Securities Dealers and the Authors Guild and is also involved with the Council on Foreign Relations. His family has been involved in the production and distribution of commodities for more than three generations.

Amine holds a degree in economics from Middlebury College. In his spare time, he enjoys playing golf, traveling, and socializing with friends. This is his third book. You can stay up-to-date on Amine's perspective on the market through the website www.commodities-investors.com.

Dedication

This book is dedicated to my most steadfast supporters — my family. You have always been there for me when I needed you and have always supported me in every endeavor I've decided to undertake. I would not have been able to accomplish half the things I've done without your tremendous support, and for that I am deeply grateful.

Author's Acknowledgments

I'd like to acknowledge the first-rate editorial team at Wiley for their input and assistance through every stage of this process. A writer hopes for nothing more than to have a team of editors who will support his or her general creative vision, and I was extremely fortunate to be able to follow through on my vision for the book — from the drafting of the Table of Contents down to the inclusion of technical charts and figures — with the guidance of a knowledgeable group of editors. Specifically, I'd like to thank Elizabeth Rea, my project editor, for providing valuable insight every step of the way. I'd also like to express thanks to Stacy Kennedy for helping launch the project early on and for her continuous input throughout the writing period. I would like to show my gratitude to the graphics department for helping me express my ideas and illustrate my points with the help of charts, graphs, and other helpful visuals. Finally, I would like to thank McLean D. Giles, who served as technical editor.

Since the financial markets in general, and the commodities markets in particular, are so broad and deep, getting insight on all the different aspects of the markets is absolutely critical. I was very fortunate that I could turn to some of the sharpest minds in finance for their insight on the markets. I'd like to thank Dr. Scott Pardee, at Middlebury College, for providing me with cutting-edge analysis on the cyclicality of the markets. I'd also like to acknowledge the contributions of Ray Strong, at Goldman Sachs, regarding all aspects of the energy markets. Thanks to Karen Treanton, at the International Energy Agency in Paris, for giving me all the vital statistical information on the energy industry. I would like to express my appreciation to John D. Phillips and Neil McMahon, at Alliance Bernstein, for their world-class research. Kevin Rich, at Deutsche Bank, shared with me his knowledge of managed funds, and thanks to everyone at the NYMEX for their insights on the futures market. Additional thanks go to Frank Ahmed, at Bear Stearns, and Richard Adler for their general guidance. I also need to acknowledge the contributions of Elisa Castro, Heather Balke, and, of course, my agent, Mark Sullivan.

Finally, I'd like to express my gratitude to my family, whose support was instrumental throughout this process.

Publisher's Acknowledgments

We're proud of this book; please send us your comments at http://dummies.custhelp.com. For other comments, please contact our Customer Care Department within the U.S. at 877-762-2974, outside the U.S. at 317-572-3993, or fax 317-572-4002.

Some of the people who helped bring this book to market include the following:

Acquisitions, Editorial, and Media Development

Project Editor: Elizabeth Rea
    (Previous Edition: Laura Peterson Nussbaum)

Acquisitions Editor: Stacy Kennedy

Copy Editor: Krista Hansing

Assistant Editor: David Lutton

Technical Editor: McLean D. Giles

Editorial Manager: Michelle Hacker

Editorial Assistants: Rachelle Amick,
    Alexa Koschier

Cover Photo: ©istockphoto.com/
Justin Horrocks

Cartoons: Rich Tennant
(www.the5thwave.com)

Composition Services

Project Coordinator: Nikki Gee

Layout and Graphics: Melanee Habig,
    Corrie Socolovitch

Proofreader: Bonnie Mikkelson

Indexer: BIM Indexing & Proofreading Services

Publishing and Editorial for Consumer Dummies

    Diane Graves Steele, Vice President and Publisher, Consumer Dummies

    Kristin Ferguson-Wagstaffe, Product Development Director, Consumer Dummies

    Ensley Eikenburg, Associate Publisher, Travel

    Kelly Regan, Editorial Director, Travel

Publishing for Technology Dummies

    Andy Cummings, Vice President and Publisher, Dummies Technology/General User

Composition Services

    Debbie Stailey, Director of Composition Services

Contents at a Glance

Table of Contents

Introduction

● ●

*W*hen I wrote the first edition of *Commodities For Dummies,* commodities were certainly not a mainstream asset class. However, five years later, commodities have grown into their own legitimate and respected asset class. Trade magazines and financial newsletters frequently include feature-length articles on the topic. Financial TV stations regularly report oil, gold, and copper prices on the crawling ticker. And no global macro money manager can claim continued success without constantly keeping a pulse on commodities. This situation wasn't true at the beginning of the century, and it's a testament to the growing importance of commodities in our globalized and globalizing world.

Why are commodities, long regarded as an inferior asset class, quickly moving to the investing mainstream? Good performance. Investors like to reward good performance, and commodities have performed well in recent years. In addition, investors can more easily access these markets: Plenty of new investment vehicles, from exchange-traded funds (ETFs) to master limited partnerships (MLPs), have been introduced to satisfy investor demand.

As commodities have been generating more interest, there's a large demand for a product to help average investors get a grip on the market fundamentals. Commodities as an asset class have been plagued by a lot of misinformation, and it's sometimes difficult to separate fact from fiction or outright fantasy. The aim of *Commodities For Dummies* is to help you figure out what commodities are all about and, more important, develop an intelligent investment strategy to profit in this market. Of course, as with every other asset class, commodities are subject to market swings and disruptions, which can be a source of risk but also an opportunity. As the 2008 Global Financial Crisis demonstrated, even the most savvy investors with the latest up-to-date market information can struggle with unique investment events.

These disruptions are part of the market process. Investors who protect themselves through a "margin of safety" philosophy will be able to protect their downside during periods of extreme volatility. Using this book, you'll better equip yourself to avoid the pitfalls inherent in any investment activity.

About This Book

My aim in writing *Commodities For Dummies,* 2nd Edition, is to offer you a comprehensive guide to the commodities markets and show you a number of investment strategies to help you profit in this market. You don't have to invest in just crude oil or gold futures contracts to benefit. You can trade ETFs, invest in companies that process commodities such as uranium, buy precious metals ownership certificates, or invest in master limited partnerships. The commodities markets are global in nature, and so are the investment opportunities. My goal is to help you uncover these global opportunities and offer you investment ideas and tools to unlock and unleash the power of the commodities markets. Best of all, I do all of this in plain English!

Anyone who's been around commodities, even for a short period of time, realizes that folks in the business are prone to engage in linguistic acrobatics. Words like *molybdenum, backwardation,* and *contango* are thrown around like "hello" and "thank you." Sometimes these words seem intimidating and confusing. Don't be intimidated. Language is powerful, after all, and getting a grip on the concepts behind the words is critical, especially if you want to come out ahead in the markets. That's why I use everyday language to explain even the most abstract and arcane concepts.

Here are some of the trading and investing ideas you discover in the book:

- ✔ **Get more bang for your buck by investing through master limited partnerships, investment vehicles used by only the most sophisticated investors.** *Master limited partnerships* (MLPs), which invest in energy infrastructure such as pipelines and storage facilities, are a unique investment because they trade publicly, like a corporation, but offer the tax benefits of a partnership. Unlike corporations, which are subject to double taxation (on the corporate and shareholder levels), MLPs can pass their income to shareholders *tax free,* so shareholders are responsible for taxes only at the individual level. Because the primary mandate of MLPs is to distribute practically all the cash flow directly to shareholders, you can't afford not to invest in these hybrid vehicles. Find out how in Chapter 6.

- ✔ **Capitalize on the increasing popularity of nuclear power by investing in uranium, an investment-grade material.** The use of nuclear power to generate electricity is on the rise. As a result, the price of uranium, the primary fuel used in nuclear power plants, has been in an extended — albeit quiet — bull market for more than a decade, *quadrupling* from $10 in 1994 to $40 in 2006. Find out which companies mine this unique commodity and how to profit from this trend in Chapter 13.

✓ **Benefit from the commodity trading craze without trading a single futures contract.** As more investors flock toward the commodities markets, the exchanges that provide futures contracts, options, and other derivatives to commodity traders have seen their business expand exponentially. The Chicago Mercantile Exchange (NYSE: CME), one of the largest commodity exchanges, has seen its stock price rise from $40 since its 2003 initial public offering to more than $310 in 2011. (See Chapter 8 for more on how to capitalize on the success of exchanges.)

✓ **Capitalize on the relationship between digital cameras and the silver markets.** You may be surprised to find that the photographic industry is a major consumer of silver, accounting for almost 20 percent of total silver consumption. Traditional cameras use silver halide, a silver and halogen compound, to create photographic film. However, digital cameras, which don't require silver halide, have decreased the demand for silver in photography. Find out how to profit from this by betting against the price of silver, using a trading technique known as *going short,* which I cover in Chapter 9. (Turn to Chapter 15 for more on the silver markets.)

✓ **Generate a gushing stream of dividend income by investing in oil tanker stocks.** One of the best-kept secrets on Wall Street is oil tanker stocks, which provide some of the highest dividend yields in the market. Average dividend yields for some of the industry's top performers are more than 12 percent, higher than even for diversified and electric utilities (which I cover in Chapter 13).

Conventions Used in This Book

To help you make the best use of this book, I use the following conventions:

✓ *Italic* is used for emphasis and to highlight new words or terms.

✓ **Boldfaced text** is used to indicate key words in bulleted lists or the action parts of numbered steps.

✓ `Monofont` is used to make Web addresses stand out for your ease.

Trading commodities requires mastering a wide variety of technical terms. The glossary tells you what all those high-sounding financial terms actually mean so you can talk the talk, too!

Foolish Assumptions

In writing *Commodities For Dummies,* I made the following assumptions about you:

- ✔ You have some previous investing experience but are looking to diversify your holdings.

- ✔ You're familiar with commodities trading but want to brush up on your knowledge.

- ✔ Your traditional investments (stocks/bonds/mutual funds) haven't performed according to your expectations, and you're looking for alternatives to maximize your returns.

- ✔ You're a new investor or someone with minimal trading experience, and you're interested in a broad-based investment approach that includes commodities and other assets.

- ✔ You understand the attractiveness of commodities and want a comprehensive and easy-to-use guide to help you get started.

- ✔ You're skeptical about the benefits of commodities but want to read about them anyway. Please do — I'm confident that this book will change your mind!

- ✔ You have little or no investment experience but are eager to find out more about investing. This book not only explores investing in commodities, but also includes explanations of general investing guidelines that apply to any market.

How This Book Is Organized

I've organized the book in a way that helps you look up essential information and analysis on the world's most important commodities and trading techniques. The following sections break down each part.

Part 1: Commodities: Just the Facts

The first part of *Commodities For Dummies,* 2nd Edition, gives you good general investing principles. Whether you're an experienced trader or a new investor, having a good grasp of basic portfolio allocation methods is crucial for your success. Find out here how to create and design an investing road map that's specifically tailored to your financial needs and goals. You also discover how commodities stack up against other investment vehicles, such as stocks and bonds.

In addition, I explain and dispel some of the common misconceptions regarding the commodities markets, particularly relating to risk and volatility. I also include a whole chapter on identifying, managing, and overcoming risk, which may be the single most important issue you face as an investor. The fact of the matter is that any investment entails a certain degree of risk — overcoming that risk separates successful investors from the rest. Find out how you, too, can successfully minimize risk and maximize your returns with the help of commodities.

Part II: Getting Started with Types of Investment Vehicles

Get the lowdown on the best investment methods you have at your disposal to invest in commodities. I analyze the pros and cons of investing through the futures markets, the equity markets, ETFs, and mutual funds. In addition, I examine the role of the market regulators so you can know your rights as an investor, and I cover specific trading techniques and analyses, such as technical and fundamental analysis. Read this part to find out how to start trading commodities.

Part III: The Power House: How to Make Money in Energy

Energy is the largest subasset class in the commodities universe. Crude oil, for example, is the most widely traded commodity in the world today. Natural gas, coal, and nuclear power are also major commodities. In addition, I uncover investment opportunities in the alternative energy space (wind and solar power) and examine the companies responsible for providing energy to the world.

Part IV: Pedal to the Metal: Investing in Metals

Metals are grouped using two criteria: whether they contain iron and, more important, whether they resist corrosion. Metals that contain iron are called *ferrous metals,* and these include metals such as zinc. *Nonferrous metals,* such as gold, silver, and platinum, don't contain iron. On the corrosion side, the metals that don't corrode easily are usually the precious metals: gold, silver, platinum, and palladium. Base metals, like copper, nickel, and zinc, are major industrial metals. As you can tell, you find out everything you ever wanted to know about metals in this part.

Part V: Going Down to the Farm: Trading Agricultural Products

Nothing is more fundamental to human life than food. In this part, find out how you can nourish and grow your portfolio by investing in this most basic commodity. Some of the most commonly traded agricultural products include coffee, sugar, and orange juice. I help you decipher the seasonal nature of the business, analyze import/export activities, and consider potential obstacles so that you can design and execute a rock-solid investment approach. Some of the commodities I discuss in this part include orange juice, cocoa, feeder cattle, soybeans, and wheat.

Part VI: The Part of Tens

The legendary *For Dummies* Part of Tens chapters give you tips on how to become a better investor and trader. Follow the ten time-tested rules that successful commodities investors have used to make substantial profits in this area. You also get acquainted with ten of the best resources to help you become a successful commodities investor.

This book also includes a detailed glossary that covers all the major technical terminology in these pages. Investing in commodities can get fairly technical, so understanding the concepts behind the words is critical for your success as an investor.

Icons Used in This Book

One of the pleasures of writing a *For Dummies* book is that you get to use all sorts of fun, interactive tools to highlight or illustrate a point. Here are some icons that I use throughout the book:

I use this icon to highlight information that you want to keep in mind or that's referenced in other parts of the book.

When you see this icon, make sure that you read the accompanying text carefully: It includes information, analysis, or insight that will help you successfully implement an investment strategy.

I explain more technical information with this icon. The commodities markets are complex, and the vocabulary and concepts are quite tricky. You can skip these paragraphs if you just want a quick overview of the commodities world, but be sure to read them before seriously investing. They give you a better grasp of the concepts discussed.

Investing can be an extremely rewarding enterprise, but it can also be a hazardous endeavor if you're not careful. I use this icon to warn you of potential pitfalls. Stay alert for these icons because they contain information that may help you avoid losing money.

Sometimes a potential investment requires a little extra research. When you see this icon, get ready to analyze the investment with a fine-toothed comb. This icon lets you know that extensive due diligence is in order.

Where to Go from Here

I've organized this book in a way that gives you the most accurate and relevant information related to investing in general and commodity investing in particular. The book is modular in nature, meaning that although it reads like a book from start to finish, you can read one chapter or even a section at a time without needing to read the whole book to understand the topic that's discussed.

If you're a true beginner, however, I recommend that you read Parts I and II carefully before you start skipping around in the chapters on particular commodities.

Part I
Commodities: Just the Facts

The 5th Wave   By Rich Tennant

"It's this trend that leads us to believe we should supplement our oil commodities with investments in some of the Earth's rich vinegar and crouton reserves."

In this part . . .

The chapters in this part give you everything you've ever wanted to know about commodities. I introduce the commodities markets and go through some of the individual commodities and how they interact with each other. I also look at the risks of commodities investing, as well as how commodities as an asset class compare to other assets, such as stocks and bonds.

Chapter 1

Investors, Start Your Engines! An Overview of Commodities

The commodities markets are broad and deep, presenting both challenges and opportunities. Investors are often overwhelmed simply by the number of commodities out there: more than 30 tradable commodities to choose from. (I cover almost all of them — 32, to be exact — more than any other introductory book on the topic.) How do you decide whether to trade crude oil or gold, sugar or palladium, natural gas or frozen concentrated orange juice, soybeans or aluminum? What about corn, feeder cattle, and silver — should you trade these commodities as well? And if you do, what's the best way to invest in them? Should you go through the futures markets, go through the equity markets, or buy the physical stuff (such as silver coins or gold bullion)? And do all commodities move in tandem, or do they perform independently of each other?

With so many variables to keep track of and options to choose from, just getting started in commodities can be daunting. Have no fear — this book provides you with the actionable information, knowledge, insight, and analysis to help you grab the commodities market by the horns. You've maybe heard a lot of myths and fantasies about commodities. I shatter some of these myths and, in the process, clear the way to help you identify the real money-making opportunities.

For example, a lot of folks equate (incorrectly) commodities exclusively with the futures markets. Undoubtedly, the two are inextricably linked — the futures markets offer a way for commercial users to hedge against commodity price risks and a means for investors and traders to profit from this price risk. However, the futures market is only one planet in the commodities universe.

Commodities throughout history

The history of commodities tells the story of civilization itself. Ever since man first appeared on earth, his existence has been defined by a perpetual and brutal quest for control over the world's natural resources. Civilizations rise and fall, nations prosper and perish, and societies survive and subside based on their ability to harness energy, develop metals, and cultivate agricultural products — in short, based on their capacity to control commodities. It's interesting to note that prehistoric times are still defined today by the subsequent stages of man's mastery of the metals production process: the Stone Age, the Bronze Age, and the Iron Age. Nations that have been able to master natural resources have survived, while those that failed have faced extinction. This sobering reality has led to some of the most epic clashes among civilizations.

History reveals that the most devastating battles have been fought over crude oil, gold, uranium, and other precious natural resources (all covered in this book). When Francisco Pizarro's first expedition to South America in 1524 led him to the discovery of vast amounts of gold deposits, his conquistadors proceeded to wipe out the whole Inca civilization that stood between them and the gold. As a matter of fact, it's probably unlikely that Christopher Columbus would have come across to the North American continent in the first place were it not for an unquenchable desire to find the shortest and most secure route to transport spices and other commodities from India to Europe.

A few centuries later, this continuous quest for commodities resulted in the deadly South African Boer Wars at the end of the 19th century, which pitted the British Empire's armed forces against local fighters in a bloody battle over South Africa's precious metals and minerals. The 20th century, which heralded a new historical phase — the Hydrocarbon Age, shortly followed by the Nuclear Age — marks a turning point in humans' ability to utilize and exploit the earth's raw materials and the extent to which they will go to preserve this control. The Persian Gulf War of 1991, which, at its essence, was an effort to stabilize global oil markets after the Iraqi invasion of oil-rich Kuwait in the Middle East, is another manifestation of this historical reality. To this day, international players in the geopolitical world take into account access to the world's vast deposits of oil, gold, copper, and other resources. Commodities have thus determined the fate and wealth of nations throughout history and will continue to do so in the future.

The equity markets are also deeply involved in commodities. Companies such as ExxonMobil (NYSE: XOM) focus exclusively on the production of crude oil, natural gas, and other energy products; Anglo-American PLC (NASDAQ: AAUK) focuses on mining precious metals and minerals across the globe; and Starbucks (NASDAQ: SBUX) offers investors access to the coffee markets. Ignoring these companies that process commodities isn't only narrow minded, but it's also a bit foolish because they provide exposure to the very same commodities traded on the futures market.

In addition to the futures and equity markets, a number of investment vehicles allow you to access the commodities markets. These vehicles include master limited partnerships (MLPs), exchange-traded funds (ETFs), and commodity mutual funds (all covered in Chapter 6). So although I do focus on the futures markets, I also examine investment opportunities in the equity markets and beyond.

The commodities universe is large, and investment opportunities abound. In this book, I help you explore this universe inside and out, from the open outcry trading pits on the floor of the New York Mercantile Exchange to the labor-intensive cocoa fields of the Ivory Coast; from the vast palladium mining operations in northeastern Russia to the corn-growing farms of Iowa; from the Ultra Large Crude Carriers that transport crude oil across vast oceans to the nickel mines of Papua New Guinea; from the sugar plantations of Brazil to the steel mills of China.

By exploring this fascinating universe, not only do you get insight into the world's most crucial commodities — and get a glimpse of how the global capital markets operate — but you also find out how to capitalize on this information to generate profits.

Defining Commodities and Their Investment Characteristics

Just what, exactly, are commodities? Put simply, commodities are the raw materials humans use to create a livable world. Humans have been exploiting earth's natural resources since the beginning of time. They use agricultural products to feed themselves, metals to build weapons and tools, and energy to sustain themselves. Energy, metals, and agricultural products are the three classes of commodities, and they are the essential building blocks of the global economy.

For the purposes of this book, I present 32 commodities that fit a very specific definition, which I define in the following bulleted list. For example, the commodities I present must be raw materials. I don't discuss currencies — even though they trade in the futures markets — because they're not a raw material; they can't be physically used to build anything. In addition, the commodities must present real moneymaking opportunities to investors.

All the commodities I cover in the book have to meet the following criteria:

✔ **Tradability:** The commodity has to be tradable, meaning that there needs to be a viable investment vehicle to help you trade it. For example, I include a commodity if it has a futures contract assigned to it on one of the major exchanges, if a company processes it, or if an ETF tracks it.

Uranium, which is an important energy commodity, isn't tracked by a futures contract, but several companies specialize in mining and processing this mineral. By investing in these companies, you get exposure to uranium.

✔ **Deliverability:** All the commodities have to be physically deliverable. I include crude oil because it can be delivered in barrels, and I include wheat because it can be delivered by the bushel. However, I don't include currencies, interest rates, and other financial futures contracts because they're not physical commodities.

✔ **Liquidity:** I don't include any commodities that trade in illiquid markets. Every commodity in the book has an active market, with buyers and sellers constantly transacting with each other. Liquidity is critical because it gives you the option of getting in and out of an investment without having to face the difficulty of trying to find a buyer or seller for your securities.

Follow the money

Commodities have allowed nations to survive and thrive, but they've also given individuals tremendous wealth-accumulation possibilities. Some of the world's most enduring fortunes have been built around commodities. Mayer Rothschild, patriarch of the European Rothschild banking family, made a fortune during the Napoleonic Wars by storing and distributing gold bullion to fund the British side of the war effort.

Andrew Carnegie, the self-made industrialist and founder of the eponymous steel company that eventually became U.S. Steel, consolidated the American steel industry and, in the process, became the second-richest man of his time, behind only John D. Rockefeller, Sr. And what better illustration of the power of commodities as wealth-building vehicles is there than John Rockefeller himself, whose impact on the global oil industry through the creation of the Standard Oil Company is still felt today? (See Daniel Yergin's *The Prize: The Epic Quest for Oil, Money and Power*.) Abdel-Aziz Al-Saud, Saudi Arabia's first monarch, consolidated and created an entire nation through the control of crude oil and natural gas riches.

To this day, individuals involved in commodities have been able to generate tremendous wealth. Legendary oilman T. Boone Pickens, for instance, made $1.4 billion in 2005 by betting on the price of oil and natural gas. Lakshmi Mittal, the Indian-born steel magnate, became the world's fourth-richest person in 2004 as a result of his business activities in the steel industry. Clearly, individuals who have the foresight to invest in commodities have profited handsomely from this enterprise. You may not be able to build as much wealth as Rockefeller or Al-Saud, but I'm confident that you can benefit by opening up to investing in commodities.

Going for a Spin: Choosing the Right Investment Vehicle

The two most critical questions to ask yourself before getting started in commodities are the following: What commodity should I invest in? How do I invest in it? I answer the second question first and then examine which commodities to choose.

The futures markets

In the futures markets, individuals, institutions, and sometimes governments transact with each other for price-hedging and speculating purposes. An airline company, for instance, may want to use futures to enter into an agreement with a fuel company to buy a fixed amount of jet fuel for a fixed price for a fixed period of time. This transaction in the futures markets allows the airline to hedge against the volatility associated with the price of jet fuel. Although commercial users are the main players in the futures arena, traders and investors also use the futures market to profit from price volatility through various trading techniques.

One such trading technique is *arbitrage,* which takes advantage of price discrepancies between different futures markets. For example, in an arbitrage trade, you purchase and sell the crude oil futures contract simultaneously in different trading venues, for the purpose of capturing price discrepancies between these venues. I take a look at some arbitrage opportunities in Chapter 9.

The futures markets are administered by the various commodity exchanges, such as the Chicago Mercantile Exchange (CME) and the Intercontinental Exchange (ICE). I discuss the major exchanges, the role they play in the markets, and the products they offer in Chapter 8.

Investing through the futures markets requires a good understanding of futures contracts, options on futures, forwards, spreads, and other derivative products. I examine these products in depth in Chapter 9.

The most direct way of investing in the futures markets is to open an account with a *futures commission merchant* (FCM). The FCM is much like a traditional stock brokerage house (such as Schwab, Fidelity, or Merrill Lynch), except that it's allowed to offer products that trade on the futures markets. Here are some other ways to get involved in futures:

- ✔ **Commodity trading advisor (CTA):** The CTA is an individual or company licensed to trade futures contracts on your behalf.

- ✔ **Commodity pool operator (CPO):** The CPO is similar to a CTA, except that the CPO can manage the funds of multiple clients under one account. This pooling provides additional leverage when trading futures.

- ✔ **Commodity indexes:** A commodity index is a benchmark, similar to the Dow Jones Industrial Average or the S&P 500, that tracks a basket of the most liquid commodities. You can track the performance of a commodity index, which allows you to essentially "buy the market." A number of commodity indexes are available, including the Goldman Sachs Commodity Index and the Reuters/Jefferies CRB Index, which I cover in Chapter 6.

These examples are only a few ways to access the futures markets. Be sure to read Chapters 5 and 6 for additional methods.

A number of organizations regulate the futures markets, including the Securities and Exchange Commission (SEC) and the Commodity Futures Trading Commission (CFTC). These organizations monitor the markets to prevent market fraud and manipulation and to protect investors from such activity. Check out Chapter 8 for an in-depth analysis of the role these regulators play and how to use them to protect yourself from market fraud.

Trading futures isn't for everyone. By their very nature, futures markets, contracts, and products are extremely complex and require a great deal of mastery by even the most seasoned investors. If you don't feel that you have a good handle on all the concepts involved in trading futures, don't simply jump into futures — you could lose a lot more than your principal (because of the use of leverage and other characteristics unique to the futures markets). If you're not comfortable trading futures, don't sweat it. You can invest in commodities in multiple other ways.

The equity markets

Although the futures markets offer the most direct investment gateway to the commodities markets, the equity markets also offer access to these raw materials. You can invest in companies that specialize in the production, transformation, and distribution of these natural resources. If you're a stock investor familiar with the equity markets, this may be a good route for you to access the commodities markets. The only drawback of the equity markets is that you have to take into account external factors, such as management competence, tax situation, debt levels, and profit margins, which have nothing to do with the underlying commodity. That said, investing in companies that process commodities still allows you to profit from the commodities boom.

Publicly traded companies

The size, structure, and scope of the companies involved in the business are varied, and I cover most of these companies throughout the book. I offer a description of the company, including a snapshot of its financial situation, future growth prospects, and areas of operation. I then make a recommendation based on the market fundamentals of the company.

You encounter these types of companies in the book:

- **Diversified mining companies:** A number of companies focus exclusively on mining metals and minerals. Some of these companies, such as Anglo-American PLC (NASDAQ: AAUK) and BHP Billiton (NYSE: BHP), have operations across the spectrum of the metals complex, mining metals that range from gold to zinc. I look at these companies in Chapter 18.

- **Electric utilities:** Utilities are an integral part of modern life because they provide one of life's most essential necessities: electricity. They're also a good investment because they have historically offered large dividends to shareholders. Read Chapter 13 to figure out whether these companies are right for you.

- **Integrated energy companies:** These companies, such as ExxonMobil (NYSE: XOM) and Chevron (NYSE: CVX), are involved in all aspects of the energy industry, from the extraction of crude oil to the distribution of liquefied natural gas (LNG). They give you broad exposure to the energy complex (see Chapter 14).

This list is only a small sampling of the commodity companies I cover in these pages. I also analyze highly specialized companies, such as coal-mining companies (Chapter 13), oil refiners (Chapter 14), platinum-mining companies (Chapter 15), and purveyors of gourmet coffee products (Chapter 19).

Master limited partnerships

Master limited partnerships (MLPs) invest in energy infrastructure such as oil pipelines and natural gas storage facilities. I'm a big fan of MLPs because they're a *publicly traded partnership.* They offer the benefit of trading like a corporation on a public exchange, while offering the tax advantages of a private partnership. MLPs are required to transfer all cash flow back to shareholders, which makes them an attractive investment. I dissect the structure of MLPs in Chapter 7 and introduce you to some of the biggest names in the business so you can take advantage of this unique investment.

Managed funds

Sometimes it's just easier to have someone else manage your investments for you. Luckily, you can count on professional money managers who specialize in commodity trading to handle your investments.

Consider a few of these options:

- **Exchange-traded funds (ETFs):** ETFs are an increasingly popular investment because they're managed funds that offer the convenience of trading like stocks. In recent years, a plethora of ETFs has appeared to track everything from crude oil and gold to diversified commodity indexes. Find out how to benefit from these vehicles in Chapter 5.

- **Mutual funds:** If you've previously invested in mutual funds and are comfortable with them, look into adding a mutual fund that gives you exposure to the commodities markets. A number of funds are available that invest solely in commodities. I examine these commodity mutual funds in Chapter 6.

If you have a pet or a child, sometimes you hire a pet sitter or babysitter to look out after your loved ones. Before you hire this individual, you interview candidates, check their references, and examine their previous experience. When you're satisfied with the top candidate's competency, only then do you entrust that person with the responsibility of looking after your cat, daughter, or both. The same thing applies when you're shopping for a money manager, or money sitter. If you already have a money manager you trust and are happy with, stick with him. If you're looking for a new investment professional to look after your investments, you need to investigate him as thoroughly as possible. In Chapter 7, I examine the selection criteria to use when shopping for a money manager.

Physical commodity purchases

The most direct way of investing in certain commodities is to actually buy them outright. Precious metals such as gold, silver, and platinum are a great example of this. As the price of gold and silver has skyrocketed recently, you may have seen ads on TV or in newspapers from companies offering to buy your gold or silver jewelry. As gold and silver prices increase in the futures markets, they also cause prices in the spot markets to rise (and vice versa). You can cash in on this trend by buying coins, bullion, or even jewelry. I present this unique investment strategy in Chapter 15.

This investment strategy is suitable for only a limited number of commodities, mostly precious metals like gold, silver, and platinum. Unless you own a farm, keeping live cattle or feeder cattle to profit from price increases doesn't make much sense. And I won't even mention commodities like crude oil or uranium!

Checking Out What's on the Menu

I cover 32 commodities in the book. Here's a listing of all the commodities you can expect to encounter while going through these pages. (Although the book is modular in nature, I list the commodities here in order of their appearance in the text.)

Energy

Energy has always been indispensable for human survival and also makes for a great investment. Energy, whether fossil fuels or renewable energy sources, has attracted a lot of attention from investors as they seek to profit from the world's seemingly unquenchable thirst for energy. I present in this book all the major forms of energy, from crude oil and coal to electricity and solar power, and show you how to profit in this arena.

- ✔ **Crude oil:** Crude oil is the undisputed heavyweight champion in the commodities world. More barrels of crude oil are traded every single day (87 million and growing) than any other commodity. Accounting for 40 percent of total global energy consumption, coal provides some terrific investment opportunities.

- ✔ **Natural gas:** Natural gas, the gaseous fossil fuel, is often overshadowed by crude oil. Nevertheless, it's a major commodity in its own right, used for everything from cooking food to heating houses during the winter. I also take a look at the prospects of liquefied natural gas (LNG).

- ✔ **Coal:** Coal accounts for more than 20 percent of total world energy consumption. In the United States, the largest energy market, 50 percent of electricity is generated through coal. Because of abundant supply, coal is making a resurgence.

- ✔ **Uranium/nuclear power:** Because of improved environmental standards within the industry, nuclear power use is on the rise. I show you how to develop an investment strategy to capitalize on this trend.

- ✔ **Electricity:** Electricity is a necessity of modern life, and the companies responsible for generating this special commodity have some unique characteristics. I examine how to start trading this electrifying commodity.

- ✔ **Solar power:** For a number of reasons that range from environmental to geopolitical, demand for renewable energy sources such as solar power is increasing.

- ✔ **Wind power:** Wind power is getting a lot of attention from investors as a viable alternative source of energy.

- ✔ **Ethanol:** Ethanol, which is produced primarily from corn or sugar, is an increasingly popular fuel additive that offers investment potential.

Other commodities are in the energy complex, such as heating oil, propane, and gasoline. Although I do provide insight into some of these other members of the energy family, I focus a lot more on the resources in the previous list.

Metals

Metallurgy has been essential to human development since the beginning of time. Societies that have mastered the production of metals have been able to thrive and survive. Similarly, investors who have incorporated metals into their portfolios have been able to generate significant returns. I cover all the major metals, from gold and platinum to nickel and zinc.

- **Gold:** Gold is perhaps the most coveted resource on the planet. For centuries, people have been attracted to its quasi-indestructibility and have used it as a store of value. Gold is a good asset for hedging against inflation and also for asset preservation during times of global turmoil.

- **Silver:** Silver, like gold, is another precious metal that has monetary applications. The British currency, the pound sterling, is still named after this metal. Silver also has applications in industry (such as electrical wiring) that places it in a unique position of being coveted for both its precious metal status and its industrial uses.

- **Platinum:** Platinum, the rich man's gold, is one of the most valuable metals in the world, used for everything from jewelry to the manufacture of catalytic converters.

- **Steel:** Steel, which is created by alloying iron and other materials, is the most widely used metal in the world. Used to build everything from cars to buildings, it's a metal endowed with unique characteristics and offers good investment potential.

- **Aluminum:** Perhaps no other metal has the versatility of aluminum; it's lightweight yet surprisingly robust. These unique characteristics mean that it's a metal worth adding to your portfolio, especially because it's the second most widely used metal (right behind steel).

- **Copper:** Copper, the third most widely used metal, is the metal of choice for industrial uses. Because it's a great conductor of heat and electricity, its applications in industry are wide and deep, making this base metal a very attractive investment.

- **Palladium:** Palladium is part of the platinum group of metals, and almost half of the palladium that's mined goes toward building automobile catalytic converters. As the number of cars with these emission-reducing devices increases, the demand for palladium will increase as well, making this an attractive investment.

- **Nickel:** Nickel is a ferrous metal that's in high demand because of its resistance to corrosion and oxidation. Steel is usually alloyed with nickel to create stainless steel, which ensures that nickel will play an important role for years to come.

✔ **Zinc:** The fourth most widely used metal in the world, zinc is sought after for its resistance to corrosion. It's used in the process of galvanization, in which zinc coating is applied to other metals, such as steel, to prevent rust.

Agricultural products

Food is the most essential element of human life, and the production of food presents solid money-making opportunities. In *Commodities For Dummies,* 2nd Edition, you find out how to invest in the agricultural sector in everything from coffee and orange juice to cattle and soybeans.

✔ **Coffee:** Coffee is the second most widely produced commodity in the world, in terms of physical volume, behind only crude oil. Folks just seem to love a good cup of coffee, and this provides good investment opportunities.

✔ **Cocoa:** Cocoa production, which is dominated by a handful of countries, is a major agricultural commodity, primarily because it's used to create chocolate.

✔ **Sugar #11:** Sugar is a popular food sweetener, and it can be a sweet investment as well. Sugar #11 represents a futures contract for global sugar.

✔ **Sugar #14:** Sugar #14 is specific to the United States and is a widely traded commodity.

✔ **Frozen concentrated orange juice — type A:** FCOJ-A, for short, is the benchmark for North American orange juice prices because it's grown in the hemisphere's two largest regions: Florida and Brazil.

✔ **Frozen concentrated orange juice — type B:** FCOJ-B, like FCOJ-A, is a widely traded contract that represents global orange juice prices. This contract gives you exposure to orange juice activity on a world scale.

✔ **Corn:** Corn's use for culinary purposes is perhaps unrivaled by any other grain, which makes this a potentially lucrative investment. Check out how to trade it in Chapter 20.

✔ **Wheat:** According to archaeological evidence, wheat was one of the first agricultural products grown by man. It's an essential staple of human life and makes for a great investment.

✔ **Soybeans:** Soybeans have many applications, including as feedstock and for cooking purposes. The soybean market is a large market and presents some good investment opportunities.

- ✔ **Soybean oil:** Soybean oil, also known as vegetable oil, is derived from actual soybeans. It's used for cooking purposes and has become popular in recent years with the health-conscious dietary movement.

- ✔ **Soybean meal:** Soybean meal is another derivative of soybeans that's used as feedstock for poultry and cattle. It may not sound sexy, but it can be a good investment.

- ✔ **Live cattle:** For investors involved in agriculture, using the live cattle futures contract to hedge against price volatility is a good idea.

- ✔ **Feeder cattle:** Whereas the live cattle contract tracks adult cows, the feeder cattle contract hedges against the risk associated with growing calves. The markets don't widely follow this area, but it's important to figure out how this market works.

- ✔ **Lean hogs:** They may not be the sexiest commodity out there, but lean hogs are an essential commodity, making them a good trading target.

- ✔ **Frozen pork bellies:** Frozen pork bellies are essentially nothing more than good old bacon. This industry is cyclical and subject to wild price swings, which provides unique arbitrage trading opportunities.

Chapter 2

Earn, Baby, Earn! Why You Should Invest in Commodities

Commodities have traditionally been considered the black sheep in the family of asset classes; for several decades, no respectable money manager wanted anything to do with them. This traditional lack of interest (which no longer applies, by the way) has generated a lot of misinformation about commodities. As a matter of fact, probably no other asset class has suffered through so much misunderstanding and misconception.

Many investors are scared of venturing into the world of commodities. For one thing, it seems that every time the word *commodities* is uttered, someone pops up with a horrible story about losing their entire life savings trading soybeans, cocoa, or some other exotic commodity. Even though this negative perception is rapidly changing, commodities are still often misunderstood as an investment. I actually know some investors who invest in commodities (and who have made money off them) but who don't understand the fundamental reasons commodities are such a good long-term investment.

In this chapter, I show you why commodities are an attractive investment and why many investors are becoming more interested in this asset class. I also give you the goods on a number of global trends that are responsible for the recent run-up in commodity prices. Investors who are able to identify and navigate these trends are going to do extremely well. It's also important to note that no investment goes up in a straight line; any market has downturns, and that is to be expected. Identifying these trends is strategically important, but being able to tactically navigate them in the short term separates the winners from the losers.

Sometimes events have a dramatic and unexpected effect on markets. Such was the case with the Global Financial Crisis (GFC) of 2008. This event had a profound impact on all markets, and commodities were no exceptions. The most astute investors, while perhaps not able to pinpoint the exact origins and effects of such events, are able to tactically adjust their portfolios to protect their downside.

Events such as the liquidity crisis of 2008 are often characterized as Black Swan events — that is, events that take the market by surprise and have a profound and lasting impact. Best-selling author Nicholas Nassim Taleb popularized the term.

You Can't Argue with Success

In recent years, commodities as an asset class have attracted a lot of attention from the investor community. Many investors are turning to commodities because they see the value in investing in an asset class that's growing in scale and importance.

Figure 2-1, which shows the recent performance of the Reuters/Jefferies CRB Index, an index that tracks a basket of commodities, accurately portrays the major dynamics at play in the commodities markets over the last several years. Until the second half of 2008, investors piled into the commodities markets, driven by a desire to get exposure to this asset class. However, the second half of 2008 was characterized by the bankruptcy of Lehman Brothers, the implosion of the mortgage and real estate markets in the United States, and the ensuing liquidity crisis that threatened to bring down some of the country's biggest financial and industrial institutions.

Given all the tumult in the market, it's noteworthy that commodities were able to bounce back and stage a comeback in 2009. The year 2008 will go down in history as one of the most turbulent years in recorded financial markets; the liquidity crisis had profound impacts on the markets, and effects will be felt for years to come. Broadly speaking, commodities were no exception to this rule, although some bright spots emerged in certain commodities, such as precious metals in general and gold specifically (see Figure 2-3).

Other bellwether commodities, such as crude oil, reacted with linearity to the crisis, suffering equally large drops as the broader markets. In Figure 2-2, you can clearly see the oil price drop as a direct result of the GFC. Crude is a phenomenal indicator of global economic growth and the state of the world's economic health. As such, its reaction to decreased global economic growth due to the GFC is completely rational.

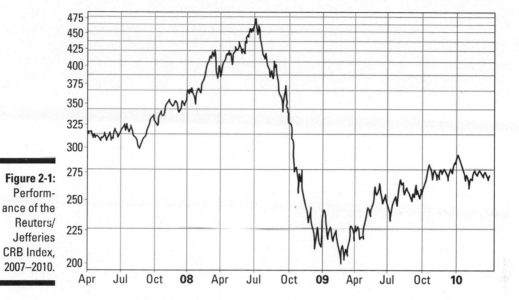

Figure 2-1:
Perform-
ance of the
Reuters/
Jefferies
CRB Index,
2007–2010.

Another important factor to note in the chart is that oil prices between 2002 and 2010 more than quadrupled, from around $20 per barrel to more than $90 per barrel. Throughout this period, the market experienced some speculative excess on the way up (2007) and a commensurate burst on the way down (2008). That said, the trend is undoubtedly in an upward mode, for reasons I outline later in this chapter, and that's one of the most important takeaways from the last several years: Although the trend is upward sloping, it doesn't necessarily mean it'll move in a straight line. You can expect lots of drops and spikes along the way.

It's also critical to isolate and examine each commodity and analyze it in its own right, separating it from the broader commodities complex. For example, although many commodities were broadly impacted by the 2008 GFC, certain commodities weren't affected as much. For example, gold didn't experience the same kind of downturn as the broader markets, as you can see in Figure 2-3. Gold has certain inherent characteristics because it's both a precious metal and an alternative monetary currency; for more on gold's special qualities, flip to Chapter 15. So although most other asset classes suffered major drops during the crisis, gold was able to perform relatively well; in fact, since 2002, gold prices have risen more than 450 percent.

Many investors, intrigued by the performance of commodities and their inherent characteristics, want in on the action. However, most investors are pouring into commodities without knowing why commodities are performing well — and this is a recipe for disaster. In this chapter and throughout the book, I lay out the case point by point on why commodities are an attractive value proposition for your portfolio.

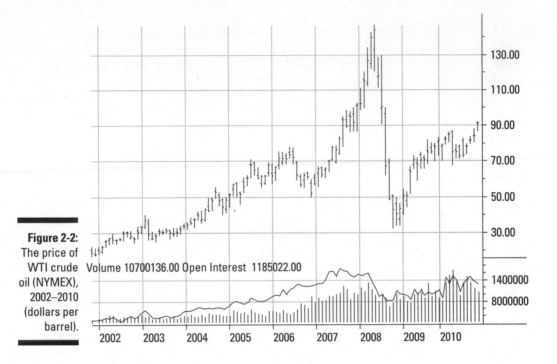

Figure 2-2:
The price of
WTI crude
oil (NYMEX),
2002–2010
(dollars per
barrel).

Figure 2-3:
The price
of gold
(COMEX),
2002–2010
(dollars per
troy ounce).

Never invest in something you don't understand. If you hear someone on TV or the radio mention an investment, perform your due diligence to get the ins and outs of the potential investment. (I talk about due diligence in Chapter 3.) Not understanding an investment before you invest in it is one of the easiest ways to lose money.

Why the 21st Century Is the Century of Commodities

Since autumn 2001, commodities have been running faster than the bulls of Pamplona. The Reuters/Jefferies CRB Index (a benchmark for commodities) nearly doubled between 2001 and 2006. During this period, oil, gold, copper, and silver hit all-time highs (although not adjusted for inflation). Other commodities also reached levels never seen before in trading sessions.

Many investors wondered what was going on. Why were commodities doing so well when other investments, such as stocks and bonds, weren't performing? I believe that we're witnessing a long-term cyclical bull market in commodities. Because of a number of fundamental factors (which I go through in the following sections), commodities are poised for a rally that will last well into the 21st century — and possibly beyond that. It's a bold statement, I know. But the facts are there to support me.

Although I'm bullish on commodities for the long term, I have to warn you that at times commodities won't perform well at all. This statement is simply the nature of the commodity cycle. Furthermore, in the history of Wall Street, no asset has ever gone up in a straight line. Minor (and, occasionally, major) pullbacks always happen before an asset makes new highs — if, in fact, it does make new highs.

Consider an example. During the first few months of 2006, commodities outperformed every asset class, with some commodities breaking record levels. Gold and copper both hit a 25-year high. Then during the week of May 15, commodities saw a big drop. The Reuters/Jefferies CRB Index fell more than 5 percent that week, with gold and copper dropping 10 and 7 percent, respectively.

Many commentators went on the offensive and started bashing commodities. "We are now seeing the beginning of the end of the rally in commodities," said one analyst. A newspaper ran the headline "Is This the End of Commodities?" An endless number of commentators hit the airwaves claiming that this was a speculative bubble about to burst. A respected economist even compared what was happening to commodities to the dotcom bubble: "There is no fundamental reason why commodity prices are going up."

Nothing could be further from fact. A couple weeks after this minor pullback, some of these commodities that were being compared to highly leveraged tech stocks had regained most, if not all, of their lost ground. Even after the GFC, most commodities are now back to their precrisis levels, with many others making all-time highs.

There's a story behind the rise in commodities — and it's a pretty compelling one.

Ka-boom! Capitalizing on the global population explosion

The 21st century is going to experience the largest population growth in the history of humankind. The United Nations (UN) estimates that the world will add a little less than 1 billion people during *each* of the first five decades of the 21st century. The global population will grow to about 9 billion people by 2050 (as of 2010, approximately 6.8 billion people live on the planet).

Also consider the following statistic: According to the UN, the average number of years it takes to add 1 billion people has shrunk from an average of 130 years in the 19th century to approximately 13 years in the 21st century! The rate at which the human population is increasing has reached exponential levels. Check out Figure 2-4 for the expected population growth in the 21st century.

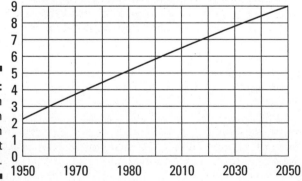

PEOPLE ON THE PLANET

Population (in billions)

Figure 2-4: Population growth in the 20th and 21st centuries.

So how is this relevant to commodities? Put simply, significant population growth translates into greater global demand for commodities. Humans are the most voracious consumers of raw materials on the planet — and the only ones who pay for them. As the number of humans in the world increases, so will the demand for natural resources. After all, people need food to eat, houses to live in, and heat to stay warm during the winter — all of this requires raw materials. This large population growth is a key driver for the increasing demand for commodities, which will continue to put upward pressure on commodity prices.

Brick by brick: Profiting from urbanization

Perhaps even more significant than population growth is the fact that it's accompanied by the largest urbanization movement the world has ever seen. In the early 20th century, according to the UN, less than 15 percent of the world's population lived in cities; by 2005, that number jumped to 50 percent — and shows no sign of decreasing. As a matter of fact, 60 percent of the world's population is expected to live in urban areas by the year 2030.

The number of large metropolitan areas with 5 million or more people (mega cities) is skyrocketing and will continue to climb for much of the century. In Figure 2-5, you can see the number of cities expected to have 5 million inhabitants by 2015. When you compare that with the growth in the number of cities with 5 million people from 1950 to 2000, you quickly realize how staggering this growth really is.

Urbanization is highly significant for commodities because people who live in urban centers consume a lot more natural resources than those who live in rural areas. In addition, more natural resources are required to expand the size of cities as more people move to them (rural to urban migration) and have more kids (indigenous urban population growth). More natural resources are required for the roads, cars, and personal appliances that are staples of city life.

Industrial metals such as copper, steel, and aluminum are going to be in high demand to construct apartment buildings, schools, hospitals, cars, and so on. So investing in industrial metals is one possible way to play the urbanization card. Be sure to read Chapter 16 for more information on these metals.

As you can see from the map in Figure 2-5, the largest urbanization is taking place in the developing world, particularly in Asia. As more Asians move from the countryside to large urban areas, expect to see huge demand from that part of the world for raw materials to fuel this growth.

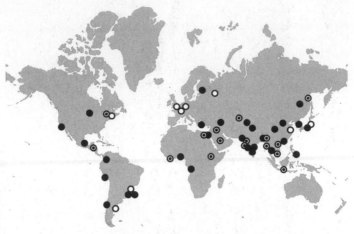

Figure 2-5:
Number of
cities with
5 million
inhabitants
in 1950,
2000, and
2015
(projected).

Size of Urban Population
o 5 million and over since 1950
● 5 million and over since 2000
◉ 5 million and over since 2015 (projected)

Full steam ahead! Benefiting from industrialization

The first industrial revolution, which took place in the 19th century, was a major transformational event primarily confined to Western Europe and North America. Major industrialization didn't spread to other corners of the globe until parts of the 20th century — even then, it was only sporadic.

A new wave of industrialization is taking place in the 21st century, and it may be the most important one in history. This wave is transforming a large number of developing countries into more industrialized countries, and raw materials are fueling this transformation.

The BRIC countries

Although many developing countries are on the fast track to industrialization, four countries need to be singled out as the frontrunners in this movement — Brazil, Russia, India, and China. They're collectively known as the *BRIC countries,* or just the BRICs.

The BRIC countries, which are now on a path toward full industrialization, are scouring the globe to secure supplies of key natural resources such as oil, natural gas, copper, and aluminum — the raw materials necessary for a country to industrialize. (See the sidebar "It's déjà vu all over again: The great game 21st century style.")

As demand from the BRIC countries for natural resources increases, expect to see increasing upward price pressures on commodities.

China

Although all four of the BRIC countries are rapidly transforming themselves, no other country is doing so as rapidly and dramatically as China. Fittingly, the saying "May you live in interesting times" is said to be an old Chinese proverb. The 21st century is undoubtedly going to be an interesting century, and China will play an increasingly important role in global economic affairs.

China's GDP has increased by 9 percent each year from 2000 to 2006. To sustain this growth, China has been consuming all sorts of commodities. Some of the highs that commodities such as oil, natural gas, cement, copper, and aluminum have experienced between 2003 and 2006 are a direct result of increased demand from China.

For example, in 2004, China gobbled up half the cement, one-third of the steel, one-quarter of the copper, and one-fifth of the aluminum produced in the world. In 2003, China overtook Japan to become the second-largest consumer of crude oil — right behind the United States. (For more information on global oil consumption, read Chapter 11.) In fact, in 2010, China surpassed Japan to become the world's second-largest economy, behind only that of the United States. In Figure 2-6, you can see the expected Chinese consumption of crude oil for the first quarter of the century.

Figure 2-6: China is expected to increase its consumption of crude oil products to approximately 12 million barrels a day by 2025.

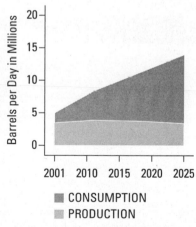

Source: Energy Information Administration

China is going to have a tremendous impact on the global economy in the 21st century and is expected to be the largest consumer of commodities in the world. For more information on China's emergence as a global economic power and the transformation of the economic playing field that this entails, I recommend the following titles:

- *China, Inc.: How the Rise of the Next Superpower Challenges America and the World,* by Ted Fishman (Scribner)
- *Three Billion New Capitalists: The Great Shift of Wealth and Power to the East,* by Clyde Prestowitz (Basic Books)
- *The End of Poverty: Economic Possibilities for Our Time,* by Jeffrey Sachs (Penguin)

Brazil

Another country that is having and will continue to have a significant impact on commodities markets worldwide is Brazil, the largest country in South America in terms of GDP, landmass, population, and abundance of natural resources.

Brazil's geography, topography, and weather patterns make it a powerhouse in the commodities space. Consider a few of the natural resources in which Brazil is a world leader or has a dominant market share:

- Coffee
- Copper
- Corn
- Crude oil (offshore)
- Eucalyptus
- Gold
- Iron ore
- Livestock
- Silver
- Soybeans
- Sugar
- Sugarcane

Blessed with large amounts of arable land, the world's largest river basin drainage systems (the Amazon), and favorable geology, Brazil is a world leader in commodities, especially agricultural commodities. Many companies are involved in the production and distribution of these natural resources, and as the world's demand for these products increases, I expect Brazil to do extremely well in the years and decades to come.

It's déjà vu all over again: The great game 21st century style

During parts of the 19th and 20th centuries, the global powers of the time were embroiled in a strategic geopolitical contest over control of the world's precious natural resources, commonly referred to as "The Great Game." The 21st century is experiencing a new great game, in which the stakes are higher and the competition fiercer. The world's industrialized and rapidly industrializing countries are prowling the investment landscape in search of secure energy and raw material sources.

China, in particular, is becoming one of the most aggressive players on the world stage when it comes to securing energy sources. As natural resources such as oil become scarcer, expect more countries and companies to act more aggressively to secure whatever supplies are left. Because demand for raw materials is fairly inelastic (see the "Gaining from inelasticity" section) and supply is limited, there is double upward pressure from both the demand and supply sides of the equation. (That's yet another reason to be bullish on commodities.)

For now, the pie is large enough that most of the global players are able to participate and get something out of this contest. To profit as an investor, keep your eye out for new companies that are making deals overseas to secure raw materials. The companies that are able to do so efficiently and aggressively will generally tend to produce higher revenues and cash flows, key ingredients to the success of any company. Keep a particularly close eye on companies from emerging China, India, South Korea, and Russia, as well as the traditional players from the United States, Great Britain, Australia, Europe, and Japan, which have the technological and capital resources to close some big deals. (For more on how to identify and evaluate these kinds of companies, flip over to Chapter 14.)

What Makes Commodities Unique

As an asset class, commodities have unique characteristics that separate them from other asset classes and make them attractive, whether as independent investments or as part of a broader investment strategy. I go through these unique characteristics in the following sections.

Gaining from inelasticity

In economics, *elasticity* seeks to determine the effects of price on supply and demand. The calculation can get pretty technical, but, essentially, elasticity quantifies how much supply and demand will change for every incremental change in price.

Goods that are elastic tend to have a high correlation between price and demand, which is usually inversely proportional: When prices of a good increase, demand tends to decrease. This relationship makes sense because you're not going to pay for a good that you don't need if it becomes too expensive. Capturing and determining that spread is what elasticity is all about.

Inelastic goods, however, are goods that are so essential to consumers that changes in price tend to have a limited effect on supply and demand. Most commodities fall in the inelastic goods category because they're essential to human existence.

For instance, if the price of ice cream increased by 25 percent, chances are, you'd stop buying ice cream. Why? Because it's not a necessity, but more of a luxury. However, if the price of unleaded gasoline at the pump increased by 25 percent (as it did during 2003–2006), you definitely wouldn't be happy about the price increase, but you'd still fill up your tank. The reason? Gas is a necessity — you need to fill up your car to go to work or school, run errands, and so on.

The demand for gasoline isn't absolutely inelastic, however — you won't keep paying for it regardless of the price. A point will come at which you'd decide that it's simply not worth it to keep paying the amount you're paying at the pump, so you'd begin looking for alternatives. (Read Chapter 13 for more information on alternative energy sources.) But the truth remains that you're willing to pay more for gasoline than for other products you don't need (such as ice cream); that's the key to understanding price inelasticity.

Most commodities are fairly inelastic because they're the raw materials that allow us to live the lives we strive for; they help us maintain a decent (and, in some cases, extravagant) standard of living. Without these precious raw materials, you wouldn't be able to heat your home in the winter — actually, without cement, copper, and other basic materials, you wouldn't even have a house to begin with! And then there's the most essential commodity of all: food. Without food, we wouldn't exist.

Because of the absolute necessity of commodities, you can be sure that as long as there are humans around, there's going to be a demand for these raw materials.

Finding a safe haven

During times of turmoil, commodities tend to act as safe havens for investors. These investors view certain commodities, such as gold and silver, as reliable stores of value, so they flock to these assets when times aren't good. When currencies slide, nations go to war, or global pandemics break out, you can rely on gold, silver, and other commodities to provide you with financial safety.

For example, after the horrible acts of September 11, 2001, the price of gold jumped as investors sought safety in the metal. You can see a clear spike in the price of gold in Figure 2-7, right after September 11.

Figure 2-7:
Investors
turned to
gold for
safety dur-
ing and
right after
the tragic
events of
September
11, 2001.
(Prices as
measured
by the
London
Gold Fix.)

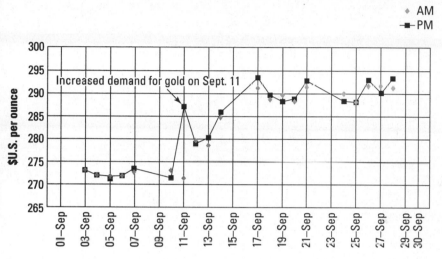

It's a good idea to have part of your portfolio in gold and other precious metals so that you can protect your assets during times of turmoil. Turn to Chapter 15 for more on investing in precious metals.

Hedging against inflation

One of the biggest factors to watch out for as an investor is the ravaging effects of inflation. Inflation can devastate your investments, particularly paper assets such as stocks. (I discuss inflation and other risks in Chapter 3.) The central bankers of the world — smart people all — spend their entire careers trying to tame inflation, but despite their efforts, inflation can easily get out of hand. You need to protect yourself against this economic enemy.

Ironically, one of the only asset classes that *benefits* from inflation is, you guessed it, commodities. Perhaps the biggest irony of all is that increases in the prices of basic goods (commodities such as oil and gas) actually contribute to the increase of inflation.

As you can see in Figure 2-8, for example, there's a positive correlation between gold and the inflation rate. During times of high inflation, investors load up on gold because it's considered a good store of value.

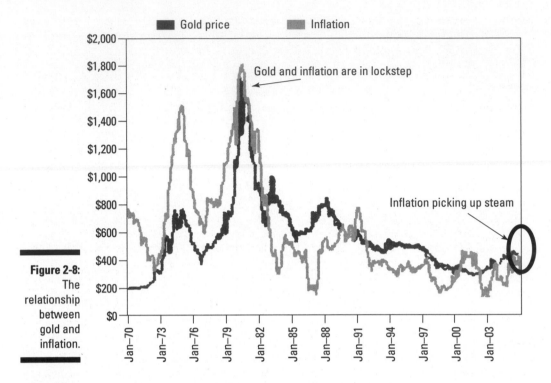

Figure 2-8:
The
relationship
between
gold and
inflation.

One way to not only protect yourself from inflation, but also profit from it, is to invest in gold. I discuss the inflation-hedging opportunities that gold provides in Chapter 15.

Taking time to bring new sources online

The business of commodities is a time- and capital-intensive business. Unlike investments in high-tech companies or other "new economy" investments (such as e-commerce), bringing commodity projects online takes a lot of time.

For example, it can take up to a decade to bring new sources of oil online. First, a company must identify potentially promising areas to explore for oil. After locating an area, the company has to actually start drilling and prospecting for the oil. If it's lucky, this process of discovering significantly recoverable sources of oil takes only three to five years. The company must then develop infrastructure and bring in machinery to extract the oil, which must be transported to a refining facility to be transformed into consumable energy products such as gasoline or jet fuel. After it goes through the lengthy refining stage, the end product must finally be transported to consumers.

Constructing the BTC pipeline

A good example of the capital- and time-intensive aspect of commodity projects is the construction of the Baku-Tbilisi-Ceyhan oil pipeline that links a large Azerbaijan offshore oil field located in the Caspian Sea (the Azeri-Chirag-Guneshi oil field) to the Turkish port city of Ceyhan in the Mediterranean Sea.

Talks about building a pipeline to deliver Azerbaijan's 32 billion barrels of oil to consumer markets started in 1996. Many Western countries and energy companies supported the project because the pipeline would tap into a vast new source of oil (thereby lowering dependence on the volatile Persian Gulf region) and would pass through Azerbaijan, recently independent Georgia, and democratic Turkey (thereby bypassing the Russians and the Iranians).

The project faced immediate opposition because of strategic geopolitical maneuvering; in other words, the Russians weren't happy that a pipeline would be built in what they considered their backyard. Environmentalists also quickly expressed their discontent, fearing the pipeline would disturb precious environmental and ecological zones.

Talks among the various interested parties stretched from 1996 until 1999, when a mutually agreeable solution was reached and the project got the green light. Planning for the construction of the pipeline then began, but actual construction didn't start until late 2002. The pipeline construction finished in 2006, and oil started flowing from the Caspian Sea to the Mediterranean Sea on May 28, 2006.

In all, it took about ten years to create, design, and execute this project, which has cost $4 billion and employed thousands of workers. The BTC pipeline is a good example of how long it can take to bring new sources of energy and other precious commodities to consumer markets. And I'm not even counting the decades it took to prospect and explore the Caspian Sea to discover the oil in the first place!

The point is that the world is in serious need of oil and other raw materials to fuel global economic growth. However, the projects that are now being developed will need many years before they're able to deliver products. Make sure you consider these factors before you invest in commodities.

So what does this all mean to you as an investor? When you're investing in commodities, you have to think long term! If you're used to investing in tech stocks or if you're an entrepreneur involved in e-commerce, you need to radically change the way you think about investing when you approach commodities. If you're able to recognize the long-term nature of commodities, you'll be on your way to becoming a successful commodities investor.

Sell in May and go away? Definitely nay!

You may have heard the saying "Sell in May and go away." This is a Wall Street adage referring to stocks. The thinking goes that because the stock market doesn't perform well during the summer months, you should sell your stocks and get back into the game in the fall.

This adage doesn't apply to commodities because commodities move in different cycles than stocks. Some commodities perform really well during the summer months. For example, because summer is the heavy driving season, there's an increase in demand for gasoline products. Thus, all things equal, unleaded gasoline tends to increase in price during the summer.

I discuss the cyclical nature of commodities in the following section. For a more in-depth comparison between the performance of commodities and that of other assets, go to Chapter 4.

Time to Get Down to Business: Commodities and the Business Cycle

Commodities are cyclical in nature. Returns on commodity investments aren't generated in a vacuum — they're influenced by a number of economic forces. In other words, the performance of commodities, like that of other major asset classes, is tied to general economic conditions. Because economies move in cycles, constantly alternating between expansions and recessions, commodities react according to the current economic phase.

The performance of commodities as an asset class is going to be different during economic expansions than during recessions.

As a general rule, commodities tend to do well during periods of late expansions and early recessions. The reason is that, as the economy slows, key interest rates are decreased to stimulate economic activity — this tends to help the performance of commodities. Stocks and bonds, on the other hand, don't perform as well during recessions. As an investor seeking returns across all phases of the business cycle, opening up to commodities enables you to generate returns during good and bad economic times.

Be sure to read Chapter 3 for a comprehensive comparison of the performance of commodities and other asset classes. Also turn to Chapter 5 for an overview of the benefits of diversification.

The study of cycles, whether for commodities, stocks, or other assets, isn't an exact science. I don't recommend using cycles as the foundation of a trading or investment strategy. Instead, try to use the study of cycles to get a sense of what historical patterns have indicated — and where an asset class is heading.

Although the historical pattern of commodities tends to show better performance during late expansions and early recessions, this in no way guarantees that commodities will keep following this pattern. Actually, during the latest commodity bull market, commodities have acted independently of the business cycle. This performance may be attributed to the fact that, for the reasons outlined in the section "Why the 21st Century Is the Century of Commodities," this commodity bull market is a different beast than in previous cycles.

Chapter 3

Investing in Commodities: Only for the Brave?

C ommodities have a reputation for being a risky asset. Many investors are simply scared of investing in this asset class. This fear is largely unfounded because, statistically, there's no greater risk in investing in commodities than there is in investing in stocks.

For whatever reason, investors have shunned this asset class in favor of what they think are more "prudent" investments, such as stocks. This reaction is quite baffling, because the performance of commodities in recent years has exceeded that of stocks. For example, between 2002 and 2005, the Dow Jones Industrial Average returned a respectable 7 percent. However, the Dow Jones–AIG Commodity Index, which tracks a basket of commodities, was up more than 21 percent! In fact, in 2002 alone, whereas the Dow Jones Industrial Average had negative returns (–7 percent), the Dow Jones–AIG Commodity Index had returns of 26 percent.

I once attended a lecture with a world-renowned market psychologist who made this simple argument: Investors are afraid of what they don't know. Many investors prefer to stick with an investment they know even if that investment doesn't perform well for them. For example, during 2000 and 2001, the investing public lost a total of $5 trillion in stocks (remember the bursting of the dotcom bubble?). Yet you never hear the kinds of warnings about stocks that you hear about commodities. Is this a double standard? You can judge for yourself.

I believe that many investors are afraid of commodities because they don't know much about them. My aim in this chapter is to shed some light on the issues surrounding commodities so that you can invest with confidence. However, I'm not denying that commodities present some risk — all investments do. I give you some tools in the following sections to minimize and manage those risks.

Biting Off More Than You Can Chew: The Pitfalls of Using Leverage

In finance, *leverage* refers to the act of magnifying returns through the use of borrowed capital. Leverage is a powerful tool that gives you the opportunity to control large market positions with relatively little upfront capital. However, leverage is the ultimate double-edged sword because both your profits and losses are magnified to outrageous proportions.

If you invest in stocks, you know that you're able to trade on margin. You have to qualify for a margin account, but when you do, you're able to use leverage (margin) to get into stock positions. You can also trade commodities on margin. However, the biggest difference between using margin with stocks and using margin with commodities is that margin requirement for commodities is much lower than margins for stocks, which means the potential for losses (and profits) is much greater in commodities.

If you qualify for trading stocks on margin, you need to have at least 50 percent of the capital in your account before you can enter into a stock position on margin.

The minimum margin requirements for commodity futures vary but, on average, are lower than those for stocks. For example, the margin requirement for soybeans in the Chicago Board of Trade is 4 percent. This means that, with only $400 in your account, you can buy $10,000 worth of soybeans futures contracts! If the trade goes your way, you're a happy camper. But if you're on the losing side of a trade on margin, you can lose much more than your principal.

Another big difference between stock and commodity futures accounts is that the balance on futures accounts is calculated at the end of the trading session. So if you get a margin call, you need to take care of it immediately.

When you're trading on margin, which is essentially trading on borrowed capital, you may get a margin call from your broker requiring you to deposit additional capital in your account to cover the borrowed amount.

Because of the use of margin and the extraordinary amounts of leverage you have at your disposal in the futures markets, you need to be extremely careful when trading commodity futures contracts. To be a responsible investor, I recommend using margin only if you have the necessary capital reserves to cover any subsequent margin calls you may receive if the market moves adversely. For more on trading futures and margin requirements, turn to Chapter 9.

Watch Your Step: Understanding the Real Risks behind Commodities

Investing is all about managing the risk involved in generating returns. In this section, I lay out some common risks you face when investing in commodities and some small steps you can take to minimize these risks.

Sovereign government risk

In the era following the 2008 credit crisis, a more acute risk emerged: the sovereign government risk. This type of risk is more important than other types of risks because it involves the balance sheet of sovereign governments. During the financial crisis, banks were in a position to bail out consumers; when banks started to fail, governments began to bail out the banks. However, when governments start to fail, few institutions can bail them out.

This type of risk became more evident in the European countries, accustomed to single-digit gross domestic profit (GDP) growth rates and relaxed lifestyles due to generous government programs and pensions. For a number of reasons (geographic, demographic, and economic), these countries no longer enjoy the place in the sun they once occupied, which is leading to the risk that these states may start defaulting. In addition to liquidity risks, these states pose a solvency risk — in other words, they simply cannot pay back their borrowers.

Many countries in Europe, such as Greece, Portugal, Spain, Ireland, and, to some extent, Italy and France (Germany being the main exception) — are facing severe budget cuts and unprecedented decreases in government expenditure programs. This situation caused riots and violence across Europe in 2010. As their unfavorable demographic trends further accelerate and their manufacturing base is eroded by more competitive spheres in Asia and other emerging markets, expect to see more belt-tightening in Europe over the next five years. In a post-2008 world, it's necessary to carefully examine the countries you're investing in.

Geopolitical risk

One of the inherent risks of commodities is that the world's natural resources are located on various continents, and the jurisdiction over these commodities lies with sovereign governments, international companies, and many other entities. For example, to access the large deposits of oil located in the Persian Gulf region, oil companies have to deal with the sovereign countries of the Middle East that have jurisdiction over this oil.

Negotiations for natural resource extractions can get pretty tense pretty quickly, with disagreements arising over licensing agreements, tax structures, environmental concerns, employment of indigenous workers, access to technology, and many other complex issues.

International disagreements over the control of natural resources are common. Sometimes a host country simply kicks out foreign companies involved in the production and distribution of the country's natural resources. In 2006, Bolivia, which contains South America's second-largest deposits of natural gas, nationalized its natural gas industry and kicked out the foreign companies involved. In a day, a number of companies, such as Brazil's Petrobras and Spain's Repsol, were left without a mandate in a country where they had spent billions of dollars developing the natural gas industry. Investors in Petrobras and Repsol paid the price.

So how do you protect yourself from this geopolitical uncertainty? Unfortunately, you can't wave a magic wand to eliminate this type of risk. However, one way to minimize it is to invest in companies with experience and economies of scale. For example, if you're interested in investing in an international oil company, go with one that has an established international track record. A company like ExxonMobil, for instance, has the scale, breadth, and experience in international markets to manage the geopolitical risk it faces. A smaller company without this sort of experience faces more risk than a bigger one. In commodities, size does matter.

Speculative risk

Similar to the bond or stock markets, the commodities are populated by traders whose primary interest is making short-term profits by speculating whether the price of a security will go up or down.

Unlike commercial users who are using the markets for hedging purposes, speculators are simply interested in making profits; thus, they tend to move the markets in different ways. Although speculators provide much-needed liquidity to the markets (particularly in commodity futures markets), they tend to increase market volatility, especially when they begin exhibiting what former Federal Reserve Chairman Alan Greenspan termed "irrational exuberance." Because speculators can get out of control, as they did during the dotcom bubble, you need to always be aware of the amount of speculative activity going on in the markets. The amount of speculative money involved in commodity markets is in constant flux, but as a general rule, most commodity futures markets consist of about 75 percent commercial users and 25 percent speculators.

Although I'm bullish on commodities because of the fundamental supply-and-demand story (which I present in Chapter 2), too much speculative money coming into the commodities markets can have detrimental effects. I anticipate that, at times, speculators will drive the prices of commodities beyond the fundamentals. If you see too much speculative activity, it's probably a good idea to simply get out of the markets.

If you trade commodities, constantly check the pulse of the markets; find out as much as possible about who the market participants are so that you can distinguish between the commercial users and the speculators. One resource I recommend is the Commitment of Traders report, put out by the Commodity Futures Trading Commission (CFTC). This report, available online at www.cftc.gov/cftc/cftccotreports.htm, gives you a detailed look at the market participants. For more information on the CFTC and other regulatory bodies, check out Chapter 8.

Corporate governance risk

As if you didn't have enough to worry about, you also need to watch out for plain and simple fraud. The CFTC and other regulatory bodies (see Chapter 8) do a decent job of protecting investors from market fraud, but the possibility of becoming a victim of fraud does exist. For example, your broker may hide debts or losses in offshore accounts, as was the case with Refco (see the nearby sidebar).

One way to prevent being taken advantage of is to be extremely vigilant about where you're putting your money. Thoroughly research a firm before you hand over your money. I go through the due diligence process to follow when selecting managers in Chapter 7. Unfortunately, sometimes no amount of research or due diligence can protect you from fraud — it's just a fact of the investment game.

The unraveling of Refco

Refco was one of the largest commodity brokers in the world. In moves not unlike the ones followed by Enron executives, the company's management hid about $400 million in debts from the public in offshore accounts right before it launched an initial public offering, to make itself attractive to public investors. When these losses were uncovered, things got completely out of hand and the company was forced into bankruptcy in 2005. This unraveling affected many individual and institutional investors.

Tracking Commodities and the 2008 Global Financial Crisis

The Global Financial Crisis (GFC) of 2008 was the equivalent of a cardiac arrest for the world economy. Just as humans need blood to survive and thrive, the global economy requires a constant stream of capital liquidity to remain robust. What started as the bursting of the real estate bubble in the United States caused a chain reaction that threatened the very foundations of the global economic system.

Origins of the crisis

The bursting of the real estate bubble had disastrous consequences in the U.S. because many consumers and households depended on stable and high real estate prices for their well-being. However, as prices dropped, so did consumer confidence and, more important, credit availability to the economy. What should have been a nasty but contained event spilled over into the capital markets in ways very few people could foresee.

A lethal combination of Wall Street's securitization machine — bundling mortgages into tradable derivative instruments — and the dissemination of such products across the world's financial institutions made this situation one of the first and worst global crises in the modern world.

When real estate prices began to drop and consumers were no longer able to afford their mortgage payments, banks holding this paper became dangerously exposed to this falling market. As prices continued to drop and bank losses continued to rise, credit availability and liquidity dried up. Banks with the worst exposure to the real estate sector were writing off assets in the tens of billions of dollars. At the height of the crisis, Citigroup alone had written off more than $60 billion in bad loans related to the real estate sector and subprime exposure. In Table 3-1, I list the top ten bank losses that are directly attributable to the housing sector.

Table 3-1 Banks' Asset Writedowns and Credit Losses, 2008

Financial Institution	Value of Writedown and Loss
Citigroup	$60.8 billion
Wachovia	$52.7 billion
Merrill Lynch	$52.2 billion
Washington Mutual	$45.6 billion
UBS	$44.2 billion
HSBC	$27.4 billion
Bank of America	$21.2 billion
JPMorgan Chase	$18.8 billion
Morgan Stanley	$15.7 billion
IKB Deutsche Industriebank	$14.8 billion

Source: Bloomberg, data up to Q4 2008

All told, total bank losses related to the subprime mess may have exceeded $2 *trillion!* And this figure is more likely much higher because many of these loan portfolios were leveraged through the use of derivatives. Indeed, the collateralized debt obligation (CDO) was a major instrument that helped spread this risk throughout the global financial system. It polluted and clogged the arteries through which global commerce takes place, with disastrous consequences for the economy.

The crisis permanently altered the banking landscape in the United States and beyond. Lehman Brothers was forced into bankruptcy on September 15, 2008, the largest bankruptcy ever recorded. JPMorgan swallowed up Bear Stearns, Bank of America gobbled up Merrill Lynch, and Goldman Sachs and Morgan Stanley were forced into becoming bank holding companies.

Overview of the crisis

Because banks provide the necessary liquidity and credit availability for the proper functioning of the global economy, this structural disruption generated massive disruptions in the real economy, the capital markets, and other asset classes, commodities included. What started as several delinquent accounts in a subsection of the real estate market ended up disrupting the world economy — and, with it, prices for everything from crude oil and aluminum to corn and soybeans.

The Lehman Brothers bankruptcy

When Lehman Brothers filed for bankruptcy on September 15, 2008, it had a devastating effect on the global economy. At one point, Lehman had been the fourth-largest investment bank in the United States, with activities in stockbrokering, bond trading, investment banking, hedge funds, real estate, and private equity. Lehman had big exposure to the real estate sector — and to subprime specifically. Because Lehman was a pure investment bank, unlike commercial banks such as JPMorgan or Citigroup, it didn't have a stable base of deposits from which to draw additional liquidity. In other words, it was highly leveraged — at one point, more than 40:1, meaning it had borrowed $40 for every $1 of assets it held — and didn't have adequate capital reserve ratios.

In the months before its bankruptcy, Lehman tried different measures to save itself, including issuing preferred stock, issuing bonds, selling a piece of itself to investors, and selling off parts of its various businesses. In the end, it wasn't able to raise enough capital, and the U.S. government (via the Treasury Department and the Federal Reserve Bank) didn't come to the rescue. Of all the controversial, shocking, and influential events of the credit crisis, the Lehman bankruptcy stands out as one of the most important events of the time. A lot of analysis has been conducted on what could have been done to save Lehman. We can only hope that the regulators and other concerned parties have learned valuable lessons to prevent future events of this nature.

As the darkest days of the crisis began to subside, the U.S. government (followed by governments around the globe) took unprecedented steps to try to stabilize the financial system. These actions included nationalizing the banks, a step so foreign in America and so incompatible with American values that many were abhorred by the government's intervention in the private sector. Figure 3-1 shows some of the steps the U.S. government — via the Federal Reserve and the Treasury — undertook to save the financial system.

Other governments also took steps to contain the crisis around the world. Iceland opted for nationalization by having the government own the banks, and Ireland, Spain, Greece, and Germany guaranteed deposits. Russia chose extra government funding, whereas Australia cut interest rates.

The purpose of this book isn't to study the credit crisis, but you need to be familiar with the events because they've had a major impact on the economy in general and commodities in particular. However, if you're interested in researching the root causes of the crisis, and for more information on the GFC and its aftermath, I recommend reading the following books:

- *The Big Short: Inside the Doomsday Machine,* by Michael Lewis (W. W. Norton & Company)
- *Too Big to Fail: The Inside Story of How Wall Street and Washington Fought to Save the Financial System — and Themselves,* by Andrew Ross Sorkin (Viking Adult)

▶ *The Greatest Trade Ever: The Behind-the-Scenes Story of How John Paulson Defied Wall Street and Made Financial History,* by Gregory Zuckerman (Crown Business)

US Bail-Out Plan

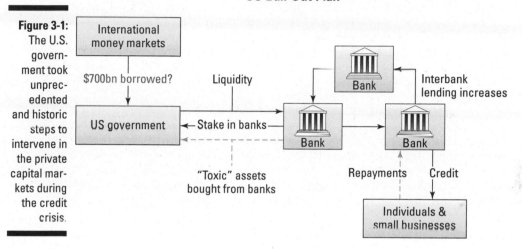

Figure 3-1: The U.S. government took unprecedented and historic steps to intervene in the private capital markets during the credit crisis.

Source: Federal Reserve Bank

In the next section, I give you some tricks of the trade and pointers to help you manage risk. That said, sometimes even the greatest risk-management techniques can't replace common sense. Many industry practitioners claim that 2008 was an unforeseeable event, one that occurs only every generation or century.

However, many industry insiders who followed the markets closely applied common sense and saw that the real estate sector was in a bubble. Investors shrewd enough saw that this housing bubble was going to have a ripple effect across asset classes because many assets were now interlinked through complex derivative instruments. And those astute investors were able to appropriately manage this risk and position their portfolios to actually benefit from this event. John Paulson, the hedge fund manager of Paulson & Co. (no relation to former Treasury Secretary Henry "Hank" Paulson), was able to manage the housing bubble risk and handsomely benefit from the downturn, returning more than 570 percent in 2008 while most other financial institutions were hemorrhaging billions of dollars in losses. Therefore, with the right judgment, analysis, and approach (and, yes, a little bit of luck), the astute and wise investor can still successfully navigate even this large-scale risk.

Managing Risk

You cannot completely eliminate risk, but you can sure take steps to help you reduce it. In this section, I go through time-proven and market-tested ways to minimize risk.

Due diligence: Just do it

One way to minimize risk is to research all aspects of the investment you're about to undertake — before you undertake it. Too often, investors don't start doing research until after they invest in commodities contracts or companies.

 Many investors buy on hype; they hear a certain commodity mentioned in the press, and they buy just because everyone else is buying. Buying on impulse is one of the most detrimental habits you can develop as an investor. Before you put your money into anything, you need to find out as much as possible about this potential investment.

Because you have a number of ways to invest in commodities (which I discuss in Chapter 5), the type of research you perform depends on the approach you take. The following sections go over the due diligence to perform for each investment methodology.

Commodity companies

One way to get exposure to commodities is to invest in companies that process commodities. Although this is an indirect way to access raw materials, it's a good approach for investors who are comfortable in the equity environment.

Ask a few questions before you buy the company's stock:

- What are the company's assets and liabilities?
- How effective is the management with the firm's capital?
- Where will the firm generate future growth?
- Where does the company generate its revenue?
- Has the company run into any regulatory problems in the past?
- What is the company's structure? (Some commodity companies are corporations, whereas others act as limited partnerships — more on these in Chapter 7.)

✔ How does the company compare with competitors?

✔ Does the company operate in regions of the world that are politically unstable?

✔ What is the company's performance across business cycles?

Of course, this list gives only a few questions to ask before making an equity investment. I go through a series of other facts and figures to gather about commodity companies in Chapter 14 (for energy companies) and Chapter 18 (for mining companies).

You can get the answers to these questions by looking through the company's annual report (Form 10K) and quarterly reports (Form 8K).

Managed funds

If you're not a hands-on investor or you simply don't have the time to actively manage your portfolio, you may want to choose a manager to do the investing for you. You can choose from a number of different managers, including the following:

✔ **Commodity mutual fund:** Manager of mutual funds that invest in commodities

✔ **Commodity pool operator:** Manager of group futures accounts

✔ **Commodity trading advisor:** Manager of individual futures accounts

Before you invest with a manager, find out as much as you can about him. Ask a few questions:

✔ What is the manager's track record?

✔ What's his investing style? Is it conservative or aggressive, and are you comfortable with it?

✔ Does he have any disciplinary actions against him?

✔ What do clients have to say about him? (It's okay to ask a manager if you can speak to one of his existing clients.)

✔ Is he registered with the appropriate regulatory bodies? (Turn to Chapter 8 for information on the regulators.)

✔ What fees does he charge? (Ask whether some fees aren't disclosed: Always watch out for hidden fees!)

✔ How much in assets does he have under management?

✔ What are his after-tax returns? (Make sure that you specify *after*-tax returns, because many managers post returns only before taxes are considered.)

✔ Are minimum time commitments involved?

✔ Are penalties assessed if you choose to withdraw your money early?

✔ Are minimum investment requirements applied?

In Chapter 7, I go through other qualifying questions to ask before choosing a manager to invest money for you.

Futures market

The futures markets play an important role in the world of commodities. They provide liquidity and allow hedgers and speculators to establish benchmark prices for the world's commodities.

If you're interested in investing through commodity futures, you need to ask a lot of questions before you get started. Consider some of these questions:

✔ On what exchange is the futures contract traded?

✔ Is there an accompanying option contract for the commodity?

✔ Is the market for the contract liquid or illiquid? (You want it to be liquid, just in case you're wondering.)

✔ Who are the main market participants?

✔ What's the expiration date for the contract you're interested in?

✔ What's the open interest for the commodity?

✔ Are there any margin requirements? If so, what are they?

To find out more about trading futures contracts, as well as options, be sure to read Chapter 9.

Commodity fundamentals

Whether you decide to invest through futures contracts, commodity companies, or managed funds, you need to gather as much information as possible about the underlying commodity itself. This caveat is perhaps the most important piece of the commodities puzzle because the performance of any investment vehicle you choose depends on the actual fundamental supply-and-demand story of the commodity.

Ask yourself a few questions before you start investing in a commodity, whether it's coffee or copper:

✔ Which country or countries hold the largest reserves of the commodity?

✔ Is the country politically stable, or is it vulnerable to turmoil?

✔ How much of the commodity is actually produced on a regular basis? (Ideally, you want to get data for the daily, monthly, quarterly, and annual basis.)

✔ Which industries or countries are the largest consumers of the commodity?

✔ What are the primary uses of the commodity?

✔ Are there any alternatives to the commodity? If so, what are they, and do they pose a significant risk to the production value of the target commodity?

✔ Do seasonal factors affect the commodity?

✔ What's the correlation between the commodity and comparable commodities in the same category?

✔ What are the historical production and consumption cycles for the commodity?

These questions are only a few to ask before you invest in any commodity. Ideally, you want to be able to gather this information before you start trading.

Diversify, diversify, diversify

One of the best ways to manage risk is to diversify. This strategy applies on a number of levels: both diversification *among* asset classes, such as bonds, stocks, and commodities; and diversification *within* an asset class, such as diversifying commodity holdings among energy and metals.

For diversification to have the desired effects on your portfolio (to minimize risk), you want to have asset classes that perform differently. One of the benefits of using commodities to minimize your overall portfolio risk is that commodities tend to behave differently than stocks and bonds. For example, as you can see in Figure 3-2, the performance of commodities and equities is remarkably different. This fact means that when stocks aren't doing well, you'll at least have your portfolio exposed to an asset class that is performing.

Managed funds: Another one (or two) bites the dust

While I was writing *Commodities For Dummies,* 1st Edition the prices of certain commodities, such as crude oil, natural gas, and gold, were in an upward trend line that seemed endless. Of course, every rally eventually comes to an end, either to take a breather before rallying again or to falter and break down completely. Such was the case with natural gas prices during the summer and early fall of 2006. Natural gas prices, which are notoriously volatile because natural gas is hard to store (see Chapter 12), broke down after a six-month rally. Several hedge funds were forced to close because of their exposure to natural gas futures.

Hedge funds, and a number of other financial institutions, poured billions of dollars into commodities such as natural gas and copper to profit from — and, naturally, contribute to — the bull market in commodities. Hedge funds generally have a high tolerance for risk and aren't afraid to enter into highly leveraged positions (through the use of high margin). Two funds that were exposed to heavy losses were caught against the tide trading natural gas futures contracts in the middle of 2006.

The first fund to suffer massive losses was MotherRock Energy Fund, a half-billion-dollar hedge fund that specializes in energy futures. MotherRock placed huge bets that the price of natural gas was going to drop; it was correct, of course, except that it got the timing wrong — natural gas prices rallied a few more weeks before they dropped. MotherRock's unfortunate timing meant that the fund lost $100 million in June 2006 and another $100 million in July 2006. Having lost half its total capital in two months, the fund was forced to shut down.

The second fund that fell victim to wild natural gas price swings was a much larger, multistrategy hedge fund based in Greenwich, Connecticut, called Amaranth Advisors. Amaranth, a fund with approximately $10 billion in assets, invests in various markets, not simply commodities. Its multistrategy focus allows it to enter any market it believes is promising. The company entered the natural gas market, hoping that its previous successes would allow it to profit in this market as well. Amaranth bet that the prices of natural gas futures would increase; unfortunately for Amaranth (and its investors), natural gas prices decreased, and it was caught on the wrong side of the natural gas tide. As a result, Amaranth lost a whopping $3 billion!

A number of lessons can be gleamed from these hedge fund debacles. First, natural gas futures are extremely volatile. Second, use leverage at your own risk. Third, overconcentration (putting all your eggs in one basket) can be devastating. These sorts of losses are few and far between, but they remind the investor that investing can be very rewarding but also very dangerous if not done properly. At the end of the day, if you're going to invest by using margin in volatile commodities, you need to be ready for both spectacular wins and devastating losses.

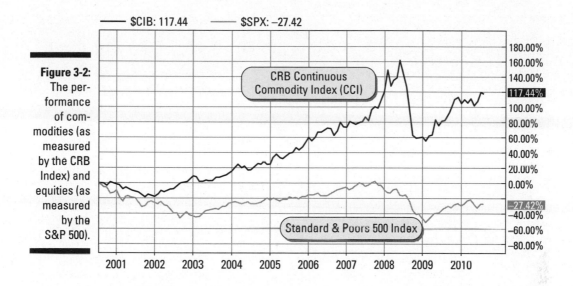

Figure 3-2: The performance of commodities (as measured by the CRB Index) and equities (as measured by the S&P 500).

To find out more about how the performance of commodities compares to that of other assets and how this benefits you, check out Chapter 4.

Chapter 4

Feel the Love: Welcoming Commodities into Your Portfolio

*W*hether you're an experienced investor or a first-time trader, it's important to have a good grasp on how to use your portfolio to improve your overall financial situation. When designing your portfolio, you need to consider factors such as your risk tolerance, tax bracket, and level of liabilities. I start off this chapter by going through these basic portfolio-management techniques so that you can synchronize your portfolio with your personal financial profile.

In the second half of the chapter, I show you how to introduce commodities into your portfolio. I go through basic portfolio-allocation methods and include an overview of the benefits of diversification. In the last part of the chapter, I list the different investment methods you have at your disposal to get exposure to commodities, from index funds to master limited partnerships.

If you've ever wondered how to actually include commodities in your portfolio, you can't afford to skip this chapter!

The Color of Money: Taking Control of Your Financial Life

You invest because you've realized that it's better to have your money working for you than to have it sit in a bank account earning so little interest that you end up losing money when you factor in inflation. Most people end up working for their money all their lives, and they get stuck in a vicious cycle where they become servants to money.

If you're caught in this vicious cycle, you want your relationship with money to do a 180-degree reversal: Instead of working hard for your money, you need to have your money work hard for you! Investing allows you to build and, more important, maintain your wealth. (In the following sections, I show you how to use commodities to achieve this goal.)

Building wealth isn't easy, but with a little discipline and self-control, it can be a fun and rewarding process. If you're new to investing in general, check out Eric Tyson's *Personal Finance For Dummies* and *Investing For Dummies* (Wiley) for foundational information and guidance.

Often the accumulation phase isn't the biggest challenge to building wealth; many times being able to preserve wealth is more difficult. Keep in mind these factors that can negatively impact your bottom line:

- ✔ **Inflation:** *Inflation,* an increase in prices or the money supply, which can result in a quick deterioration of value, is one of the most detrimental forces you face as an investor. Inflation keeps some of the brightest minds up at night; among them is the Chairman of the Federal Reserve, whose main priority is making sure that the economy doesn't grow so fast that it creates bad inflation. When inflation gets out of control, the currency literally isn't worth the paper it's printed on. This state, known as *hyperinflation,* occurred in Weimar Germany in the 1920s. At its worst, people placed paper money in their stoves to heat themselves during the winter because the money burned longer than wood. Conveniently, one way to protect yourself from inflation is to invest in commodities such as gold and silver. (Turn to Chapter 15 for more on using precious metals as a hedge against inflation.)

- ✔ **Business cycles:** In the world of investing, nothing ever goes up in a straight line. Minor turbulence always arises along the way, and most investments usually experience some drops before they reach new highs — that is, if they ever reach new highs! The economy moves in the same way, alternating between expansions and recessions. Certain assets that perform well during expansions (such as stocks) don't do so well during recessions. Alternatively, assets such as commodities do fairly well during late expansionary and early recessionary phases of the business cycle. As an investor interested in preserving and growing your capital base, you need to be able to identify and invest in assets that are going to perform and generate returns, regardless of the current business cycle. I discuss the performance of commodities across the business cycle in Chapter 2.

You can minimize these risks and others, such as risks posed by fraud, the markets, and geopolitics, with some due diligence and a few wise decisions. I look at risk as it relates to both commodities and investing in general in Chapter 3.

Looking Ahead: Creating a Financial Road Map

Building wealth through investing takes a lot of time, effort, and discipline — unlike winning the lottery or getting a large inheritance. Achieving your financial goals takes a conscious and systematic effort. Of course, the first part is identifying and establishing your financial goals. These goals may be as diverse as amassing enough money to retire by age 50 and travel the world, to gathering enough money to pay for college, or to making enough money to pass on to your children or grandchildren. Before you start investing in commodities (or any other asset), sit down and figure out clear financial goals. Every individual has different needs and interests. In the following sections, I outline some key points to help you establish your financial goals.

After you identify your goals, you can begin figuring out how to use commodities to achieve those goals. I show you how in the section "Making Room in Your Portfolio for Commodities."

Figuring out your net worth

You need to know where you are before you can determine where you want to go. From a personal finance perspective, you need to know how much you're worth so that you can determine how much capital to allocate to investments, living expenses, retirement, and so on.

You calculate your net worth by subtracting your total liabilities from your total assets. (*Assets* put money in your pocket, whereas *liabilities* remove money from your pocket.)

Fill in the blanks in Table 4-1 to determine the total value of your assets.

Table 4-1 Total Assets	
Assets	*Value*
Annuities	$_____
Bonds and other fixed income	$_____
Cash in all checking and savings accounts	$_____
Cash on hand	$_____
Certificates of deposit (CDs)	$_____
Commodity investments	$_____
Futures and options	$_____
Individual retirement accounts (IRAs)	$_____
Life insurance	$_____
Money market funds	$_____
Market value of home	$_____
Market value of other real estate	$_____
Mutual funds	$_____
Pension plans (401(k) and/or 403(b))	$_____
Personal belongings (home furnishings, jewelry, and so on)	$_____
Stocks and other equity	$_____
Vehicles (car, boat, and so on)	$_____
Other investment assets	$_____
TOTAL VALUE OF ASSETS	$_____

Assets are only one part of the net worth equation. After you calculate your total assets, you need to determine how many liabilities you have. Use Table 4-2 to help you determine your total liabilities.

Table 4-2 Total Liabilities	
Liabilities	*Value*
Car loans	$_____
College loans	$_____
Credit card loans	$_____
Mortgage(s)	$_____

Liabilities	Value
Mortgage equity line	$_____
Other loans	$_____
TOTAL VALUE OF LIABILITIES	$_____

After you determine both your total assets and total liabilities, use the following formula to determine your total net worth:

Total net worth = Total assets – Total liabilities

 Determining your net worth on a regular basis is important because it allows you to keep track of the balance between your assets and liabilities. Knowing your net worth allows you to then determine which investment strategy to pursue.

 Based on this simple mathematical formula, the key to increasing your net worth is to increase your assets while reducing your liabilities. Investing helps you increase your assets. Cutting down on living expenses may help you reduce your liabilities.

Identifying your tax bracket

Taxes have a direct impact on how much of your assets you get to keep at the end of the day. You must understand the implications that taxes can have on your portfolio.

How much you pay in taxes is based on your tax bracket. Table 4-3 lists the individual income tax brackets to help you determine how much you'll end up paying in taxes based on your income.

Table 4-3   2010 Income Tax Rate Schedule (Federal Level)

Annual Taxable Income	Tax Level
$0–$8,375	10%
$8,375–$34,000	15%
$34,000–$82,400	25%
$82,400–$171,850	28%
$171,850–$373,650	33%
$373,650+	35%

The tax rate schedule in Table 4-3 is known as Schedule X, and it applies to you if you're filing your tax return as a single person. The Internal Revenue Service (IRS) has a number of different schedules, depending on how you're filing your returns.

- ✔ **Schedule Y-1:** Married and filing jointly *or* qualifying widow(er)
- ✔ **Schedule Y-2:** Married and filing separately
- ✔ **Schedule Z:** Head of household

Tax rates change depending on which schedule you file under. Visit the IRS Web site, at www.irs.gov, or talk to your accountant to find out the tax rates under the different schedules. Because tax rates may change on an annual basis, inquire about these tax issues regularly.

Where you live can also have a big impact on how taxes affect your investments. Did you know that a number of states within the continental United States don't have income taxes? As a resident of one of these states, you pay federal income taxes but no state income taxes, so no one will blame you for considering relocation. These states have absolutely no income tax, which means you get to keep more of what you earn!

- ✔ Alaska
- ✔ Florida
- ✔ Nevada
- ✔ New Hampshire
- ✔ South Dakota
- ✔ Tennessee
- ✔ Texas
- ✔ Washington
- ✔ Wyoming

Out of the nine states that don't have personal income taxes, Florida does place a tax on intangible personal property. Thus, items such as stocks, bonds, and mutual funds are subject to taxes. Also note that New Hampshire and Tennessee both tax income earned on interest and dividends.

Investing in commodities, as in any other asset class, has tax implications. I'm not an accountant, and the aim of this book isn't to offer you tax advice, so I recommend that you talk to your accountant before you invest in commodities. Knowing the tax implications before you invest may save you a lot of heartache down the road.

Determining your appetite for risk

Risk is perhaps the single greatest enemy you face as an investor. How wonderful would life be if you could have guaranteed returns without risk? Because that's not possible (and has never been possible), you have to find how to manage, tame, and minimize risk. I devote a whole chapter to managing risk related to commodities (see Chapter 3), but I briefly discuss general portfolio risk in this section.

Your risk tolerance depends on a number of factors that are unique to you as an individual. The first step in determining your risk tolerance is deciding how much risk you're willing to take on. Although no equation or formula can determine risk (it would be nice if there were one), you can use a general rule to identify the percentage of your assets to dedicate to aggressive investments with an elevated risk/reward ratio.

As a general rule, the younger you are, the higher your percentage of assets should be devoted to higher-risk investments. This approach makes sense because if you lose a lot of value, you still have a lot of time ahead of you to recoup your losses. When you're older, however, you don't have as much time to get back your investments.

Table 4-4 gives you a simple guideline to help you determine the percentage of assets that should go into investments with higher returns (and risks), such as stocks, commodities, and real estate. This is *not* a percentage of how much of your portfolio you should invest in commodities; I discuss that percentage in the following section.

Table 4-4	Recommended Percentage of Assets in Growth Investments by Age Group
Age Group	**Percentage in Growth Investments**
0–20	Up to 90%
20–30	80%–90%
31–40	70%–80%
41–50	60%–70%
51–64	45%–60%
65 and over	Less than 45%

The rules in Table 4-4 aren't set in stone, but you can use them to approximate how much of your assets to place in investments that have a high risk/reward ratio. If your investments are increasing just fine with the percentages you're working with, don't change them! As the saying goes, if it's not broken, don't try to fix it.

Making Room in Your Portfolio for Commodities

One of the most common questions I get from investors is, "How much of my portfolio should I have in commodities?" My answer is usually simple: It depends. To answer that question, you have to take into account a number of factors to determine how much capital to dedicate to commodities.

Personally, my portfolio may include at any one point anywhere between 35 and 50 percent commodities. However, sometimes it's much lower than that — and sometimes almost 90 percent of my portfolio is in commodities!

If you're new to commodities, I recommend starting out with a relatively modest amount — anywhere between 3 and 5 percent of your portfolio — to see how comfortable you feel with this new member of your financial family. Test how commodities contribute to your overall portfolio's performance during one or two investing quarters. If you're satisfied, I recommend that you gradually increase your percentage.

Many investors who like the way commodities anchor their portfolios settle at about 15 percent exposure to commodities. I find that's a pretty good place to be if you're still getting used to commodities. When you see the benefits and realize how much value commodities can provide, I'll bet that number will steadily increase.

Figure 4-1 shows a hypothetical portfolio that includes commodities along with other asset classes. This could be a sample portfolio for an average investor who wants exposure to both liquid and nonliquid (real estate) assets. A diversified portfolio such as this one helps reduce the overall volatility of your market exposures. Having unrelated assets increases your chances of maintaining good returns when a certain asset underperforms.

Modern Portfolio Theory and the benefits of diversification

The idea that diversification is a good strategy in portfolio allocation is the cornerstone of Modern Portfolio Theory (MPT). MPT is the brainchild of Nobel Prize–winning economist Harry Markowitz. In a paper he wrote in 1952 for his doctoral thesis, Markowitz argued that investors must look at a portfolio's overall risk/reward ratio. Although this sounds like common sense today, it was a groundbreaking idea at the time.

Before Markowitz's paper, most investors constructed their portfolios based on a risk/reward ratio analysis of individual securities. Investors chose a security based on its individual risk profile and ignored how that risk profile fit within a broader portfolio. Markowitz argued (successfully) that investors could construct more profitable portfolios if they looked at the overall risk/reward ratio of their portfolios.

Therefore, when considering an individual security, you need to not only assess its individual risk profile, but also take into account how that risk profile fits within your general investment strategy. Markowitz's idea that holding a group of different securities reduces a portfolio's overall volatility is one of the most important ideas in portfolio allocation.

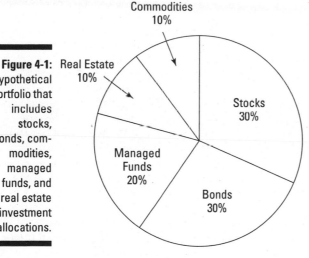

Figure 4-1: Hypothetical portfolio that includes stocks, bonds, commodities, managed funds, and real estate investment allocations.

Commodities 10%

Real Estate 10%

Stocks 30%

Managed Funds 20%

Bonds 30%

Fully Exposed: The Top Ways to Get Exposure to Commodities

You have several methods at your disposal, both direct and indirect, for getting exposure to commodities. In this section, I go through the different ways you can invest in commodities. You can find more information on these investment options in Part II.

Looking toward the future with commodity futures

The futures markets are the most direct way to get exposure to commodities. Futures contracts allow you to purchase an underlying commodity for an agreed-upon price in the future. I talk about futures contracts in depth in Chapter 9. In this section, I list some ways you can play the futures markets.

Commodity index

Commodity indexes track a basket of commodity futures contracts. Each index uses a different methodology and performs differently than its peers. Commodity indexes are known as passive, long-only investments because they're not actively managed and they can only buy the underlying commodity; they can't short it. (For more on going long and going short, turn to Chapter 9.)

You can choose from these five major commodity indexes:

- Deutsche Bank Liquid Commodity Index (DBLCI)
- Dow Jones–AIG Commodity Index (DJ-AIGCI)
- Goldman Sachs Commodity Index (GSCI)
- Reuters/Jefferies Commodity Research Bureau Index (R/J-CRBI)
- Rogers International Commodity Index (RICI)

I analyze the components, performance, and construction methodology of each of these indexes in Chapter 6.

Futures commission merchant

Don't be intimidated by the name — a *futures commission merchant* (FCM) is much like a regular stockbroker. However, instead of selling stocks, an FCM is licensed to sell futures contracts, options, and other derivatives to the public.

If you're comfortable trading futures and options contracts, opening an account with an FCM gives you the most direct access to the commodity futures markets. Make sure that you read Chapter 6 to find out the pros and cons of investing through an FCM.

Commodity trading advisor

A *commodity trading advisor* (CTA) is an individual who manages accounts for clients who trade futures contracts. The CTA may provide advice on how to place your trades, but he may also manage your account on your behalf. Be sure to research the CTA's track record and investment philosophy so that you know whether it squares with yours.

CTAs may manage accounts for more than one client. However, they're not allowed to "pool" accounts and share all profits and losses among clients equally. (This is one of the main differences between a CTA and a CPO, discussed in the next section.)

Chapter 6 can help you identify key elements to look for when shopping for a CTA.

Commodity pool operator

The *commodity pool operator* (CPO) acts a lot like a CTA, except that, instead of managing separate accounts, the CPO has the authority to "pool" all client funds in one account and trade them as if she were trading one account.

Investing through a CPO offers two advantages over investing through a CTA:

- ✔ Because CPOs can pool funds, they have access to more funds to invest. This pooling provides both leverage and diversification opportunities that smaller accounts don't offer. You can buy a lot more assets with $100,000 than with $10,000.

- ✔ Most CPOs are structured as partnerships, which means that the only money you can lose is your principal. In the world of futures, this is pretty good because, due to margin and the use of leverage, you can end up owing a lot more than the principal if a trade goes sour. Be sure to read Chapter 9 for more on margin and leverage.

I walk through the pros and cons of investing through a CPO in Chapter 7.

Funding your account with commodity funds

If you think delving into commodity derivatives isn't for you, you can access the commodity markets through funds. If you've invested before, you may be familiar with these two investment vehicles.

Commodity mutual funds

Commodity mutual funds are exactly like average, run-of-the-mill mutual funds, except that they focus specifically on investing in commodities. You can choose from several funds, although the two biggest ones are the PIMCO and the Oppenheimer funds. (I examine commodity mutual funds in Chapter 7.)

A 2005 ruling by the Securities and Exchange Commission (SEC) changed the way mutual funds account for qualifying income. This ruling has put some pressure on funds, particularly PIMCO, to come up with different accounting methods. Make sure you find out how such rulings affect your investments.

Exchange-traded funds

Exchange-traded funds (ETFs) have become popular with investors because they provide the benefits of investing in a fund with the ease of trading a stock. This hybrid instrument is becoming one of the best ways for investors to access the commodities markets.

The world of commodity ETFs is fairly new and is constantly changing. Because this is such a dynamic field, I have a section called ETF Watch on my Web site (www.commodities-investors.com) that I encourage you to check out, to stay up-to-date on everything that's happening in the world of ETFs.

You currently have at your disposal ETFs that track baskets of commodities through commodity indexes, as well as ETFs that track single commodities such as oil, gold, and silver. I list some popular commodity ETFs in Table 4-5.

Table 4-5	Commodity ETFs
ETF	**Description**
Deutsche Bank Commodity Index Tracking Fund (DBC)	Tracks the performance of the Deutsche Bank Commodity Index
US Oil Fund (USO)	Mirrors the movements of the WTI crude oil on the NYMEX
Street Tracks Gold Shares (GLD)	Tracks the performance of gold bullion
iShares COMEX Gold Trust (IAU)	Tracks the performance of gold futures contracts on the COMEX
iShares Silver Trust (SLV)	Tracks the performance of silver

Make sure you examine all fees associated with the ETF before you invest. Check out Chapter 5 for more information on this investment vehicle.

You're in good company: Investing in commodity companies

Another route you can take to get exposure to commodities is to buy stocks of commodity companies. These companies are generally involved in the production, transformation, or distribution of various commodities.

This route is perhaps the most indirect way of accessing the commodity markets because, in buying a company's stock, you're getting exposure not only to the performance of the underlying commodity that the company is involved in, but also other factors, such as the company's management skills, creditworthiness, and ability to generate cash flow and minimize expenses.

Publicly traded companies

Publicly traded companies can give you exposure to specific sectors of commodities, such as metals, energy, or agricultural products. Within these three categories, you can choose companies that deal with specific methods or commodities, such as refiners of crude oil into finished products or gold-mining companies.

If you're considering an equity stake in a commodity company, you need to determine how the company's stock performs relative to the price of the underlying commodity that company is involved in.

Although there's no hard rule, I've found a relatively strong correlation between the performance of commodity futures contracts and the performance of companies that use these commodities as inputs.

So investing in the stock of commodity companies actually gives you pretty good exposure to the underlying commodities themselves. However, you want to be extra careful and to perform thorough due diligence before you invest in these companies. I show you some keys to look for before you invest in such companies in Chapters 14 and 18.

Master limited partnerships

Master limited partnerships (MLPs) are a hybrid instrument that offers you the convenience of trading a partnership like a stock. You get the best of both worlds: the liquidity that comes from being a publicly traded entity and the tax protection of being a partnership.

One of the biggest advantages of MLPs is that, as a unit holder, you are taxed at only the individual level. This structure is different than if you invest in a corporation, because cash back to shareholders (in the form of dividends) is taxed at both the corporate level and the individual level. MLPs don't pay any corporate tax, which is a huge benefit for your bottom line.

For an MLP to qualify for these tax breaks, it must generate 90 percent of its income from qualifying sources that relate to commodities, particularly in the oil and gas industry.

Some of the popular assets that MLPs invest in include oil and gas storage facilities and transportation infrastructure such as pipelines. I cover MLPs in detail in Chapter 7.

Part II
Getting Started with Types of Investment Vehicles

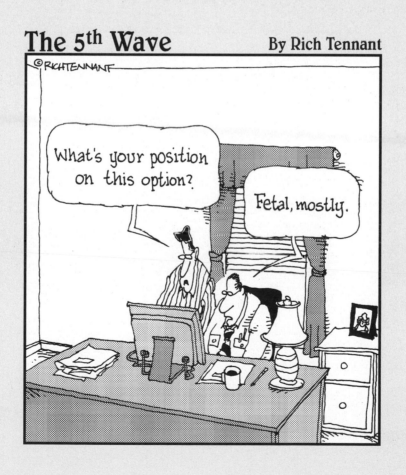

The 5th Wave   By Rich Tennant

In this part . . .

*W*hether you're an experienced investor or a beginning trader, having a good grasp of portfolio allocation and design methodology is critical for your success. In this part, you discover the best strategies, trading techniques, and investment vehicles to help you profit in the commodities markets.

Chapter 5

Benefiting from Exchange-Traded Funds

Driven by growing investor demand for commodities, many financial institutions are now offering the commodities *exchange-traded fund* (ETF). This new breed of fund enables you to buy into a fund that offers the diversification inherent in a mutual fund and the added benefit of being able to trade that fund like a regular stock. Thus, you get a powerful combination of diversification and liquidity. ETFs are becoming popular with investors because they provide the benefits of investing in a fund with the ease of trading a stock. This hybrid instrument is becoming one of the best ways for investors to access the commodities markets.

Getting to Know ETFs

ETFs offer many advantages to investors because they offer exposure to asset classes and specific investments that would otherwise be difficult for the average investor to access, such as uranium or palladium. In addition, they give you a broad diversification platform because they can track a basket of stocks or commodities. This characteristic is a major reason ETFs have become so popular in the last decade, increasing from several dozen to more than 2,500 ETF products.

Unlike a regular mutual fund, in which the net asset value is generally calculated at the end of the trading day, the ETF enables you to trade throughout the day. Furthermore, you can go both long and short the ETF, something you can't do with regular mutual funds. (For more on going long and short, turn to Chapter 9.)

It's critical to perform extensive due diligence on any ETF product you're considering for your portfolio. You need a solid understanding of the underlying assets in the ETF. Often beginning investors simply browse the description without getting a good grip on what they're actually buying. For example, the current uranium ETF URA (NYSE: URA) isn't a product that tracks uranium metal prices; it tracks a basket of uranium-mining equities. Folks who don't get into the fine print may miss basic yet critical pieces of information regarding ETFs specifically and broader investment products in general. Make sure you go beyond the headlines and into the fine print!

ETFs aren't free, in the sense that they're actively managed products associated with a financial institution. ETF sponsors generally charge an added layer of fees for the convenience of using their products. Therefore, it's imperative to know the types of fees associated with each ETF you purchase. This information is conveniently located in the fund's prospectus.

Deutsche Bank launched the first commodity index ETF in the United States in February 2006. The *Deutsche Bank Commodity Index Tracking Fund* (AMEX: DBC) is listed on the American Stock and Options Exchange (AMEX) and tracks the Deutsche Bank Liquid Commodity Index (DBLCI). The DBLCI, in turn, tracks a basket of six liquid commodities:

- ✔ Light, sweet crude oil (35 percent)
- ✔ Heating oil (20 percent)
- ✔ Aluminum (12.5 percent)
- ✔ Corn (11.25 percent)
- ✔ Wheat (11.25 percent)
- ✔ Gold (10 percent)

You can see the performance of the DBC in Figure 5-1; clearly, the DBC is a superb indicator of the broader commodity markets. The story of commodities since 2005 is characterized by a massive run-up in prices, driven partly by large consumption demands from emerging markets such as China and by speculative activity. That price run-up resulted in a massive bursting of asset bubbles in 2008 during the Global Financial Crisis. Commodities, like almost every other tradable asset class, suffered a shocking downward dislocation when liquidity dried up; the DBC accurately portrays this turn of events.

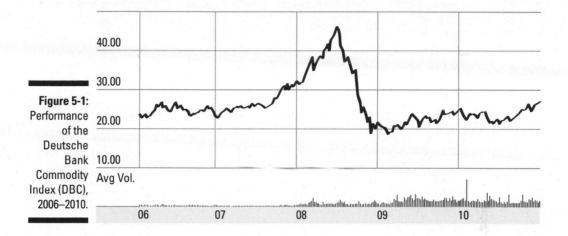

Figure 5-1:
Performance
of the
Deutsche
Bank
Commodity
Index (DBC),
2006–2010.

The DBC ETF is structured as a commodity pool operator (CPO), and the fund invests directly in commodity futures contracts. (See Chapter 7 for more on commodity pools.) To capture additional yields, the energy contracts are rolled monthly; the rest of the contracts are rolled annually. (Chapter 9 gives you more on rolling futures contracts.) The fund also invests in fixed-income products, including the three-month Treasury bill, which provides an additional yield for investors. With an expense ratio of 1.5 percent, it's a reasonably priced investment.

Accessing a Variety of Commodity Markets through ETFs

One of the downsides of investing in ETFs is that they can be fairly volatile because they track derivative instruments that trade in the futures markets. A downside of the DBC specifically (see the preceding section) is that it tracks a basket of only six commodities. However, more commodity ETFs are in the pipeline that will offer greater diversification benefits. In Table 5-1, I list some of the more common ETFs available. As you can see, you can now access a broad variety of commodity markets through ETFs, ranging from livestock and natural gas all the way to uranium and palladium.

Table 5-1	List of Commodity ETFs	
ETF	*Category*	*Ticker*
Dow Jones–AIG Commodity Index Total Return	Broad index	NYSE: DJP
Deutsche Bank Commodity Index Tracking Fund	Broad index	NYSE: DBC
Goldman Sachs Commodity Index Total Return	Broad index	NYSE: GSG
Dow Jones–AIG Agriculture Total Return ETN	Agriculture index	NYSE: JJA
streetTRACKS Gold Shares ETF	Gold	NYSE: GLD
iShares Gold Trust ETF	Gold	NYSE: IAU
iShares Silver Trust Fund	Silver	NYSE: SLV
Dow Jones–AIG Aluminum ETN	Aluminum	NYSE: JJU
United States Natural Gas Fund	Natural gas	NYSE: UNG
United States Oil Fund	Crude oil	NYSE: USO
Dow Jones–AIG Livestock Total Return ETN	Livestock index	NYSE: COW
ETFS Physical Palladium Shares ETF	Palladium	NYSE: PALL
ETFS Physical Platinum Shares ETF	Platinum	NYSE: PPLT
Global X Global Gold Explorers ETF	Gold exploration	NYSE: GLDX
Global X Global Silver Explorers ETF	Silver exploration	NYSE: SIL
Global X Lithium ETF	Lithium metal	NYSE: LIT
Global X Uranium ETF	Uranium metal	NYSE: URA
Emerging Global Energy Titans Index	Energy companies	NYSE: EEO

As commodities become a more accepted asset class, I expect more ETFs to launch and be available for you to trade. For the latest on ETF products, check out www.commodities-investors.com.

These ETFs are some of the most popular ones in the marketplace today.

> ✔ **United States Oil Fund (AMEX: USO):** The *Unites States Oil Fund (USO)* is an ETF that seeks to mirror the performance of the West Texas Intermediate (WTI) crude oil futures contract on the New York Mercantile Exchange (NYMEX). Although the ETF doesn't reflect the movement of the WTI contract tick by tick, it does a good job of broadly mirroring its performance. It's a good way to get exposure to crude oil without going through the futures markets. You can see the performance of the USO in Figure 5-2.

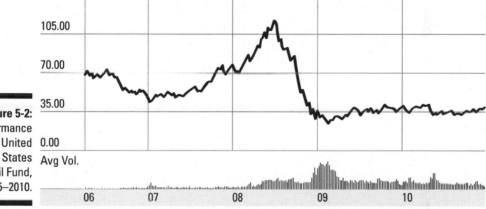

Figure 5-2: Performance of the United States Oil Fund, 2006–2010.

> ✔ **streetTRACKS Gold Shares (AMEX: GLD):** This ETF seeks to mirror the performance of the price of gold on a daily basis. The fund actually holds physical gold in vaults located in secure locations, to give investors the ability to get exposure to physical gold without having to hold gold bullion. You can see the performance of the GLD in Figure 5-3.
>
> ✔ **iShares Silver Trust (AMEX: SLV):** This ETF is the first ever to track the performance of the price of physical silver. Like the gold ETF, the silver ETF holds actual physical silver in vaults. It's a safe way to invest in the silver markets without going through the futures or physical markets. You can see the performance of the SLV in Figure 5-4.

Another newcomer to the ETF marketplace is the Aluminum ETF, launched by Dow Jones & AIG. Aluminum has always been an important metal because it's one of the building blocks of construction, industry, and infrastructure.

With many important uses and applications, investors and traders worldwide closely follow this metal. For the first time, investors can get exposure to this important metal; you can see its performance in 2010 in Figure 5-5.

I like this ETF for active traders because it's a fairly volatile metal, as you can see in Figure 5-5. You can play the momentum in your favor in order to actively trade it.

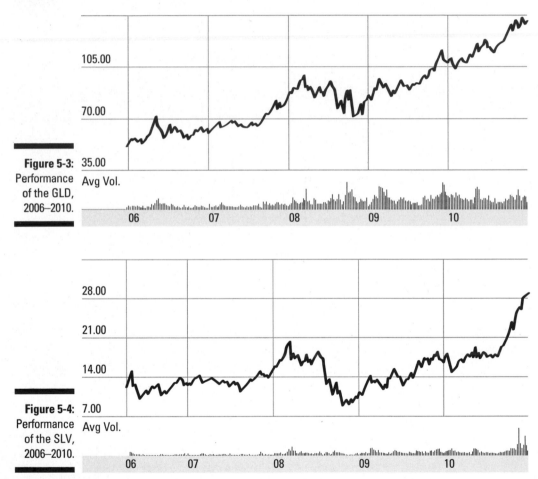

Figure 5-3:
Performance
of the GLD,
2006–2010.

Figure 5-4:
Performance
of the SLV,
2006–2010.

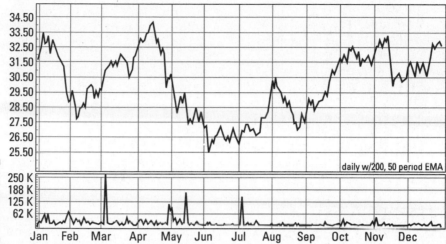

Figure 5-5:
Performance
of Aluminum
ETF, 2010.

daily w/200, 50 period EMA

Taking a Look at Leveraged ETFs

A new breed of ETFs is emerging and is having a major impact on the ETF and commodity landscapes: *leveraged* ETFs. As the name suggests, leveraged ETFs (or LETFs, for short) seek to boost the returns of the underlying asset by using an added layer of leverage. LETFs often do this through futures, options, and swaps, to enhance returns. The leverage can go both ways, both long and short, so it has a certain degree of versatility that investors find appealing and that has boosted the popularity of this new breed.

However, LETFs have also come under strong criticism by industry insiders for the massive use of leverage. Leverage is a double-edged sword, possibly enhancing your returns on the way up, but ushering in potential catastrophe on the way down. Professional investment advisors warn their clients about the responsible use of leverage, and if you're not an experienced trader, I also recommend that you tread carefully with LETFs.

If you're gung-ho about using LETFs, consult your financial advisor and carefully read the fine print in the prospectus to get a solid understanding of the type and degree of leverage used. In some cases, ETFs use *double* leverage — that's right, leverage ×2 — to further enhance returns. My advice is, if you don't have a crystal clear grasp of leverage, steer clear of products that use this mechanism.

Chapter 6

Track and Trade: Investing through Commodity Indexes

*I*ndexes are useful tools in the world of investing. If investing were similar to driving a car, the index would be the equivalent of the speedometer — it tells you how fast the car (or the market) is going. Indexes exist for all sorts of assets: The two most well-known indexes track the top 30 blue-chip companies in the United States (Dow Jones Industrial Average) and the 500 largest companies (S&P 500), but plenty of others await investors, too.

If you want to measure the performance of commodities, you also have at your disposal indexes that track baskets of commodities. These commodity indexes can be useful for two reasons. First, you can use them as market indicators, to help you gauge where the commodity markets are trading as a whole. Second, because most indexes are tradable instruments (through exchange-traded funds and other investment vehicles), you can profit by investing directly in the index.

In this chapter, I give you the goods on commodity indexes and show you how to profit by using these powerful tools.

Checking Out Commodity Indexes

A commodity index tracks the price of a futures contract of an underlying physical commodity on a designated exchange. When you invest through one of the commodity indexes I present in this chapter, you're actually investing in the futures markets. (For more on futures contracts, check out Chapter 9.)

Indexes are known as passive, long-only investments, for two reasons: No one is actively trading the index, and the index tracks only the long performance of a commodity. It doesn't track commodities that are *short* (a sophisticated strategy meant to profit when prices go down). For more on long and short positions, flip to Chapter 9.

Is it *indexes* or *indices*? I use the plural form *indexes* because that's the more traditional form, but you may also run into *indices* as a plural alternative. Dow Jones, which has its own commodity index, spells the plural form of *index* as *indexes*. On the other hand, Standard & Poor's, which also has a commodity index, spells the plural form as *indices*. No matter how you spell them, though, at the end of the day, *indexes* and *indices* refer to the same thing.

Why indexes are useful

Using commodity indexes is a good way to determine where the commodity markets are heading. Just as stock indexes allow you to identify broad market movements (which then enables you to implement and update your investment strategy accordingly), commodity indexes give you a way to measure the broad movements of the commodities markets.

In essence, a commodity index gives you a snapshot of the current state of the commodities market. You can use an index in one of three ways:

- ✔ **Benchmark:** You can use a commodity index to compare the performance of commodities as an asset class with the performance of other asset classes, such as stocks and bonds.

- ✔ **Indicator:** You can use the commodity index as an indicator of economic activity, possible inflationary pressures, and the state of global economic production.

- ✔ **Investment vehicle:** Because a commodity index tracks the performance of specific futures contracts, you can replicate the performance of the index by trading the contracts it tracks. You can invest in a commodity index both directly (by buying the contracts) and indirectly (via mutual funds); I discuss those options in depth in the following section.

How to make money by using an index

You can invest through a commodity index by using a number of methods. You can choose from five widely followed commodity indexes (I cover these in the section "Cataloguing the Five Major Indexes," later in this chapter), and each one is tracked and traded differently.

Consider a few ways you can invest through a commodity index:

- **Own the futures contracts.** One of the most direct ways of tracking the performance of an index is to own the contracts the index tracks. To do this, you must have a *futures account*. (Refer to Chapter 8 to find out how to open a futures account.)

- **Invest with a third-party manager.** Many money managers use commodity indexes as the basis of their investment strategy. Some of these vehicles include mutual funds, commodity pools, and commodity trading advisors. (For more on selecting the right manager, be sure to read Chapter 7.)

- **Own futures contracts of the index.** A few commodity indexes have futures contracts that track their performance. When you buy the futures contract of the index, it's similar to buying all the commodity futures contracts the index trades!

- **Make use of exchange-traded funds.** ETFs, as they're known on Wall Street, are a fairly new breed of investment that tracks the performance of a fund through the convenience of trading a stock. ETFs are a popular alternative for folks who don't want to trade futures. (Be sure to explore the benefits and drawbacks of ETFs in Chapter 5.)

Here I list only a few ways you can get exposure to commodity indexes. As commodities become more popular with the investing community, expect to see more ways to get access to indexes. To keep track of all the new developments in index investing, keep checking my Web site, at www.commodities-investors.com.

From Head to Toe: Uncovering the Anatomy of a Commodity Index

As an investor interested in making money through index investing, you have five commodity indexes at your disposal. Although the composition and structure of every index is different, the aim is the same: to track a basket of commodities. Before you get into the specific commodity indexes, watch out for these pitfalls when you're shopping for an index:

- ✓ **Components:** Each index follows a specific methodology to determine which commodities are part of the index. Some indexes, such as the S&P GSCI (see the following section), include commodities based on their global *production value.* Other indexes, such as the DBLCI, include commodities based on their *liquidity* and *representational value* of a component class, such as picking gold to represent metals and choosing oil as a representative of the energy market.

- ✓ **Weightings:** Some indexes follow a *production-weighted methodology,* in which weights are assigned to each commodity based on its proportional production in the world. Other indexes choose *component weightings* based on the liquidity of the commodity's futures contract. In addition, some weightings are fixed over a predetermined period of time, whereas others fluctuate to reflect changes in actual production values.

- ✓ **Rolling methodology:** Because the index's purpose is to track the performance of commodities and not take actual delivery of the commodity, the futures contracts that the index tracks must be rolled over from the *current-month contract* to the *front-month contract* (the upcoming trading month). Because this rolling process provides a *roll yield* (a yield that results from the price differential between the current and front months), you need to examine each index's policy on rolling. You can find this information in the index brochure.

- ✓ **Rebalancing features:** Every index reviews its components and their weightings on a regular basis to maintain an index that reflects actual values in the global commodities markets. Some indexes rebalance annually; other indexes rebalance more frequently. Before you invest in an index, find out when it's rebalanced and what methodology it uses to rebalance.

Although each index is constructed differently, all indexes have to follow certain criteria to determine whether a commodity will be included in the index:

- ✓ **Tradability:** The commodities have to be traded on a designated exchange and must have a futures contract assigned to them.

- ✓ **Deliverability:** The contracts that go into the index must be for an underlying commodity that has the potential to be delivered. This eliminates the inclusion of futures contracts that represent financial instruments, such as economic indicators, interest rates, and other "financials."

> ✔ **Liquidity:** The market for the underlying commodity has to be liquid enough to allow investors to move in and out of their positions without facing liquidity crunches, such as not being able to find a buyer or seller.

Cataloguing the Five Major Indexes

In the following sections, I go through each of the five major commodity indexes you can invest in. Each one is unique, so you can be sure to find one that best suits your needs.

The S&P Goldman Sachs Commodity Index

The S&P *Goldman Sachs Commodity Index* (S&P GSCI) is one of the most closely watched indexes in the market. Launched in 1992 by the investment bank Goldman Sachs, it tracks the performance of 24 commodity futures contracts. In 2007, Standard & Poor's (S&P) purchased the original GSCI from Goldman Sachs and is now responsible for its operations. The S&P GSCI is the most heavily tracked index. As of 2006, investors had poured in $50 billion to track it; by 2010, that figure was $65 billion.

The S&P GSCI is a production-weighted index because it assigns different weights to different commodities proportional to their current global production quantity, a method known as *global production weighting*. As such, the index assigns more weight to crude oil than cocoa, to reflect actual world production figures — there's a lot more crude oil produced in the world than cocoa.

 To calculate the contract production weight of each commodity (the percentage of a commodity assigned to the index), the S&P GSCI takes the average of that commodity's global production over the previous five years. The main advantage of using a five-year average over a one-year average is that the former takes into account any statistical aberrations related to the production of the specific commodity. For example, if a natural disaster affected the production of a particular commodity during one year, the five-year average would reflect that change but still maintain a heavy weighting on that commodity because that event was an aberration.

Figure 6-1 lists the main component classes that the S&P GSCI tracks. Notice that the bulk of the S&P GSCI is tied to energy contracts because energy products dominate global commodity production.

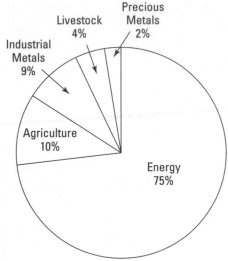

GSCI

Figure 6-1:
Component
classes of
the S&P
GSCI.

The S&P GSCI is currently overweight energy, but this can always change in the future. If energy production decreases on a global scale, the index will reflect this change. The index reviews its weightings annually and reassigns weights to the index in January.

Table 6-1 lists the actual commodity futures contracts that make up the S&P GSCI, along with their correspondent weighting in the index. I also list the exchange on which they trade, in case you want to purchase these contracts.

Table 6-1		S&P GSCI Components			
Commodity	*Exchange*	*Weight*	*Commodity*	*Exchange*	*Weight*
Chicago wheat	CME	2.47%	Gas–oil	ICE	4.41%
Kansas wheat	KBOT	0.90%	Unleaded gas	CME	7.84%
Corn	CME	2.46%	WTI crude oil	CME	30.05%
Soybeans	CME	1.77%	Brent crude oil	ICE	13.81%
Coffee	CSC	0.80%	Natural gas	CME	10.30%
Sugar	CSC	1.30%	Aluminum	LME	2.88%

Commodity	Exchange	Weight	Commodity	Exchange	Weight
Cocoa	CSC	0.23%	Copper	LME	2.37%
Cotton	NYC	0.99%	Lead	LME	0.29%
Lean hogs	CME	2.00%	Nickel	LME	0.82%
Live cattle	CME	2.88%	Zinc	LME	0.54%
Feeder cattle	CME	0.78%	Gold	CME	1.73%
Heating oil	CME	8.16%	Silver	CME	0.20%

Because futures contracts have an expiration date, they must be rolled on a regular basis. Contracts such as the crude oil futures are rolled monthly because they expire every month. However, some contracts have contract expiration dates only during certain months of the year. (I discuss monthly contract tradability in Chapter 9.) These contracts, such as the contracts for cotton or gold, are rolled according to the available monthly contract trade.

The S&P GSCI has a futures contract that tracks the index's performance. You can buy this contract on the Chicago Mercantile Exchange (CME). If you have a futures trading account (you find out how to open one in Chapter 8), you can simply buy this contract to get direct access to the S&P GSCI. The ticker symbol for the S&P GSCI on the CME is GI.

Another way to access the S&P GSCI is to invest in a managed fund that tracks its performance. One such fund is the Oppenheimer Real Asset Fund (which I discuss in Chapter 7). The Oppenheimer Fund mirrors the perfomance of the S&P GSCI. However, as a general rule, managed funds don't identically replicate the performance of an index because you have to take into consideration external factors such as loads, management fees, and other expenses related to the management of the fund.

Reuters/Jefferies Commodity Research Bureau Index

Created in 1957 as the Commodity Research Bureau's official commodity-tracking index, this index is the oldest commodity index in the world. The original index received its most recent makeover in 2005 when it was renamed the *Reuters/Jefferies Commodity Research Bureau Index* (CRB) — quite a mouthful!

The CRB index is widely followed by institutional investors and economists; of all the indexes, it's perhaps the most widely used as an economic benchmark, although the S&P GSCI and the DJ/AIGCI (introduced in the next section) are also widely used references.

The CRB index has performed well since 2002. Table 6-2 lists the total annual returns of the CRB index.

Table 6-2	Annual Returns of the CRB Index, 2002–2009
Year	*Total Return*
2002	23%
2003	8.9%
2004	11.2%
2005	16.9%
2006	–3%
2007	16.5%
2008	–32%
2009	17%

Ten-year annualized returns for the CRB are 9.02 percent, outpacing many asset classes, including some comparable commodity indexes.

The CRB index tracks all the major commodity component classes, which you can see in Figure 6-2.

**Reuters/Jefferies CRB Index
Component Classes**

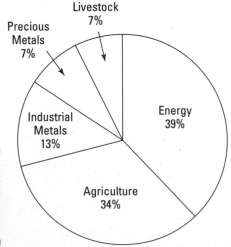

Figure 6-2:
Component
classes of
the CRB
index.

The CRB index currently tracks a basket of 19 commodities, which are selected based on their liquidity and production value. This index is unique because it is the only index that uses a *tiered methodology* of distributing weights to commodities. This hybrid approach gives a production value weight to energy products, while assigning fixed weights to other commodities. The components and their weightings are reviewed annually. Table 6-3 lists the index tiers and the commodities the index tracks.

Table 6-3	CRB Index Tiers and Components		
Tiers	*Commodity*	*Weight*	*Exchange*
Tier I	WTI crude oil	23%	CME
	Heating oil	5%	CME
	Unleaded gas	5%	CME
Tier II	Natural gas	6%	CME
	Corn	6%	CME
	Soybeans	6%	CME
	Live cattle	6%	CME
	Gold	6%	CME
	Aluminum	6%	LME
	Copper	6%	CME
Tier III	Sugar	5%	ICE
	Cotton	5%	ICE
	Cocoa	5%	ICE
	Coffee	5%	ICE
Tier IV	Nickel	1%	LME
	Wheat	1%	CME
	Lean hogs	1%	CME
	Orange juice	1%	ICE
	Silver	1%	CME

Dow Jones–AIG Commodity Index

With approximately $31 billion tracking it (2010 figures), the *Dow Jones–AIG Commodity Index* (DJ-AIGCI) is one of the most widely followed indexes in the market. The DJ-AIGCI places a premium on liquidity but also chooses commodities based on their production value.

The DJ-AIGCI is one of the few indexes that places a *floor* and *ceiling* on individual commodities and component classes. For example, no component class (such as energy or metals) is allowed to account for more than 33 percent of the index weighting. Another rule is that no single commodity may make up less than 2 percent of the index's total weighting. The DJ-AIGCI follows these rules to ensure that all commodities are well represented and that no commodity or component class dominates the index. Figure 6-3 shows the component classes of the DJ-AIGCI.

DJ-AIGCI Component Classes

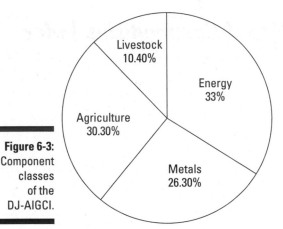

Figure 6-3:
Component
classes
of the
DJ-AIGCI.

The component weightings are rebalanced annually. Currently, the index tracks a group of 19 publicly traded commodities, listed in Table 6-4.

Table 6-4	DJ-AIGCI Components		
Commodity	*Weight*	*Commodity*	*Weight*
Natural gas	12.32%	Aluminum	6.90%
WTI crude oil	12.78%	Copper	5.88%
Unleaded gas	4.05%	Zinc	2.70%
Heating oil	3.84%	Nickel	2.66%
Live cattle	6.09%	Gold	6.22%
Lean hogs	4.35%	Silver	2.00%
Wheat	4.77%	Sugar	2.96%
Corn	5.87%	Cotton	3.16%
Soybeans	7.76%	Coffee	2.93%
Soybean oil	2.76%		

One way to access the commodities listed in the DJ-AIGCI is to invest in a mutual fund that tracks it. One of the largest commodity mutual funds, the *PIMCO Commodity Real Return Fund,* uses the DJ-AIGCI as its benchmark. Therefore, you get a very high correlation between the performance of the index and the performance of the fund. Turn to Chapter 7 to find out more about the PIMCO fund.

Another way to access the DJ-AIGCI is through the CME, which offers a futures contract that tracks the performance of the DJ-AIGCI. This is similar to the S&P GSCI contract on the CME. The ticker symbol for the DJ-AIGCI on the CME is AI.

Rogers International Commodities Index

With a grand total of 35 listed commodities, the *Rogers International Commodities Index* (RICI) tracks the most commodities among the different indexes. The RICI is the brainchild of famed commodities investor Jim Rogers, who launched the index to achieve the widest exposure to commodities.

As with the other commodity indexes, the RICI includes traditional commodities such as crude oil, natural gas, and silver. However, it also includes quite exotic commodities, including silk and adzuki beans. If you're looking for the broadest exposure to commodities, the RICI is probably your best bet.

The RICI was launched in 1998 and has performed extremely well. Between 1998 and 2006, its total return was 265.58 percent.

The RICI is a production-weighted index, assigning weightings to component classes based on their actual global production value and rebalancing the index every December. Figure 6-4 lists the main component classes of the RICI. Table 6-5 lists the RICI components and their index weighting.

Table 6-5		RICI Components	
Commodity	*Weight*	*Commodity*	*Weight*
Crude oil	35%	Sugar	2%
Wheat	7%	Platinum	1.80%
Corn	4.75%	Live hogs	1%
Aluminum	4%	Cocoa	1%
Copper	4%	Nickel	1%
Cotton	4%	Tin	1%
Heating oil	3.75%	Rubber	1%
Unleaded gas	3.75%	Lumber	1%

(continued)

Table 6-5 *(continued)*

Commodity	Weight	Commodity	Weight
Natural gas	3%	Soybean meal	0.75%
Soybeans	3%	Canola	0.67%
Gold	3%	Orange juice	0.66%
Live cattle	2%	Rice	0.50%
Coffee	2%	Adzuki beans	0.50%
Zinc	2%	Oats	0.50%
Silver	2%	Palladium	0.30%
Lead	2%	Barley	0.27%
Soybean oil	2%	Silk	0.05%

If you want to invest in the RICI, you can do so through the *RICI TRAKRS* offered by the CME. *TRAKRS* (pronounced "trackers") are similar to the futures contracts offered by the CME. To trade the RICI TRAKRS on the CME, use the ticker symbol RCI.

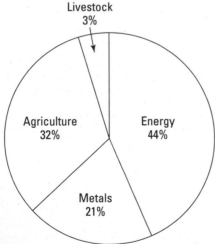

RICI Component Classes

Livestock 3%

Agriculture 32%

Energy 44%

Metals 21%

Figure 6-4: Component classes of the RICI.

Deutsche Bank Liquid Commodity Index

Launched in 2003 by Deutsche Bank, the *Deutsche Bank Liquid Commodity Index* (DBLCI) is the new kid on the index block and has the most distinct approach to tracking commodity futures contracts. The DBLCI tracks just six commodity contracts: two in energy, two in metals, and two in agricultural products. Figure 6-5 shows the weighting of each of these component classes.

DBLCI Component Classes

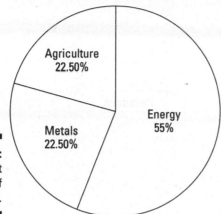

Agriculture
22.50%

Energy
55%

Metals
22.50%

Figure 6-5:
Component
classes of
the DBLCI.

The weighting of the DBLCI is done at the end of the year, and it seeks to reflect global production values. Hence, as with the other production-weighted indexes (such as the S&P GSCI), it's also overweight energy because this reflects the current production values in the world.

Table 6-6 lists the commodities that make up the component classes of the DBLCI.

Table 6-6	DBLCI Components	
Commodity	*Exchange*	*Weight*
WTI crude oil	CME	35%
Heating oil	CME	20%
Aluminum	LME	12.5%
Corn	CME	11.25%
Wheat	CME	11.25%
Gold	CME	10%

With so few underlying commodities, you may be asking whether the DBLCI offers a broad and diverse enough exposure to the commodities markets. One of the advantages of the DBLCI is that it chooses only the most *liquid* and *representative* commodities in their respective component classes.

For example, the WTI Crude Oil contract is indicative of where the energy complex is moving. So instead of including unleaded gas, propane, natural gas, and other energy contracts, the DBLCI relies on WTI as a benchmark to achieve representation in the energy market as a whole. This approach is unique in the world of commodity indexes: The index can track the commodities markets by monitoring the performance of only a small number of commodities. This "less is more" approach is also helpful for individual investors who prefer to track indexes by buying the index contracts: Instead of buying 19 contracts, you have to buy only 6 contracts to mirror the index's performance.

The energy contracts of the DBLCI are rolled monthly; the metal and agricultural contracts are rolled annually.

The DBLCI is the first commodity index to have its performance tracked by an exchange-traded fund (ETF). You can buy the ETF and get exposure to the DBLCI on the American Stock and Options Exchange (AMEX). Deutsche Bank also manages this fund, whose ticker symbol is DBC. I discuss this ETF in depth in Chapter 5.

Determining Which Index to Use

With so many indexes to choose from, how do you decide which one to follow? Generally, the S&P Goldman Sachs Commodity Index (S&P GSCI) is the most tracked index in the market — it has the most funds following, or tracking, its performance. As of 2010, more than $85 billion in assets tracked its performance, and this number is growing monthly. The index is pretty popular with institutional and, increasingly, individual investors. It's also perhaps the easiest one to follow because you can track it by investing through the Oppenheimer Real Asset Fund, as well as through the S&P GSCI futures contracts on the CME.

Although the S&P GSCI is the most widely tracked index, the most closely *watched* index (there's a difference) is the Reuters/Jefferies CRB Index. The CRB Index is a global benchmark for what the commodities markets are doing. As such, it is the equivalent of the Dow Jones Industrial Average in the commodity world: When investors want to gauge where the commodity markets are heading, they usually turn to the CRB Index. In addition, when analysts or journalists discuss the performance of the commodities markets, they usually refer to the CRB Index.

Investors who don't trade futures or don't feel comfortable investing in an index through a mutual fund can always choose to invest in an index through ETFs, which offer the convenience of trading complex financial instruments with the ease of trading stocks. Currently, the DBLCI is the only index tracked by an ETF, the DBC. Buying the DBC is as simple as logging into your brokerage account or calling your broker and placing an order for the number of DBC units you want to purchase. An ETF is in the works to track the S&P GSCI, and I expect to see more ETFs that track these commodity indexes as more investors seek access to this area of the market.

Chapter 7

Show Me the Money! Choosing the Right Manager

*I*f you're looking for ways to get involved in commodities, you have the option of hiring a trained professional to do the investing for you. As the number of investors putting their money into this asset class grows, more investment vehicles are being developed to satisfy this demand. Currently, plenty of money managers offer their services to help you invest in this market.

Of course, whenever you hand over your hard-earned money to a manager, you want to make sure that you feel confident about her ability to invest your money wisely. In this chapter, I look at some of the vehicles you have at your disposal to invest in the commodities markets, and I offer you hands-on information to help you select the most suitable money manager for you.

Mutually Beneficial: Investing in Commodity Mutual Funds

A common way to invest in commodities is through a mutual fund. It may be the simplest way for you to get involved in the commodities markets because you're relying on a trained professional to do the investing on your behalf.

A *mutual fund* is a fund managed by an investment professional for the benefit of the fund investors. Mutual funds, by definition, can follow only a specific set of trading techniques. Mutual funds don't engage in sophisticated trading techniques such as arbitrage trades, special situations, long–short strategies, or distressed asset investing. These strategies are conducted primarily by *hedge funds,* which are similar to mutual funds except that they can engage in these sophisticated investment strategies. Most mutual funds follow *long-only* strategies, which is an investment policy based on the *buy-and-hold* principle.

Many different types of mutual funds have nothing to do with commodities. You can invest in stock funds, bond funds, currency funds, and even country-specific funds. But a number of mutual funds specialize in investing in only commodities or commodity-related products.

Plain vanilla funds are your run-of-the-mill funds. If you've ever invested in a mutual fund, you should have no problem investing in these straight-forward funds. How do you get started? You write your check, purchase shares of the mutual funds either through your broker or directly from the fund providers, and voilà! Of course, I recommend asking a number of questions before you write that check. You can find these qualifying questions in the following section.

Plain vanilla funds are actively administered by a fund manager whose responsibility is to allocate capital across various subasset classes, to maximize the fund's returns. Generally, these mutual funds invest in commodity-linked derivative instruments such as futures contracts and options on futures traded on the major commodity exchanges in New York, Chicago, and elsewhere. Other mutual funds may also invest in companies that process these raw materials, such as energy companies (see Chapter 14) and mining companies (see Chapter 18).

Riddle me this, riddle me that: Asking the right questions

Before you invest in a mutual fund, you need to gather as much information as possible about the fund itself, as well as about the mechanics of investing in the fund. You can get answers to these questions directly from the fund manager or the fund's prospectus.

Call the mutual fund company directly and ask for a prospectus. A *prospectus* contains a wealth of information regarding how the fund is managed, the strategies the fund managers use, and details on fees and expenses. It's a great way to start gathering information on a prospective fund. Best of all, mutual funds send you their prospectus for free!

Some useful questions can help you zero in on the key points of mutual fund investing:

- ✔ **What is the fund's investment objective?** Different funds have radically different investment objectives. One may focus on *capital gains,* where the purpose is price appreciation, whereas another may specialize in *income investing* by buying assets, such as bonds, that generate an income stream. Knowing the fund's objective is one of the first pieces of information to look for.

- ✔ **What securities does the fund invest in?** This may seem like an obvious question when you're looking at commodities funds, but a number of funds claim that their main investment products are commodities, when in reality, only a small percentage of the fund is commodities related. I look at some of these funds in the section "Taking a look at what's out there."

- ✔ **Who manages the fund?** You want to know as much as possible about the individuals who will be managing your hard-earned money. Most money managers in the United States have to be registered with the National Association of Securities Dealers (NASD). You can get information on a manager's personal background by checking the NASD Web site, at www.nasdbrokercheck.com. Look for these key points:

  - • **Experience:** How long has he been a manager?

  - • **Track record:** What kind of returns has the manager achieved for his clients in the past?

  - • **Disciplinary actions:** Has this manager been disciplined for a past action? If so, find out more.

  - • **Registrations and certifications:** Does this manager have all the required registrations with the appropriate financial authorities to trade and invest on behalf of clients?

- ✔ **What kind of strategy does the fund use?** A fund's strategy relies on a number of factors, including the investing style of the portfolio managers, the fund's objective, and the securities it chooses to invest in. Some funds follow low-risk, steady-income strategies, while others have a more aggressive strategy that uses a lot of leverage. Identifying the fund's strategy right away is critical.

- ✔ **What is the profile of the typical investor in this fund?** The fund caters to the profile of its investors, which can be anywhere from highly conservative to extremely aggressive. You need to know what kind of individual is likely to invest in this fund and determine whether your risk tolerance squares with that of the other investors.

✔ **What are the main risks of investing in this fund?** Whenever you invest, you take on a certain degree of risk: interest rate risk, credit risk, risk of loss of principal, liquidity risk, hedging risk, and geopolitical risk. For a detailed look at a number of different risks, take a look at Chapter 3.

✔ **What is the fund's track record?** Although past performance doesn't guarantee future results, it's always important to examine the fund's track record, to get a sense of the kinds of returns the managers have achieved for their investors in the past. Most funds post their performance over a number of years; in particular, take a look at the key periods of the past three, five, and ten years.

✔ **What is the fund's *after-tax* performance?** Pay close attention to *after-tax* returns when looking at historical performance; they're a more accurate measure of the fund's performance — and how much money you get to keep after you pay Uncle Sam. Many funds use big, bold charts to advertise their performance before taxes, but these can be misleading because a significant portion of these returns ends up in the government's coffers after taxes are taken out.

✔ **What are the fund's fees and expenses?** Fees and expenses always cut into how much money you can get out of the fund. Look for funds that have lower expenses and fees. This information is available in the prospectus.

✔ **What is the minimum capital an investor must commit?** A number of mutual funds require investing a minimum amount of money, ranging anywhere from $500 to $10,000 or more. The minimum requirement may also vary according to the type of investor. Someone investing in an IRA, for example, may have to put up less money up front than someone investing through a brokerage account. Finally, many funds also require *minimum incremental amounts* after the initial investment amount. So you may invest $1,000 up front but then be required to increase your investment by at least $100 each subsequent time you want to invest in the fund.

✔ **Are there different classes of shares?** Most mutual funds offer more than one class of shares to investors. The different classes are based on several factors, including sales charges, deferred sales charges, redemption fees, and investor availability. Examine each class of shares closely to determine which one is best for you.

✔ **What are the tax implications of investing in this fund?** Talk to your accountant to determine the tax consequences of any investment you make.

As with almost everything else in finance, investing in commodity mutual funds requires mastering specific terminology. These technical terms can help you talk the talk:

- **Expense ratio:** The expense ratio is the percentage of the fund's total assets earmarked for general operational expenses. This is the amount used to run the fund, and it generally lowers total fund returns.

- **Sales load:** Some mutual funds sell their shares through brokerage houses and other financial intermediaries. A *sales load* is the commission the mutual fund pays to brokers who sell their shares to the general public. The investor pays the sales load. Some funds don't have sales load; they're called *no-load funds*.

- **Sales charge:** A sales charge, sometimes referred to as a *deferred sales charge,* is a fee that the mutual fund investor pays when she sells her mutual fund shares. This charge is also known as a *back-end charge* because you pay a fee after you sell your shares.

- **Net asset value (NAV):** A fund's net asset value (NAV) is its total assets minus total liabilities. Mutual funds calculate NAV on a per-share basis at the end of each trading day by dividing the difference between total assets and liabilities by the number of shares outstanding. A mutual fund's NAV is similar to a publicly traded company's stock price on a per-share basis.

Taking a look at what's out there

You can choose from two main commodity mutual funds: the PIMCO Commodity Real Return Strategy Fund and the Oppenheimer Real Asset Fund.

To find out more about commodity mutual funds, a useful tool is the Morningstar Web site (www.morningstar.com). This all-around excellent resource for investors includes lots of information related to commodity mutual funds, such as the latest news, updates, load charges, expense ratios, and other key data. It also uses a helpful five-star ratings system to rate mutual funds.

The PIMCO Commodity Real Return Strategy Fund

With more than $14 billion in assets under management, the *PIMCO Commodity Real Return Strategy Fund* (PCRAX) is the largest commodity-oriented fund in the market. Although the fund is actively managed, it seeks to broadly mirror the performance of the Dow Jones–AIG Commodity Index (see Chapter 6 for the goods on this index). As such, the fund invests directly in commodity-linked instruments such as futures contracts, forward contracts, and options on futures. (For more on these instruments, flip to Chapter 9.)

Because these contracts are naturally leveraged, the fund also invests in bonds and other fixed-income securities to act as collateral to the commodity instruments. This fund offers two classes of shares: A and B. I encourage you to examine each class carefully, to choose the best one for you.

> ✔ Class A shares have a minimum investment amount of $5,000, a front load of 5.5 percent, and an expense ratio of 1.24 percent.
>
> ✔ Class B shares require no front load, although they incur a deferred sales charge of 5 percent and an expense ratio of 1.99 percent.

The Oppenheimer Real Asset Fund

With a little less than $2 billion in assets, the *Oppenheimer Real Asset Fund* (QRAAX) is considerably smaller than the PIMCO fund. It tracks the performance of the Goldman Sachs Commodity Index, an index that tracks a broad basket of 24 commodities. (Flip to Chapter 6 for more on commodity indexes.)

With a $1,000 minimum investment requirement, Oppenheimer requires a little less capital up front than the PIMCO fund. It offers five classes of shares (A, B, C, N, and Y); Class A is the most popular among average individual investors. Class A shares have no deferred sales charge, although they have a front load of 5.75 percent and an expense ratio of 1.32 percent. So even though you need less initial capital to invest in the Oppenheimer fund, it's slightly more expensive than the PIMCO fund because of the front-load charges and its expense ratio.

Additional commodity funds on the market

Although Oppenheimer and PIMCO offer the two most popular commodity funds, other firms are starting to offer similar products to satisfy the growing demand from investors for funds that have wide exposure to the commodities markets. Two newcomers to the market are the *Merrill Lynch Real Investment* (MDCDX) and the *Credit Suisse Commodity Return Strategy Fund* (CRSCX). As more investors seek exposure to commodities, expect more funds of this nature to crop up in the future. This growth is good news because you'll have more funds to choose from!

Mastering MLPs

If you're interested in investing in companies that are involved in the production, transformation, and distribution of commodities, one of the best ways to do so is to invest in a *master limited partnership* (MLP). MLPs are a great investment because of their tax advantage and high cash payouts.

The ABCs of MLPs

MLPs are public entities that trade on public exchanges. Just as a company issues stock on an exchange, an MLP issues shares that trade on an exchange.

You can get involved in an MLP by simply purchasing its shares on an exchange. This is why an MLP is also called a *publicly traded partnership* (PTP).

Although most MLPs trade on the New York Stock Exchange (NYSE), a few MLPs also trade on the Nasdaq National Market (NASDAQ) and the American Stock and Options Exchange (AMEX). The section "The nuts and bolts of MLP investing," later in this chapter, lists a few MLPs and the exchanges they trade on.

The shares that an MLP issues are called *units,* and investors who own these units are known as *unit holders.* When you invest in an MLP, you're essentially investing in a public partnership. This partnership is run by a *general partner* for his benefit and, more important, for that of the *limited partners* (which you become when you buy MLP units). See the following sections "General partner" and "Limited partner."

The taxman only rings once

One of the reasons I like MLPs so much for commodities investing is that, unlike regular corporations, they're taxed only once. Many publicly traded companies are subject to double taxation: They're taxed at the corporate level as well as at the shareholder (individual) level. Not so with MLPs.

Because of congressional legislation, any MLP that derives 90 percent or more of its income from activities related to the production, distribution, and transformation of commodities qualifies for this tax-exempt status.

The income that an MLP uses to qualify for tax advantages is known as *qualifying income.* If an MLP can prove its qualifying income, it can "pass through" its income tax-free to its shareholders, who are then responsible for paying whatever taxes are appropriate for them. This is why MLPs are sometimes referred to as *pass-through entities.*

Curious to see how this tax advantage plays out in the real world? Suppose that you're in a 35 percent tax bracket. You invest $1 in an MLP and $1 in a corporation. The corporation needs to generate $2.20 in income to distribute $1 of after-tax profits to you. The MLP, thanks to its favorable tax treatment, has to generate only $1.54 in income to give you back $1 of after-tax profits.

This tax status gives MLPs a competitive advantage over other publicly traded entities when they compete for assets. An MLP simply doesn't have to generate as much cash flow as a corporation to distribute similar levels of after-tax income to shareholders — and this fact has two possible implications. First, if it wants, the MLP can afford to overpay for an asset and still generate healthy cash flows for its investors. Alternatively, it can purchase an asset at a similar price from a competing corporation but generate more cash flow to investors because of its favorable tax treatment.

MLP structure: The method behind the madness

Kinder Morgan is one of the largest energy transportation and distribution companies in the United States. The Kinder Morgan family of companies consists of three separate entities, including its successful MLP, Kinder Morgan Energy Partners, LP (NYSE: KMP). Kinder Morgan's MLP is managed by a general partner called Kinder Morgan Management, LLC (NYSE: KMR), which was established to manage the MLP. The Kinder Morgan GP is, in turn, owned by an even larger entity: Kinder Morgan, Inc. (NYSE: KMI). So the Kinder Morgan MLP (KMP) is run by the Kinder Morgan general partner (KMR), which is owned by Kinder Morgan, Inc. (KMI). If you're scratching your head trying to figure out this structure, don't worry. Because of regulatory, legal, and corporate reasons, the structures of many MLPs can get pretty convoluted — another reason for reading this book before you get started!

MLPs are required to distribute all available cash back to unit holders on a quarterly basis. When you own an MLP, you receive a K1 tax form, which is similar to the 1099 tax form you receive from a corporation.

Be sure to inform your accountant of your MLP investments in advance, because most K1 forms aren't mailed out to shareholders until February. This gives you only a few weeks to account for the MLP income in your taxes.

General partner

The main responsibility of the *general partner* (GP) is running the MLP. The GP isn't always an individual. In fact, most GPs are actually other corporate entities set up for the specific purpose of running the MLP. These entities are sometimes set up in the form of corporations or limited liability companies (LLCs) and are often owned by an even larger corporation.

Besides managing the MLP, the GP generally has a financial stake in the MLP itself (usually 2 percent) and is eligible to receive *incentive distribution rights* (IDRs) based on performance. IDRs are a percentage of the total payout the GP gets to keep after hitting specific targets. Because the *raison d'être* of the MLP is to distribute cash back to its unit holders, most MLPs include incentives for the GP if and when it distributes certain levels of cash back to the LPs.

The distribution rights that an MLP grants the general partners are disclosed in the MLP's *partnership agreement* with the GP. Before investing in an MLP, comb through the partnership agreement carefully to understand the incentive rights granted to the GP. This is important because IDRs have a direct impact on how much money you get to keep at the end of the day. The most important piece of information to look for in the partnership agreement is the MLP's IDR structure.

To understand the MLP structure, you need to fully appreciate the degree of autonomy that the GP has in running the MLP. Keep a few points in mind:

- ✔ Limited partners have limited voting rights.

- ✔ LPs have no say in day-to-day operations, which the general partner carries out.

- ✔ The GP often has no fiduciary duty to the LPs.

- ✔ An MLP isn't required to hold annual meetings for unit holders.

Essentially, when you invest in an MLP, you turn over the keys of the kingdom to the GP. The GP exercises a high degree of control over how the MLP is run, how much cash is distributed back to the unit holders, and the general governance matters relating to the MLP. It's a good idea to thoroughly investigate the general partner's track record and historical performance. At the end of the day, you can't do much if you disagree with what the GP is doing, except sell your units. In this way, an MLP is different than a corporation, where, as a shareholder, you can attend annual meetings, issue proxy statements, and generally exercise a larger degree of control. That said, most GPs do a good job of running MLPs because it's in their best financial interest to do so.

Limited partner

Although the general partner is responsible for managing the MLP, the limited partners bring in the capital that the MLP manages. To become a limited partner in an MLP, all you have to do is purchase units of that MLP on an exchange. (For more on how to do this, read the section "The nuts and bolts of MLP investing.") After you purchase the MLP units, you are officially a limited partner in that MLP.

As a limited partner, you have virtually no say in how the partnership is managed, but you get to participate in the MLP's cash flow distribution, which is probably the most important reason you want to own MLP units in the first place.

When you purchase MLP units, you can make money from two sources: quarterly cash flow distributions and appreciation of the unit price. Because units are publicly traded, they may appreciate in value as the partnership expands and grows over time. In addition, because the MLP is obligated to distribute all available cash back to its unit holders on a quarterly basis, your units generate quarterly income for you as well.

As a matter of fact, the MLP *yields* (the amount of cash distributed back to shareholders) are among the highest of any asset class, with an average yield of 6 percent. Some MLPs actually have yields as high as 10 percent! MLP yields are similar to stock dividends, except that they're slightly more advantageous, thanks to the favorable tax treatment they enjoy. (More on that in the following section.)

The biggest drawback of being an LP is that you don't get to make any decisions about where the partnership is heading. You essentially transfer power to the GP, who makes all operational decisions. However, because certain incentives are built into the MLP agreement, it is in the GP's own interest to make sure that the MLP generates as much cash flow as possible.

Cash flow is king

The whole reason MLPs exist is to distribute all available cash back to the MLP unit holders, which has to be done on a quarterly basis. These factors determine how much cash is distributed to each investor:

- ✔ How many units the investors hold
- ✔ The incentive distribution rights (IDRs) created for the GP
- ✔ The difference between distributable and discretionary cash flow

The GP is responsible for distributing cash back to the LPs proportionally to their holdings. In other words, an investor who owns 1,000 units gets twice as much cash as an investor who owns 500 units in the same MLP. (But remember, this doesn't mean that the investor with the greater number of units gets to keep all that cash — she still has to pay taxes on this income, based on her tax profile.)

To promote the GP's efforts to increase cash flow for shareholders, many MLPs include incentives for the GP. Generally, the more cash flow the GP generates back to shareholders, the more cash he gets to keep. Although IDRs are different for each MLP, they're always based on a *tier system*. A typical IDR incentive structure for GPs increases the distribution rate to unit holders, as the following table illustrates.

Distribution Tier	Dollar Distribution	LP Payout	GP Participation
Tier 1	$0.50	98%	2%
Tier 2	$1.00	85%	15%
Tier 3	$1.50	75%	25%
Tier 4	$2.00	50%	50%

Using this tier distribution system, if the GP generates $1 of cash flow per unit (Tier 2), the LP gets 85¢ and the GP gets 15¢ of that dollar. However, if the GP is able to generate $2 of cash flow per unit (Tier 4), he gets to keep 50 percent of that amount, or $1; the LP gets a smaller percentage amount (50 percent, down from 85 percent) but gets a higher cash payout ($1) than other tiers. The GP is thus encouraged to generate as much cash flow as possible because he gets a higher cut of the profits. This example shows the incentive behind this elegant and sophisticated tiered distribution system.

The distribution of cash flow is known as *splits* because the LPs split their share of cash flow with the GP. Tier 4, where the GP participates on equal footing with the LPs, is known as a *high split*.

Therefore, it's in the best interest of the GP to maximize the cash flow to the investor. This point is important because the GP has a lot of discretion over how much of the available cash is actually redistributed to shareholders and how much will be used for operations related to the MLP — the difference between *distributable cash flow* and *discretionary cash flow*.

Distributable cash flow

As its name implies, *distributable cash flow* describes the amount of cash that's available to redistribute to shareholders. Generally, most MLPs calculate distributable cash flow by using the following formula:

> MLP distributable cash flow = Income + (Depreciation and amortization) – Capital expenditures

This amount is the cash available to all members of the MLP, including both the GP and the LP. To calculate how much cash is distributed back to the LPs only, use the following formula:

> LP distributable cash flow = Income + (Depreciation and amortization) – Capital expenditures – GP distribution

This formula takes into account the cash flow participation of the GP and is a more accurate indicator of how much cash will flow back to the regular investors — the LPs.

Discretionary cash flow

The GP has a lot of discretion over how much cash flow is distributed to shareholders. Although he could theoretically distribute all available cash flow back to shareholders, he's unlikely to do so because the GP has to have cash to operate the MLP. He may need some cash handy to finance growth projects, acquisitions, or other investments. This cash is known as *discretionary cash flow,* and, as the name implies, the GP can use it at his discretion. Whereas distributable cash flow is a measure of how much cash could *theoretically* be distributed back, *actual* cash flow is calculated by factoring in discretionary cash flow. This simple equation gives you a more accurate way to calculate how much money you'll end up with:

> Actual cash flow = Distributable cash flow – Discretionary cash flow

This amount is the difference between how much can be paid and how much is actually paid.

The nuts and bolts of MLP investing

So how do you actually go about investing in an MLP? It's quite simple, really. Because MLPs are publicly traded, you can purchase any of them on the exchange on which it's traded by calling your broker to purchase MLP units or by buying them through an online trading account, if you have one. Either way, buying MLP units is as simple as buying stocks.

In Table 7-1, I list some MLPs along with the exchanges they're traded on.

Table 7-1	Exchange-Traded MLPs	
MLP Name	*Investments*	*Exchange*
Kinder Morgan (KMP)	Energy transportation, storage, and distribution	NYSE
Enterprise Products (EPD)	Oil and gas pipelines, storage and drilling platforms	NYSE
Enbridge Energy (EEP)	Energy pipelines	NYSE
Alliance Resources (ARLP)	Coal production and marketing	NASDAQ

Although most MLPs in the United States trade on the NYSE, a few trade on the NASDAQ and the AMEX.

For a complete list of MLPs, check out the Web site www.ptpcoalition. org. Although this is a lobbying group for the industry, the site includes a complete listing of all available MLPs. I also recommend checking whether your brokerage firm has published any research on MLPs you're interested in.

About 50 MLPs are publicly traded in the United States; out of these, 40 are involved in the energy industry, with a focus on storage terminals, pipelines/ transportation, refining, and distribution. Remember, MLPs invest in these assets because 90 percent of their income must come from infrastructure related to the production and distribution of commodities for them to be exempt from double taxation. In addition, many MLPs invest in pipelines and other energy infrastructure because they offer steady cash flow streams, which can then be distributed back to shareholders.

Before you invest in an MLP, ask your broker the following questions:

- ✔ What's the historical payout?
- ✔ How much is cash flow?
- ✔ What is the GP's IDR?
- ✔ What are the operational activities?
- ✔ How much assets are under management?

Heads up! Risk and MLPs

Investing in MLPs comes with a number of risks. Here's a quick list of some of those risks so that you don't come upon any surprises when you get your K-1 tax form in February:

- ✔ **Management risk:** Because as a limited partner you have no say in the way the business is run, you're essentially handing over control to the general partner to manage the MLP as she sees fit. If you're not satisfied with the GP's performance, you can't do anything about it except withdraw your money from the MLP.

- ✔ **Environmental risk:** Many MLPs operate sophisticated infrastructures such as pipelines and drilling rigs, which are often vulnerable to natural disasters such as hurricanes and earthquakes. Any of these may have a negative impact on your bottom line.

- ✔ **Liquidity risk:** Because the MLP market is still fairly small compared to other assets such as stocks and bonds, you may face liquidity issues if you want to dispose of your units. Until liquidity increases in the MLP market, you risk not finding a buyer for your units.

- ✔ **Terrorism risk:** MLPs' assets often include sensitive infrastructures that may be vulnerable to a terrorist attack.

These risks are a few of the risks associated with MLPs, which is still a growing market. However, because of the beneficial structure and scope of operations of these entities, I believe they have a place in any diversified portfolio.

Relying on a Commodity Trading Advisor

If you're interested in investing in commodities through the futures markets or on a commodity exchange, getting the help of a trained professional to guide you down this path is always a good idea. One option is to hire the services of a *commodity trading advisor,* or CTA. The CTA is like a traditional stockbroker who specializes in the futures markets. He can help you open a futures account, trade futures contracts, and develop an investment strategy based on your personal financial profile.

CTAs have to pass a rigorous financial, trading, and portfolio-management exam called the Series 3. Administered by the National Association of Securities Dealers (NASD), this exam tests the candidate's knowledge of the commodities markets inside and out. By virtue of passing this exam and working at a commodities firm, most CTAs have a good fundamental understanding of the futures markets. CTAs are also licensed by the Commodity Futures Trading Commission (CFTC) and registered with the National Futures Association (NFA).

I've used these resources and found them helpful in finding the right CTAs:

- www.autumngold.com
- www.barclaygrp.com
- www.iasg.com

Each CTA has his own investment approach and trading philosophy. Before you select a CTA, find out about each candidate's investment style to see whether it squares with your investment goals. You also have to decide how much of a role you want the CTA to play in your investment life. Do you want someone to actively manage your funds or simply someone who will give you advice?

To answer these questions, you must first decide how involved you want to be in running your portfolio. If you're a hands-on kind of investor with free time to invest, you may consider investing on your own but keeping a CTA close by to answer questions.

On the other hand, if you don't have a lot of time or in-depth knowledge of commodities and prefer to have the CTA manage your funds for you, ask yourself a few questions to determine which CTA is right for you.

Consider these points when looking for a CTA:

- **Track record:** Web sites like Autumngold.com and IASG.com rank CTAs by their historical track record. I recommend that you take a look at the longest historical track record, which is the annualized return since the CTA began trading. However, it can also be useful to look at one-, three-, or six-month returns, as well as one-, three-, and five-year annualized returns.

- **Disciplinary actions:** The National Futures Association (NFA) maintains a comprehensive database of all registered CTAs, including a record of any disciplinary action the CTA may have faced. Make sure that the CTA you may be doing business with has a clean record. The NFA database that tracks CTAs is called the *Background Affiliation Status Information*

Center (BASIC), and you can access it through the NFA Web site, at `www.nfa.futures.org/basicnet`. An additional resource is the National Association of Securities Dealers (NASD), which also maintains a comprehensive database of CTAs and other securities professionals. You can order a report on a CTA from the NASD by going to `www.nasdbrokercheck.com`.

- **Management fee:** Similar to most money managers, most CTAs charge a flat management fee. The industry average is 2 percent, although, depending on their track record, some CTAs charge higher management fees. These fees generally go toward operational expenses: paying employees, taking care of rent, mailing and printing marketing material, running a trading platform, maintaining a 1-800 number, and so on.

- **Performance fee:** Although a large portion of the management fee goes toward running the CTA's business, the performance fee provides an incentive for the CTA to generate the highest returns possible. This is the CTA's bread and butter. Again, performance fees differ among CTAs, although I've found that 20 percent seems to be a benchmark for most CTAs. Some CTAs with good track records may have higher performance fees, in which case you want to compare historical and actual returns among different CTAs to find the one with the highest distribution back to investors. However, if the CTA doesn't reach certain levels, she shouldn't get any performance fee. In other words, the CTA should be rewarded only for good performance; if she doesn't hit her numbers, she doesn't get to participate in the profits.

- **Miscellaneous fees:** Watch out for these fees, because they can add up really quickly — just like the miscellaneous fees you get on your cell-phone bill. Ever opened your phone bill and found that miscellaneous fees increased your bill by 10 or 15 percent or higher? Your CTA may charge you for such items as express mail deliveries, check and wiring fees, night desk charges (a fee you pay if the CTA trades your account after trading hours), and maintenance fees. For example, if you don't maintain a minimum amount in your account — such as $500 — you can be charged a fee!

- **Margin requirements:** If you decide to open a *margin account* (as opposed to a cash account), you can borrow money from your CTA to purchase securities. Buying on margin gives you a lot of leverage (on both the upside and the downside), so knowing the details of the margin requirement is absolutely critical. (For more on using margin, take a look at Chapter 3.)

- **Minimum investment requirement:** Many CTAs require that you invest a minimum amount of money with them. This can be as low as $1,000 and as high as $200,000. I recommend investing no more than 5 to 10 percent of your investing capital with a CTA. This way, you diversify your holding to include managed futures, but it won't come back to haunt you if the CTA performs badly. (For more on how to construct a balanced, diversified portfolio, flip to Chapter 5.)

Jumping into a Commodity Pool

Another way you can get access to the commodities futures markets is to join a *commodity pool*. As its name suggests, a commodity pool is a pool of funds that trades in the commodities futures markets. The commodity pool is managed and operated by a designated *commodity pool operator* (CPO), who is licensed with the National Futures Association and registered with the Commodity Futures Trading Commission. All investors share in the profits (and losses) of the commodity pool based on how much capital they've contributed to the pool.

Investing in a commodity pool has two main advantages over opening an individual trading account with a CTA. First, because you're joining a pool with a number of different investors, your purchasing power increases significantly. You get a lot more leverage and diversification if you're trading a $1 million account as opposed to a $10,000 account.

The second benefit, which may not seem obvious at first, is that commodity pools tend to be structured as limited partnerships. This means that, as an investor with a stake in the pool, the most you can lose is the principal you invested in the first place. Losing your entire principal may seem like a bad deal, but for the futures markets, it's pretty good!

Let me explain. With an individual account, you can purchase securities on margin. That is, you can borrow funds to buy futures contracts. What happens if the position you entered into with the borrowed funds does the opposite of what you expected it to? Now not only have you lost your principal, but you also have to pay back your broker, who lent you the money to open the position. This means that you lose your principal and you still owe money, which is known as a *margin call.*

Now, because commodity pools are registered as limited partnerships, even if the fund uses leverage to buy securities and the fund gets a margin call, you're not responsible for that margin call. Hence, the only capital you risk is your principal! Of course, you want to perform due diligence on the CPO to keep the likelihood of the pool going bust as small as possible!

A good place to start looking for commodity pools is the Web site www.commodities-investors.com.

Chapter 8

Exploring Commodity Exchanges, Brokers, and Trading Accounts

The first commodity exchanges appeared in the United States during the 1800s, and their role was to match buyers and sellers interested in acquiring and selling commodities. The first traded commodities included wheat, butter, milk, cheese, and other agricultural products. Commodity exchanges soon evolved from simple places of commerce to highly regulated marketplaces where prices were established for all sorts of commodities.

The first image that usually comes to mind when you think of a commodity exchange is a group of brokers standing in a large circle, wearing bright-colored jackets and shouting at each other while making funny gestures. If you've ever visited or seen television footage of a commodity exchange, you've probably wondered what all the fuss was about. Why are these guys yelling? What are they saying? Can anyone actually hear anything down there, anyway?

Behind all this apparent chaos is a very rational, efficient, and orderly process that is responsible for setting global benchmark prices for the world's most important commodities. The prices established in the exchanges have a direct impact on our lives, from the price we pay to fill our gas tanks to how much we pay to heat our homes.

In this chapter, I give you an overview of commodity exchanges, those important institutions that not only are responsible for setting global prices of all sorts of commodities, but also give investors a direct and transparent way to participate in the commodities markets. I start off by giving you a quick rundown of the main exchanges out there, the structure of the industry, and the important role the exchanges play. Then I give you the necessary tools to actually open a trading account and start trading commodities via the exchanges themselves.

Why Do We Have Commodities Exchanges, Anyway?

Whether you're an individual seeking to hedge commodity prices for the future or an investor interested in capturing price discrepancies and fluctuations in the global commodity markets, the commodity exchange will help you achieve your goals.

Commodity exchanges give investors and traders the opportunity to invest in commodities by trading futures contracts, options on futures, and other derivative products. (See Chapter 9 for more on these products.) By their very nature, these products are extremely sophisticated financial instruments used by only the savviest investors and the most experienced traders.

Although independent traders like you and me can and do trade the futures markets, most players in the futures markets are large commercial entities that use the futures markets for price hedging. For example, Hershey Foods Corporation is an active participant in cocoa futures because it wants to hedge against the price risk of cocoa, a primary input for making its chocolates. If you decide to trade cocoa futures contracts (covered in Chapter 19), remember that you're up against some large and experienced market players.

At the end of the day, the commodity futures exchanges are your gateway to the futures markets; in fact, they *are* the commodity futures markets. However, because of the fierce competition in these markets and the complexity of exchange-traded products, you want to trade directly in the commodity futures markets only if you have an iron-clad grasp of the technical aspects of the markets and a rock-solid understanding of the market fundamentals. If you don't have either, I recommend staying out of these markets because you may be subjecting yourself to disastrous losses. That said, you can hire a trained professional with experience trading commodity futures to do the trading for you; I cover that option in the following sections and also in depth in Chapter 7.

Commodity futures exchanges serve an important role in establishing global benchmark prices for crucial commodities such as crude oil, gold, copper, orange juice, and coffee. The exchanges are crucial for both producers and consumers of commodities. Producers, who use commodities as inputs to create finished goods, want to shelter themselves from the daily fluctuations of global commodity prices. Producers may use the commodity exchange to lock in prices for these raw materials for fixed periods of time by using futures contracts (more on these in Chapter 9). This process is known as *hedging*. Similarly, traders may use the commodity exchange to profit from these fluctuations, sometimes known as *speculation*.

Whether you're an individual seeking to hedge commodity prices for the future or an investor interested in capturing price discrepancies and fluctuations in the global commodity markets, the commodity exchange will help you achieve your goals. A number of commodity exchanges operate worldwide, specializing in all sorts of commodities. In the following sections, I identify the major commodity exchanges and list the commodities traded in them.

Identifying the Major Commodity Exchanges

A number of commodity exchanges operate worldwide and specialize in all sorts of commodities. Before 2007, the industry was characterized by several players, each dominant in a particular segment of the market. Although some overlap existed among some of the commodities the exchanges offered — for example, gold contracts were traded on both the *New York Mercantile Exchange* (NYMEX) and the *Chicago Board of Trade* (CBOT) — most exchanges offered unique contracts. As such, every exchange specialized in certain commodities. For instance, the NYMEX focused on products to trade energy and metals; it had contracts for crude oil, propane, and heating oil, as well as gold, silver, and palladium.

The *New York Board of Trade* (NYBOT), on the other hand, focused primarily on tropical or "soft" commodities, such as coffee, cocoa, sugar, and frozen concentrated orange juice (covered in Chapter 19). The *Chicago Mercantile Exchange* (CME) offered a wide range of products but specialized in livestock, offering contracts for live cattle, feeder cattle, lean hogs, and frozen pork bellies.

Beginning in 2007, the industry experienced a significant and game-changing consolidation period during which the number of players decreased and the number of product offerings from each remaining body increased significantly. This consolidation permanently altered the exchange landscape and, in a certain way, made it easier for investors and traders to get access to these markets: The remaining exchanges became one-stop shops offering a variety of different products.

Although the industry had been ripe for consolidation for some time, the latest catalyst for change has been the advent of electronic and Internet-based trading platforms. Indeed, one of the main factors of the digital revolution has been the migration of trade flow from floor exchanges to electronic platforms. This shift has resulted in decreased volumes on traditional floor exchanges (such as the NYMEX) and increased flow in electronic-based exchanges such as the *Intercontinental Exchange* (ICE).

The consolidation era saw two main players emerge: the CME and the ICE. The CME acquired the CBOT and the NYMEX, including the COMEX division, making it the largest commodities exchange globally. The ICE had made a bid for the CBOT but failed in its acquisition; instead, it acquired the NYBOT and the *Winnipeg Commodity Exchange* (WCE). The ICE is a dominant player in energy (crude oil, coal, natural gas) and agricultural commodities (cocoa, coffee, cotton). Note that both the ICE and the CME offer interactive, online-based trading platforms.

The main commodity exchanges in the United States are located in New York and Chicago, with a few other exchanges in other parts of the country. In Table 8-1, I list the major commodity exchanges in the United States, along with the commodities traded in each one. *Note:* This list is only a small sampling of the commodities these exchanges offer. The CME, for example, offers more than 100 futures products that track everything from milk and feeder cattle to nonfarm payrolls and currencies. I recommend visiting the exchange Web sites for a comprehensive listing of their product offerings.

Table 8-1	**The Major U.S. Commodity Exchanges**
Exchange Name	*Commodities Traded*
Chicago Board of Trade (CBOT)	Corn, ethanol, oats, rice, soybeans, wheat, gold, silver
Chicago Mercantile Exchange (CME)	Feeder cattle, frozen pork bellies, lean hogs, live cattle, butter, milk, lumber
Intercontinental Exchange (ICE)	Crude oil, electricity, natural gas
Kansas City Board of Trade (KCBT)	Natural gas, wheat
Minneapolis Grain Exchange (MGE)	Corn, soybeans, wheat
New York Board of Trade (NYBOT)	Cocoa, coffee, cotton, frozen concentrated orange juice, sugar, ethanol
New York Mercantile Exchange (NYMEX)	Aluminum, copper, gold, palladium, platinum, silver, crude oil, electricity, gasoline, heating oil, natural gas, propane

The technical name for a commodity exchange is a *Designated Contract Market* (DCM). DCM is a designation that the *Commodity Futures Trading Commission* (CFTC) assigns to exchanges that offer commodity products to the public. (More on the CFTC in the following section.) If an exchange doesn't have the designation DCM, stay away from it!

Fighting back against fraud

The first contracts began trading on U.S. commodity exchanges in the middle of the 19th century. In the early part of the 20th century, the U.S. government decided to regulate these exchanges, to prevent market fraud and abuse. So in 1936, Congress passed the Commodity Exchange Act (CEA), providing federal oversight and regulation of all commodity exchanges operating in the United States. In 2000, Congress passed the Commodity Futures Modernization Act (CFMA) to overhaul the CEA and adapt it to the modern financial marketplace.

Most commodities in the United States are traded on only one exchange. The feeder cattle contract is traded only on the CME, and frozen concentrated orange juice is traded only on the NYBOT. However, certain commodities are traded on more than one exchange. For example, the WTI crude oil contract is traded on both the NYMEX and the ICE. In this case, you want to trade the most liquid market. You can find the most liquid market for a commodity by consulting the CFTC, which keeps information on all the exchanges and their products.

Commodity exchanges are under strict oversight, to protect all market participants and ensure transparency in the exchanges. These main regulatory organizations have oversight of commodity exchanges in the United States:

✔ **Commodity Futures Trading Commission (CFTC):** The CFTC is a federal regulatory agency created by Congress in 1974. Its main purpose is to regulate the commodity markets and protect all market participants from fraud, manipulation, and abusive practices. Any exchange that conducts business with the public must be registered with the CFTC. You can visit its Web site at www.cftc.gov.

✔ **National Futures Association (NFA):** The NFA is the industry's self-regulatory body. It conducts audits, launches investigations to root out corrupt practices in the industry, and enforces the rules related to trading commodities on the various exchanges. It also regulates every firm or individual who conducts business with you as an investor — including floor traders and brokers, futures commission merchants, commodity trading advisors, commodity pool operators, and introducing brokers.

You can check out the work of the NFA, as well as research individual commodities professionals, at the NFA Web site: www.nfa.futures.org.

Commodity exchanges are responsible for setting global benchmark prices for some of the world's most important commodities. As a result, the amount of liquidity they generate is enormous. For example, more than $1.5 trillion worth of contracts are traded in the commodity exchanges mentioned previously — each day!

Reading between the crude oil price lines

Have you ever picked up the newspaper and read that crude oil prices reached a new high? Have you ever asked yourself how these prices are determined? Well, they're determined on an exchange. The global benchmark for crude oil prices is a type of crude traded on the CME/NYMEX, called West Texas Intermediate (WTI). WTI comes from where its name suggests — West Texas. WTI is a light, sweet crude oil, and it's a benchmark because refiners prefer light, sweet crude to heavy, sour crude; they can get a lot more products out of that type of oil. (I take an in-depth look at the different types of crude oil in Chapter 10.)

Because the WTI is traded on the CME/NYMEX as a futures contract, the price you read in the

newspaper usually refers to the front-month delivery of the contract. (For more on futures delivery dates, turn to Chapter 9.) So when you read that oil is now at $62 a barrel, this refers to WTI crude oil traded on the CME/NYMEX for next month's delivery. This is very different than the current *spot market* price — the price you would pay if you purchased a barrel of oil right away, or on the *spot*. Additionally, the North Sea Brent — another light, sweet crude — which trades in London on the International Petroleum Exchange (now part of the Intercontinental Exchange), is used as a secondary global benchmark.

Although the bulk of commodity trading is done in the United States — the largest consumer market of commodities — commodity exchanges are located in other countries. If you're in the United States, you may want to consider investing in overseas exchanges for liquidity purposes. For example, both the American CME/NYMEX and the British *London Metal Exchange* (LME) offer aluminum futures contracts. However, the aluminum contract in the LME is more liquid, so you may get a better price by buying aluminum contracts in London rather than Chicago. In Table 8-2, I list some of these international commodity exchanges.

Table 8-2	International Commodity Exchanges	
Exchange Name	*Country*	*Commodities Traded*
European Energy Exchange	Germany	Electricity
London Metal Exchange	United Kingdom	Aluminum, copper, lead, nickel, tin, zinc
Natural Gas Exchange	Canada	Natural gas
Tokyo Commodity Exchange	Japan	Aluminum, gold, palladium, platinum, silver, crude oil, gasoline, kerosene, rubber

Ready, Set, Invest: Opening an Account and Placing Orders

When you're ready to start trading exchange-traded products, you have to choose the most suitable way for you to do so. Unless you're a member of an exchange or have a seat on the exchange floor, you have to open a trading account with a commodity broker who's licensed to conduct business on behalf of clients at the exchange.

The technical term for a commodity broker is a *futures commission merchant* (FCM). The FCM is licensed to solicit and execute commodity orders and accept payments for this service. Another term for FCM is *introducing broker* (IB).

Before choosing a commodity broker to handle your account, you have to perform a thorough and comprehensive analysis of the trading platform. You want to get as much information as possible about the firm and its activities. A few things to consider are firm history, clients, licensing information, trading platform, regulatory data, and employee information. Chapter 7 gives you a detailed analysis of the criteria you want to use in selecting a broker.

Choosing the right account

After you select a commodity brokerage firm you're comfortable with, it's time to open an account and start trading! You can choose from a number of different brokerage accounts. Most firms will offer you at least two types of accounts, depending on the level of control you want to exercise over the account.

If you feel confident about your trading abilities, a *self-directed account,* in which you call the shots, is the most suitable account for you. On the other hand, if you prefer to have a professional make the trading decisions for you, a *managed account* is your best bet. In this section, I go through the pros and cons of self-directed and managed accounts so you can determine which one is best for you.

Self-directed account

If you feel comfortable with exchange-traded products and are ready to take direct control of your account, consider opening a self-directed account, also known as a *nondiscretionary individual account*. With this account, you take matters into your own hands and make all the trading decisions. If you have a good understanding of market fundamentals and want to get direct access to commodity exchange products, a self-directed account is for you.

Before you open a self-directed account, talk to a few commodity brokers. Each firm offers different account features. This is similar to buying a car — you want to test-drive as many cars as possible to get the biggest bang for your buck.

Specifically, ask about any minimum capital requirements the firm has. Some commodity brokers require that you invest a minimum amount of $10,000 or more. You also want to become familiar with account maintenance fees and the commission scale the firm uses. Knowing this information up front can save you a lot of heartache down the road. After you gather all the relevant information and open your account, you're finally ready to start trading and placing orders!

Managed account

In a managed account, you're essentially transferring the responsibility of making all buying and selling decisions to a trained professional.

Open a managed account in these cases:

- ✔ You don't follow the markets on a regular (that is, daily) basis but are interested in getting exposure to commodities.
- ✔ You follow the markets regularly but are unsure about which trading strategy will maximize your returns.
- ✔ You don't have the time to manage a personal account.
- ✔ You feel comfortable knowing that someone else is making trading decisions for you.

If these statements apply to you, you're ready to open a managed account. So how do you get started? First, you need to determine your investment goals, time horizon, and risk tolerance. (For help in determining your investment strategy, flip over to Chapter 7.) Then you need to find out about any minimum capital requirements, commissions, or management fees you may face. (I cover these in depth in Chapter 7 also.) When you have this information, you can move on to choosing a commodity trading advisor (CTA) to manage the account.

If you have mutual funds, the CTA is similar to a fund manager. The FCM, on the other hand, is more like a stock brokerage house. The FCM provides you with a trading platform, whereas the CTA actually manages your accounts for you.

A CTA is a securities professional who is licensed by the National Association of Securities Dealers (NASD) and the National Futures Association (NFA) to offer advice on commodities and to accept compensation for investment and management services. Before you select a CTA, I recommend that you perform a rigorous background check. Because a CTA is required to register with the NFA to transact with the public, you can find out a lot about a CTA by simply visiting the NFA Web site (`www.nfa.futures.org`). (Also check out Chapter 7 for more info on selecting CTAs and other money managers.)

You want to find out this info about your CTA:

- ✔ How many years of market experience does he have?

- ✔ What is his long-term performance record?

- ✔ What is his trading strategy, and does it square with your investment goals?

- ✔ Does he have any complaints filed against him? (This information is publicly available through the NFA.)

- ✔ Many CTAs manage more than one account. Try to find out how many accounts he's currently managing. If the number seems too high (more than 100), maybe your account won't be a high priority for him.

- ✔ Does he have a criminal record? If so, find out the details of any arrests or convictions he has. This information is also available through the NFA.

If you perform due diligence on your CTA and feel comfortable with him, you're ready to turn over trading privileges to him. How do you do that? You have to sign a *power of attorney* document. After you sign that document, your CTA gets full trading discretion and complete control over the buying and selling of commodities in your account. He then makes all the decisions, and you have to live with the good (and sometimes bad) decisions he makes. If you trade stocks, this account is similar to having a discretionary individual stock account, in which your stockbroker makes trading decisions for you. The main benefit of the managed account is that you get a trained professional managing your investments. The drawback is that you can't blame anyone but yourself if you incur any losses.

A CTA is allowed by law to manage more than one account and have more than one client. However, a CTA must keep all managed accounts separate. Thus, there's no commingling of funds allowed and no transferring profits or losses between accounts. A managed account differs from a *commodity pool,* in which your funds are "pooled" with those of other investors and you all share profits or losses. When you choose a managed account, make sure you get a CTA who will manage your account based on your personal risk profile. (I cover commodity pool operators [CPOs]) and examine the differences between the CPO and the CTA more closely in Chapter 7.)

Placing orders

Your trading account is your link to the commodity exchange. The broker's trading platform gives you access to the exchange's main products, such as futures contracts, options on futures, and other derivative products. Because the products traded on commodity exchanges are fairly sophisticated financial instruments, you need to specify a number of parameters to purchase the product you want.

Understanding contract parameters

The lifeblood of the exchange is the contract. As an investor, you can choose from a number of contracts, from plain vanilla futures contracts to exotic swaps and spreads. (I discuss these products in depth in Chapter 9.) Whether you're buying a forward contract or engaging in a swap, you need to follow specific entry order procedures.

Here's a list of the parameters you need to indicate to place an order at the exchange:

- ✔ **Action:** Indicate whether you're buying or selling.

- ✔ **Quantity:** Specify the number of contracts you're interested in either buying or selling.

- ✔ **Time:** By definition, commodity futures contracts represent an underlying commodity traded at a specific price for delivery at a specific point in the future. Futures contracts have delivery months, and you must specify the delivery month. Additionally, you need to specify the year, because many contracts represent delivery points for periods of up to five years (or more).

- ✔ **Commodity:** This is the underlying commodity that the contract represents, such as crude oil, gold, or soybeans. Sometimes it's also helpful to indicate the exchange on which you want to place your order. (This information is fairly significant because more of the same commodities are being offered on different exchanges. For example, the benchmark WTI crude oil, which used to be traded only on the CME/NYMEX, is now available on both the CME/NYMEX floor and the ICE electronic exchange.)

- ✔ **Price:** This info may be the most important piece of the contract: the price at which you're willing to buy or sell the contract. Unless you're placing a market order (which is executed at current market prices), you need to indicate the price at which you want your order to be filled.

- ✔ **Type of order:** A lot of different types of orders exist, from plain vanilla market orders to more exotic ones such as *fill or kill* (FOK). See Table 8-3 for a list of the different order types. This info is an important piece of the order because you're indicating how you want to buy or sell the contract.

- ✔ **Day or open order:** Market orders relate to price, and day or open orders relate to how long you want your order to remain open. In a *day order,* your order expires if it isn't filled by the end of the trading day. An *open order,* however, remains open unless you cancel the order, the order is filled, or the contract expires.

Defining different types of orders

One of the most important pieces of information you need to indicate is the order type. This indicates how you want your order to be placed and executed. Table 8-3 lists the major types of orders, along with a brief description of each one.

Table 8-3	Defining Different Types of Orders
Order Type	**What It Means**
Fill or kill (FOK)	Use this order if you want your order to be filled right away at a specific price. If a matching offer isn't found within three attempts, your order is cancelled, or "killed."
Limit (LMT)	A limit order is placed when you want your order to be filled only at a specified price or better. If you're on the buy side of a transaction, you want your limit buy order placed at or below the market price. Conversely, if you're on the sell side, you want your limit sell order at or above market price.
Market (MKT)	A market order is perhaps the simplest type of order. When you choose a market order, you're saying you want your order filled at the current market price.
Market if touched (MIT)	A market if touched order sounds intimidating, but it's not. When you place an MIT, you specify the price at which you want to buy or sell a commodity. When that price is reached (or "touched"), your order is automatically filled at the current market price. A buy MIT order is placed below the market; a sell MIT order is placed above the market. In other words, you buy low and sell high.
Market on close (MOC)	When you place a market on close order, you're selecting not a specific price, but a specific time to execute your order. Your order is executed at whatever price that particular commodity happens to close at the end of the trading session.
Stop (STP)	A stop order is a lot like a market if touched order because your order is placed when trading occurs at or through a specified price. However, unlike an MIT order, a buy stop order is placed above the market, and a sell stop order is placed below market levels.
Stop close only (SCO)	If you choose a stop close only order, your stop order is executed only at the closing of trading and only if the closing trading range is at or through your designated stop price.
Stop limit (STL)	A stop limit order combines both a stop order and a limit order. When the stop price is reached, the order becomes a limit order and the transaction is executed only if the specified price at which you want the order to go through has been reached.

To put theory into practice, consider a couple sample orders:

"Buy ten June 2011 CME/COMEX Gold at $1,380 Limit Day Order." This means you're buying ten contracts for gold on the CME/COMEX (the metals complex of the CME), with a delivery date of June 2011. You're willing to pay $1,380 per troy ounce per contract or better. (A troy ounce is the measurement unit for gold at the CME/COMEX.) Because this is a day order, if your order isn't filled by the end of the trading day, it will expire.

"Sell 100 September 2011 CME/NYMEX Crude at Market Open Order." Through this order, you're selling 100 contracts of crude oil on the CME/NYMEX, with a delivery date of September 2011. You're willing to sell them at the current market price. Because this is an open order, your order will remain open for multiple trading sessions until it's filled.

Suppose that Mary is an investor who has recently opened a self-directed account with Infinity Brokers, a commodity brokerage firm. She keeps track of the markets and is comfortable placing orders that will take advantage of current market fundamentals. Mary picks up her newspaper one morning and reads about political turmoil in Nigeria, one of the world's top oil exporters. Rebels have seized a major pipeline, and Nigeria's oil exports will be cut by 15 percent. This revolt will have a significant impact on global oil prices, which are already sensitive to any supply disruptions.

Anticipating higher oil prices due to this latest development, Mary picks up the phone and calls her broker (sometimes known as an *account executive*), and instructs him to buy a contract for 1,000 barrels of oil at current market prices on the NYMEX for next month's delivery. The account executive takes down her order and informs her that he'll notify her as soon as her order is executed.

What happens between the time the orders are placed and the time they're executed? In the following section, I give you a behind-the-scenes look at what actually goes on at the exchange that enables your orders to go through. I introduce you to some of the players who are responsible for seeing the orders through from start to finish.

Tracking your order from start to finish

When you pick up the phone or log in to your online account and place an order, it's sometimes easy to forget that your order isn't placed in a vacuum. You place the order and wait for the confirmation number. Seems simple, right? Not quite. A number of people are involved in making sure that your order is executed as smoothly and efficiently as possible, and your order goes through an extensive supply chain before it's executed. In this section, I shed some light on how your orders are executed and introduce you to some of the people who make this possible.

The clerk

The exchange's first point of contact with the outside world is the clerk. The *clerk* isn't an employee of the exchange, but is employed by the various commodity brokers who are licensed to conduct business at the exchange. The clerk works the phones and is responsible for taking down client orders. When the clerk receives an order by phone (and now, increasingly, through e-mail as well), he fills out an order ticket, which he then passes on to the floor broker.

The floor broker

The *floor broker* (FB) is the one in the large ring shouting and making funny gestures. The FB is responsible for actually executing the order and is on the front lines of every transaction that goes through the exchange during the open outcry sessions. When the FB receives the order ticket from the clerk, it's her responsibility to find a matching offer and fill the order. The FB shouts and makes gestures (which are actually derived from American Sign Language) to interact with other brokers and traders in the ring. When she finds a broker or trader who is willing to fill the order, she writes down on the order ticket the time the agreement was entered into.

The floor trader

The *floor trader* (FT) is different than a floor broker because the FB is licensed to buy and sell commodities on behalf of clients. The trader may trade only on behalf of his personal account. The FT, sometimes known as a "local," provides much-needed liquidity to the exchange. An FT may be the person who sells or buys a contract from the FB.

When both buyer and seller at the exchange agree on price and other contractual terms, both must write down that the transaction went through on their tickets. However, only the *seller* is responsible for notifying the exchange that the transaction went through. How does he do that? He fills out an order ticket with the price, quality, and quantity of the contract, along with the time the transaction took place. He must then physically throw the ticket order to the card clocker.

The card clocker

The *card clocker* sits in the middle of the ring, where she's literally at the center of the action. The clocker must time-stamp every ticket order and record the time of each transaction that takes place on the exchange floor.

She is an employee of the exchange and processes about 1,000 tickets every minute! Because brokers and traders are throwing order tickets at her, the card clocker must wear eye goggles for protection.

The floor runner

The *floor runner* is also employed by the exchange, and his responsibility is to gather all time-stamped ticket orders from the card clocker and hand them to the data-entry folks at the exchange. He's called a floor runner because he has to literally run between the card clocker and data-entry personnel to deliver the ticket orders. The data-entry folks are responsible for recording the exact time and nature of the contract for the exchange's internal compliance records.

The price reporter

The *price reporter* is a major link between what goes on inside the trading rings and the outside world. The price reporter is responsible for noting the price and time of every transaction that takes place inside the ring. The price reporter notes this information on a hand-held computer that's directly linked to the exchange's floor board. The price the reporter notes flashes directly and instantaneously on the board; various news and wire services then disseminate it to the outside public.

The price you read in a crawling news ticker is the price recorded by the price reporter during trading hours, and it represents the settlement price of the latest transaction for a given contract. However, unless you subscribe to a wire service that gives you "real-time access" to the prices on the exchange, the price you read is usually delayed by 15 to 20 minutes. This is because news providers such as Bloomberg, Dow Jones, and Reuters pay a premium to get access to exchange prices in real time.

If you want real-time exchange quotes, you have to subscribe to one of these business news services. Cameras, cellphones, and other recording devices are strictly prohibited at exchanges: The news providers and exchanges don't want you to get access to the latest information, fearing that you might disseminate it to the outside world for free!

The ring supervisor

Every exchange has a floor with more than one ring in it. A ring, sometimes known as a *pit*, is where specific commodity contracts are bought and sold during the open outcry sessions. For example, the floor of the CME/NYMEX has a natural gas ring, a crude oil ring, and a heating oil ring. The brokers and traders in each ring may buy and sell only the specific commodity that's traded in that ring. Every ring has a supervisor who's responsible for overseeing trading activity and maintaining orderly conduct in the ring. (I know, it's a little hard to imagine order in a trading pit, but that's the job!) The ring supervisor is similar to the umpire in a tennis game — she oversees the game to make sure that all the rules are followed and intervenes when they're not.

Keeping up at the exchange

Working at the commodity exchange isn't for the fainthearted! Many people are attracted by the energy (pun intended) and fast pace of the exchanges, but remember that in this high-pressure environment, the competition is ruthless. Brokers are paid by how many transactions they successfully complete, so the pressure to close as many deals as possible is intense. If you ever consider a career working on the exchange floor, keep this in mind.

The preceding section covers only some of the people involved in making the exchanges run as smoothly and efficiently as possible. As an investor with a brokerage account, all you see after you place your order is a confirmation number, and most investors fail to recognize the complexity behind placing orders at the commodity exchanges. Understanding the mechanism behind the order-placement procedure goes a long way toward making you a better investor. The more information you have on the mechanics of the exchange, the better off you are placing your trades with confidence.

It's also important to note that the *open outcry system* (in which brokers stand in a trading pit filling and executing orders manually) has faced increased competition from electronic trading platforms, where orders are matched electronically. As a matter of fact, out of the major exchanges in the United States, only the CME/NYMEX, CME/COMEX, and ICE/NYBOT still rely heavily on the open outcry system to conduct business. Most exchanges now use a combination of electronic and open outcry, and many believe that the open outcry system is in jeopardy of being retired altogether. For example, in 2005, the open outcry at the CME accounted for only 30 percent of the exchange's total volume — 70 percent of orders were placed electronically.

Owning a Piece of an Exchange

Savvy investors always keep their pulse on the markets and seek to develop investment strategies that take advantage of the market fundamentals. One of the biggest trends in the global investment game in the beginning of the 21st century is the increasing popularity of commodities in investor portfolios. Driven by high commodity prices, many investors are looking for ways to profit in this sector — after all, that's why you're reading this book! (For an in-depth analysis of this trend, turn to Chapter 4.)

Commodity exchanges are becoming popular vehicles through which investors access the commodity markets. Because of their unique position, commodity exchanges stand to gain tremendously from this interest from the investing public. Interested in cashing in on this trend without trading a single contract on a single commodity exchange?

Sometimes, with all the commotion associated with the trading floors on commodity exchanges, it's easy to forget that an exchange is a business like any other business. Exchanges have employees, board members, revenues, earnings, expenses, and so on. Exchanges aren't charitable organizations; a commodity exchange is a for-profit enterprise. Just as a car manufacturer sells cars to customers, commodity exchanges sell commodity contracts to customers. That's their bread and butter — their business is to sell financial instruments to the investing public. As with any company, exchanges charge a fee for this service.

For most of their existence, exchanges have been privately held companies whose business side has remained under close wraps. However, because of the increasing popularity of commodities and the rise of the electronic trading platform, many commodity exchanges are now going public. That is, they're becoming public companies with shareholders and outside investors. Most of the commodity exchanges are now traded on stock exchanges just like Microsoft, Ford, or Wal-Mart.

In 2003, the Chicago Mercantile Exchange (the nation's largest commodity exchange in terms of volume) went public. Its shares are now traded on the New York Stock Exchange under the ticker symbol CME. CME went public at a price of $43 a share. After reaching a high of $700 a share in 2007 and a low of $200 during the Global Financial Crisis, the stock price has stabilized in the $300 range since 2008 (see Figure 8-1). Encouraged by these results, a number of other commodity exchanges went public soon afterward, and more are following suit. You can cash in on this trend by becoming a shareholder in one of these exchanges.

Figure 8-1: CME historical chart.

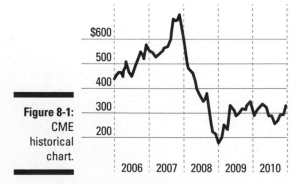

Before you purchase equity (stock) in one of the commodity exchanges, make sure that you perform a thorough analysis of the stock and the company fundamentals. A stock never goes up in a straight arrow — it always retreats before making new highs. Sometimes it doesn't make new highs at all.

I recommend that you follow a stock on paper — that is, follow its movements without actually owning the stock — for a period of at least two weeks. That way, you can get a feel for how the stock moves with the rest of the market. You can hopefully pinpoint the right entry and exit points.

Table 8-4 lists a couple of the commodity exchanges that recently have gone public.

Table 8-4	Exchanges Gone Public			
Exchange Name	**Ticker**	**Listed In**	**IPO Date**	**IPO Price**
Chicago Mercantile Exchange	CME	NYSE	December 2002	$43.60
Intercontinental Exchange	ICE	NYSE	November 2005	$39.00

If you're interested in profiting from the popularity of commodity exchanges, a unique way to do so is to purchase equity in these exchanges directly. The benefit is that you get to capitalize on the growing commodity trend without actually having to buy commodity exchange-traded products!

Chapter 9

Back to the Future: Getting a Grip on Futures and Options

Some investors think that "futures and options" and "commodities" are basically the same, but they're not. *Commodities* are a class of assets that includes energy, metals, agricultural products, and similar items. *Futures* and *options* are investment vehicles through which you can invest in commodities. Think of it this way: If commodities were a place, futures and options would be the vehicle you'd use to get there. In addition to commodities, futures and options allow you to invest in a variety of other asset classes, such as stocks, indexes, currencies, bonds, and even interest rates, often referred to as financial futures.

In Wall Street lingo, futures and options are known as *derivatives* because they *derive* their value from an underlying financial instrument such as a stock, bond, or commodity. However, futures and options are different financial instruments with singular structures and uses — but I'm getting ahead of myself.

My aim in this chapter isn't to make you an expert in trading these sophisticated financial instruments, but to introduce you to these vehicles so that you have a working knowledge of what they are. If you then choose to use them in your trading strategy, you'll at least have a good understanding of how to best utilize them. Or if you decide to hire a professional money manager to invest in the futures markets for you, you'll know the lingo and key concepts so you can ask the right questions. I include a comprehensive list of money managers who specialize in helping investors invest in the futures markets on my Web site, www.commodities-investors.com. I also discuss how to go about choosing a money manager in Chapter 7.

Taking the Mystery out of Futures and Options

Futures and options conjure up a lot of apprehension and puzzlement among investors. Most investors have never used them, and the ones who have often come back with stories about losing their life savings trading them. Their negative aspects are slightly exaggerated, but trading futures and options isn't for everyone.

By their very nature, futures and options are complex financial instruments. It's not like investing in a mutual fund, where you mail your check and wait for quarterly statements and dividends. If you invest in futures and options contracts, you need to monitor your positions daily — or even hourly. You have to keep track of the expiration date, the premium paid, the strike price, margin requirements, and other shifting variables. (I discuss these in the section "Contract specs: Keeping track of all the moving pieces.")

That said, understanding futures and options can be beneficial to you as an investor because they're powerful tools. They give you leverage and risk-management opportunities that your average financial instruments don't offer. If you can harness the power of these instruments, you can dramatically increase your leverage — and performance — in the markets.

The futures markets are only one way for you to get involved in commodities. Because they're fairly volatile, it's important that you have a solid understanding before you jump in.

Although several books deal specifically with futures and options, I recommend checking out *Trading Options For Dummies,* by George A. Fontanills (Wiley); *Trading Futures For Dummies,* by Joe Duarte, MD (Wiley); and *Derivatives Demystified,* by Andrew Chisholm (Wiley).

The Future Looks Bright: How to Trade Futures Contracts

The futures market is divided into two segments: one that's regulated and another one that's unregulated. Trading in the regulated portion of the futures market is done through designated commodity futures exchanges such as the New York Board of Trade (NYBOT) — now part of the Intercontinental Exchange (ICE) — and the Chicago Mercantile Exchange (CME), which I cover in Chapter 8. Trading in the unregulated portion of the futures market is done by individual parties outside the purview of the exchanges. This is known as the *over-the-counter (OTC) market.*

The futures market is the opposite of the cash market, often known as the *spot market,* because transactions take place right away, or on the spot.

A *futures contract* is a highly standardized financial instrument in which two parties enter into an agreement to exchange an underlying security (such as soybeans, palladium, or ethanol) at a mutually agreed-upon price at a specific time in the future — which is why it's called a futures contract.

Futures contracts, by definition, trade on designated commodity futures exchanges, such as the London Metal Exchange (LME) or the Chicago Mercantile Exchange (CME). The exchanges provide liquidity and transparency to all market participants. However, the structure of the futures market is such that only about 20 percent of market activity takes place in the exchange arena. The overwhelming majority of transactions in the futures markets take place in the OTC market. The OTC market isn't regulated or monitored by the exchanges, and it usually involves two market participants that establish the terms of their agreements through forward contracts. *Forwards* are similar to futures contracts, except that they trade in the OTC market and thus allow the parties to come up with flexible and individualized terms for their agreements. Generally, the OTC market isn't suitable for individual investors who seek speculative opportunities because it consists primarily of large commercial users (such as oil companies and airlines) who use it solely for hedging purposes.

In this chapter, I focus on derivatives that trade on the commodity exchanges. I don't focus on the OTC market because it doesn't lend itself to trading by individual investors. So when I refer to the "futures market" in this chapter, I'm talking about the trading activity in the designated commodity futures exchanges.

Despite the fact that futures contracts are designed to accommodate delivery of physical commodities, such delivery rarely takes place because the primary purpose of the futures markets is to minimize risk and maximize profits. The futures market, unlike the cash or spot market, isn't intended to serve as the primary exchange of physical commodities. Instead, it's a market where buyers and sellers transact with each other for hedging and speculative purposes. Out of the billions of contracts traded on commodity futures exchanges each year, only about 2 percent of these contracts result in the actual physical delivery of a commodity.

In the land of futures contracts, both the buyer and the seller have the right *and* the obligation to fulfill the contract's terms. This process works differently than in the realm of options: With options, the buyer has the right but *not* the obligation to exercise the option, and the seller has the obligation but *not* the right to fulfill her contractual obligations. This scenario can get a little confusing, I know! I dig deeper into these issues in the section "Keeping Your Options Open: Trading with Options."

Commodity exchanges: The great consolidation

For decades, the world of commodity exchanges was populated by a broad range of participants centered on major commercial centers, such as New York and Chicago. The Chicago Board of Trade (CBOT) specialized in soft commodities such as wheat, corn, and soybeans, and the New York Mercantile Exchange (NYMEX) had offerings in energy and metals, including crude oil, natural gas, gold, and platinum. Since the first edition of this book, most of these independent exchanges have been swept up under the great consolidation wave of 2007–2008. NYMEX, COMEX, and CBOT were gobbled up by the much-bigger Chicago Mercantile Exchange (CME), which now has the largest offering of commodity contracts on the market. In the meantime, the Intercontinental Exchange (ICE) — a predominantly electronic-based exchange — acquired the New York Board of Trade (NYBOT) and assumed trading for contracts such as coffee, cocoa, and cotton. Another important development is the advent of electronic trading and the migration from a predominantly human-based open outcry system to an Internet-based electronic trading platform. The advent of the electronic platform is significant because it allows investors to trade more contracts and get broader and faster exposure than ever.

The competition: Who trades futures?

Essentially, two types of folks trade futures contracts. The first are commercial producers and consumers of commodities who use the futures markets to stabilize either their costs (in the case of consumers) or their revenues (in the case of producers). The second group consists of individual traders, investment banks, and other financial institutions who are interested in using the futures markets as a way of generating trading profits. Both groups take advantage of the futures markets' liquidity and leverage (which I discuss in the following sections) to implement their trading strategies.

If you ever get involved in the futures markets, it's important to know who you're up against. I examine the role of these hedgers and speculators in the following sections so you're ready to deal with the competition.

Getting over the hedge

Hedgers are the actual producers and consumers of commodities. Both producers and consumers enter the futures markets with the aim of reducing price volatility in the commodities they buy or sell. Hedging gives these commercial enterprises the opportunity to reduce the risk associated with daily price fluctuations by establishing fixed prices of primary commodities for months, sometimes even years, in advance.

Hedgers can be on either side of a transaction in the futures market, the *buy side* or the *sell side.* Consider a few examples of entities that use the futures markets for hedging purposes:

✔ Farmers who want to establish steady prices for their products use futures contracts to sell their products to consumers at a fixed price for a fixed period of time, thus guaranteeing a fixed stream of revenues.

✔ Electric utility companies that supply power to residential customers can buy electricity on the futures markets, to keep their costs fixed and protect their bottom line.

✔ Transportation companies whose business depends on the price of fuel get involved in the futures markets to maintain fixed costs of fuel over specific periods of time.

To get a better idea of hedging in action, consider a hedging strategy that the airline industry uses.

One of airline executives' biggest worries is the unpredictable price of jet fuel, which can vary wildly from day to day on the spot market. Airlines don't like this kind of uncertainty because they want to keep their costs low and predictable. (They already have enough to worry about with rising pension and health-care costs, fears of terrorism, and other external factors.) So how do they do that? They hedge the price of jet fuel through the futures market.

Southwest Airlines (NYSE: LUV) is one of the most active hedgers in the industry. At any one point, Southwest may have up to 80 percent of a given year's jet fuel consumption fixed at a specific price. Southwest enters into agreements with producers through the futures markets, primarily through OTC agreements, to purchase fuel at a fixed price for a specific period of time in the future.

The benefit for Southwest (and its passengers) is that the company has fixed its costs and eliminated the volatility associated with the price fluctuation of jet fuel. This action has a direct impact on Southwest's bottom line. The advantage for the producer is that it now has a customer who's willing to purchase the product for a fixed time at a fixed price, thus guaranteeing a steady stream of cash flow.

However, unless prices in the cash market remain steady, one of the two parties who enters into this sort of agreement may have been better off without the hedge. If prices for jet fuel increase, the producer has to bear that cost and deliver jet fuel to the airline at the agreed-upon price, which is now below the market price. Similarly, if prices of jet fuel go down, the airline would have been better off purchasing jet fuel on the cash market. But because these are unknown variables, hedgers still see a benefit in entering into these agreements, to eliminate unpredictability.

The truth about speculators

For some reason, the term *speculator* carries some negative connotation, as if speculating is a sinful or immoral act. In reality, speculators play an important and necessary role in the global financial system. In fact, whenever you buy a stock or a bond, you're speculating. When you think prices are going up, you buy. When they're going down, you sell. The process of figuring out where prices are heading and how to profit from this is the essence of speculation. So we're all speculators!

In the futures markets, speculators provide much-needed liquidity that allows the many market players to match their buy and sell orders. Speculators, often simply known as *traders,* buy and sell futures contracts, options, and other exchange-traded products through an electronic platform or a broker, to profit from price fluctuations. A trader who thinks that the price of crude oil is going up will buy a crude oil futures contract to try to profit from his hunch. This action adds liquidity to the markets, which is valuable because liquidity is a prerequisite for the smooth and efficient functioning of the futures markets.

When markets are liquid, you know that you'll be able to find a buyer or a seller for your contracts. You also know that you'll get a reasonable price because liquidity offers you a large pool of market participants competing for your contracts. Finally, liquidity means that when a number of participants are transacting in the marketplace, prices aren't going to be subject to extremely wild and unpredictable price fluctuations. This doesn't mean that liquidity eliminates volatility, but it certainly helps reduce it.

At the end of the day, having a large number of market participants is positive, and speculators play an important role with the liquidity they add to the futures markets.

Contract specs: Keeping track of all the moving pieces

Trading futures contracts takes a lot of discipline, patience, and coordination. One of the biggest deterrents to participating in the futures markets is the number of moving pieces you have to constantly monitor. In this section, I go through the many pieces you have to keep track of if you decide to trade futures.

Because futures contracts can be traded on only designated and regulated exchanges, these contracts are highly standardized. *Standardization* simply means that these contracts are based on a uniform set of rules. For example, the CME crude oil contract is standardized because it represents a specific grade of crude (West Texas Intermediate) and a specific size (1,000 barrels). Therefore, you can expect all CME crude contracts to represent 1,000 barrels of West Texas Intermediate crude oil. In other words, the contract you purchase won't be for 1,000 barrels of Nigerian Bonny Light, another grade of crude oil.

The regulatory bodies that are responsible for overseeing and monitoring trading activities on commodity futures exchanges are the Commodity Futures Trading Commission (CFTC) and the National Futures Association (NFA). I discuss these at length in Chapter 8.

The buyer of a futures contract is known as the *holder;* when you buy a futures contract, you're essentially "going long" the commodity. The seller of a futures contract is referred to as the *underwriter* or *writer.* If you sell a futures contract, you're holding a short position. Remember that "going long" simply means you're on the buy side of a transaction; conversely, "going short" means you're on the sell side. In other words, when you "go long," you expect prices to rise, and when you "go short," you expect prices to decrease.

Underlying asset

The *underlying asset* is the financial instrument that the futures contract represents. The underlying asset can be anything from crude oil to platinum, to soybeans, to propane. Because futures contracts are traded on designated exchanges, every exchange offers different types of assets you can trade. For a list of these assets, be sure to read Chapter 8.

Futures contracts can be used to trade all sorts of assets, not just traditional commodities like oil and gold. Futures can be used to trade interest rates, indexes, currencies, equities, and a host of other assets. Some futures contracts even allow you to trade weather!

Before you place your order, make sure that you're very clear about the underlying commodity you want to trade. Specify on which exchange you want your order executed. This is important because you have contracts for the same commodities that trade on different exchanges. For example, aluminum futures contracts are traded on both the CME and the LME. When you're placing an order for an aluminum contract, it's important to specify where you want to buy the contract: either on the COMEX or on the LME.

Underlying quantity

The contract size, also known as the *trading unit,* is how much of the underlying asset the contract represents. To meet certain standards, all futures contracts have a predetermined and fixed size. For example, one futures contract for ethanol traded on the Chicago Board of Trade is the equivalent of one rail car of ethanol, which is approximately 29,000 gallons.

The light, sweet crude oil contract on the CME represents 1,000 U.S. barrels, which is the equivalent of 42,000 gallons. The futures contract for frozen pork bellies represents 40,000 pounds of pork.

Make sure that you know the exact amount of underlying commodity the contract represents before you purchase a futures contract.

Because more individual investors want to trade futures contracts, many exchanges are now offering contracts with smaller sizes, which means that the contracts cost less. The CME, for instance, now offers the miNY™ Light Sweet Crude Oil contract, which represents 500 barrels of oil and is half the price of its traditional crude oil contract.

Product grade

Imagine that you placed an order for a Ford Mustang and instead got a Ford Taurus. You'd be pretty upset, right? To avoid unpleasant surprises if delivery of a physical commodity actually takes place, exchanges require that all contracts represent a standard product grade. For instance, gasoline futures traded on the CME are based on contract specifications for New York Harbor Unleaded Gasoline. This grade is a uniform grade of gasoline widely used across the East Coast, which is transported to New York Harbor from refineries in the East Coast and the Gulf of Mexico. Thus, if delivery of a CME gasoline futures contracts takes place, you can expect to receive New York Harbor Unleaded Gas.

If your sole purpose is to speculate and you're not intending to have gasoline or soybeans delivered, knowing the product grade isn't as important as if you were taking physical delivery of the commodity. However, it's always good to know what kind of product you're actually trading.

Price quote

Most futures contracts are priced in U.S. dollars, but some contracts are priced in other currencies, such as the pound sterling or the Japanese yen. The price quote really depends on which exchange you're buying or selling the futures contract from. Keep in mind that if you're trading futures in a foreign currency, you're potentially exposing yourself to currency exchange risks.

Price limits

Price limits help you determine the value of the contract. Every contract has a minimum and maximum price increment, also known as *tick size*. Contracts move in ticks, which is the amount by which the futures contract increases or decreases with every transaction. Most stocks, for example, move in cents. In futures, most contracts move in larger dollar amounts, reflecting the size of the contract. In other words, one tick represents different values for different contracts.

For example, the *minimum tick size* of the ethanol futures contract on the CME is $29 per contract. This means every contract will move in increments of $29. On the other hand, the *maximum tick size* for ethanol on the CME is $4,350, meaning that if the tick size is greater than $4,350, trading will be halted. Exchanges step in when contracts are experiencing extreme volatility, to calm the markets.

The exchanges establish minimum and maximum tick sizes based on the set-tlement price during the previous day's trading session. Determining the value of the tick allows you to quantify the price swings of the contract on any given trading session.

Trading months

Although you can trade futures contracts practically around the clock, cer-tain commodities are available for delivery only during certain months.

For instance, frozen pork bellies on the CME are listed for the months of February, March, May, July, and August. This means that you can trade a July contract at any given point, but you cannot trade a June contract — a con-tract that's deliverable in June — because that contract doesn't exist. On the other hand, crude oil on the CME is available all 12 months of the year.

Check the contract listing before you trade so you know for which delivery months you can trade the contracts.

The *front month* is simply the upcoming delivery month. For example, June is the front month during the May trading session.

In the world of futures, trading and delivery months have specific abbrevia-tions attributed to each month. I list these abbreviations in Table 9-1.

Table 9-1		Monthly Abbreviation Codes	
Month	*Code*	*Month*	*Code*
January	F	July	N
February	G	August	Q
March	H	September	U
April	J	October	V
May	K	November	X
June	M	December	Z

Traders use these abbreviations to quickly identify the months they're inter-ested in trading. If you're placing an order with a futures broker (which I dis-cuss in Chapter 8), knowing these abbreviations is helpful.

Delivery location

In case of actual delivery, exchanges designate areas where the physical exchange of commodities actually takes place. For instance, delivery of the CME's WTI crude oil contract takes place in Cushing, Oklahoma, which is a major transportation hub for crude oil in the United States.

Last trading day

All futures contracts must expire at some point. The *last trading day* is the absolute latest time you have to trade that particular contract. Trading days change from exchange to exchange and from contract to contract. Be sure to check out the contract specifications at the different exchanges for information on the last trading day.

Trading hours

Before the days of electronic trading, contracts were traded through the open outcry system during specific time periods. Now, with the advent of electronic trading, you have more time to trade the contracts. Check the exchange Web sites (which I list in Chapter 8) for information on trading hours.

Knowing at what times to place your trades has a direct impact on your bottom line because the number of market participants varies throughout the day. Ideally, you'd like to execute your orders when there are the most buyers and sellers because this increases your chances of getting the best price for your contracts.

For a Few Dollars Less: Trading Futures on Margin

One of the unique characteristics of futures contracts is the ability to trade with margin. If you've ever traded stocks, you know that *margin* is the amount of borrowed money you use to pay for stock. Margin in the futures markets is slightly different than stock market margin.

In the futures markets, *margin* refers to the minimum amount of capital that must be available in your account for you to trade futures contracts. Think of margin as collateral that allows you to participate in the futures markets.

- ✔ **Initial margin:** The minimum amount of capital you need in your account to trade futures contracts
- ✔ **Maintenance margin:** The subsequent amount of capital you must contribute to your account to maintain the minimum margin requirements

Margin requirements are established for every type of contract by the exchange on which those contracts are traded. However, the futures broker you use to place your order may have different margin requirements. Make sure you find out what those requirements are before you start trading.

In the stock market, capital gains and losses are calculated after you close out your position. In the futures market, capital gains and losses are calculated at the end of the trading day and credited to or debited from your account. If you experience a loss in your positions on any given day, you receive a *margin call,* which means that you have to replenish your account to meet the minimum margin requirements if you want to keep trading.

Trading on margin provides you with a lot of leverage because you need to put up only relatively small amounts of capital as collateral to invest in significant dollar amounts of a commodity. For example, if you want to trade the soybean futures contracts on the CME, the initial margin requirement is $1,100. With this small amount, you can control a CME soybeans futures contract that has a value of approximately $28,400 (5,000 bushels at $5.68 per bushel)! This translates to a minimum margin requirement of less than 4 percent!

Margin is a double-edged sword because both profits and losses are amplified to large degrees. If you're on the right side of a trade, you're going to make a lot of money. However, you're also in a position to lose a lot (much more than your initial investment) if things don't go your way. Knowing how to use margin properly is absolutely critical. I discuss in depth how to use leverage responsibly in Chapter 3.

Taking a Pulse: Figuring Out Where the Futures Market Is Heading

You need to be familiar with a couple technical terms related to movements in the futures markets if you want to successfully trade futures contracts. (Even by Wall Street standards, these terms are kind of out there.)

Contango: It takes two to tango

Futures markets, by definition, are predicated on the future price of a commodity. Analyzing where the future price of a commodity is heading is what futures trading is all about. Because futures contracts are available for different months throughout the year, the price of the contracts changes from month to month. When the *front month* trades higher than the current month, this market condition is known as *contango.* The market is also in contango when the price of the front month is higher than the spot market, and also when late delivery months are higher than near delivery months. I include an example of the CME crude oil contract in contango in Table 9-2.

Table 9-2	CME Crude Oil in Contango
Month	*Settlement Price*
December 2010	$82.68
January 2011	$83.40
February 2011	$83.98
March 2011	$84.45
April 2011	$84.94
May 2011	$85.00

As the contract extends into the future, the price of the contract increases. Contango is thus a bullish indicator, showing that the market expects the price of the futures contract to increase steadily into the future.

Backwardation: One step forward, two steps back

Backwardation is the opposite of contango. When a market is experiencing backwardation, the contracts for future months are decreasing in value relative to the current and most recent months. The spot price is thus greater than the front month, which is greater than future delivery months. Table 9-3 shows the CME copper contract in backwardation.

Table 9-3	CME Copper in Backwardation
Month	*Settlement Price*
July 2006	$3.08
August 2006	$3.07
September 2006	$3.04

A market in backwardation is a bearish sign because traders expect prices over the long term to decrease.

The Metallgesellschaft debacle

Trading futures contracts certainly isn't for the fainthearted. Even the pros can run into lots of trouble in the futures markets. Consider what happened in the 1990s to a company called Metallgesellschaft. Metallgesellschaft (I've shortened it to MG so you won't have to go to the trouble of pronouncing it!) was a German company partly owned by a conglomerate led by Deutsche Bank that specialized in metals trading. In 1993, MG lost a staggering $2.2 billion trading futures contracts.

In the early 1990s, MG set up an energy division to trade futures contracts in the United States. Its motive was to profit by betting on the price fluctuations of crude oil. MG's strategy was based on taking advantage of the price differential between crude oil on the spot markets and futures markets. Specifically, MG sold long-term futures contracts to various parties and hedged its long-term risk by buying short-term contracts and rolling them on a monthly basis. This strategy works beautifully — but only when the long-term prices are lower than the short-term prices. In other words, this is a good strategy when the markets are in backwardation.

However, in 1993, long-term crude oil prices started increasing, and MG was caught short with these contracts. When the markets moved to contango (prices for future months were higher than the current month), MG found itself unable to hedge the long-term contracts and was forced to meet the obligations on those long-term contracts. Because it held such large open positions, MG eventually lost a mind-numbing $2.2 billion! The parent company pulled the plug, and MG was forced into liquidation.

The moral of this story is that futures trading can be volatile and risky, even for seasoned professionals. Fortunately for investors like you and me who are interested in commodities, the futures market is only one way you can invest in this asset class. If you're interested in accessing the futures markets, I recommend seeking the help of a commodity trading advisor (CTA) or a commodity pool operator (CPO). If you want to explore other ways to invest in commodities (such as through mutual funds or exchange-traded funds), I recommend reading Chapter 6.

Keeping Your Options Open: Trading with Options

There's a big difference between futures and options. Often folks think of futures and options as being one and the same — that's understandable, because whenever you hear "futures," "options" is never too far behind! However, as I explain in the following sections, futures and options are different financial instruments with singular structures and uses. Realizing this difference right off the bat will help you understand these financial instruments better.

Futures give the *holder* (buyer) and *underwriter* (seller) both the right *and* the obligation to fulfill the contract's obligations. Options give the holder the right (or option) but not the obligation to exercise the contract. The underwriter of the option, on the other hand, is required to fulfill the contract's obligations if the holder chooses to exercise the contract.

When you're buying an option, you're essentially paying for the right to buy or sell an underlying security at a specific point in time at an agreed-upon price. The price you pay for the right to exercise that option is known as the *premium*.

The technically correct way of thinking about options is as "options on futures contracts." In other words, the options contracts give you the option to buy futures contracts for commodities such as wheat and zinc. These options are different than stock options, which give you the option to purchase stocks. In this section, I examine options on futures contracts because that's the focus of this chapter. If you want an overview of stock options, I recommend *Stock Options For Dummies,* by Alan R. Simon (Wiley).

Following options in action

Understanding options can be challenging because they're, in fact, derivatives used to trade other derivatives (futures contracts). So here's an example that applies the concept of options to a real-world situation.

You walk into a car dealership and see the car of your dreams: It's shiny and beautiful, and you know you'll look great in it! Unfortunately, it costs $100,000, and you can't spend that amount of money on a car right now. However, you're due for a large bonus at work — or you just made a killing trading commodities, take your pick! — and you'll be able to pay for it in two weeks. So you approach the car dealer and ask him to hold the car for you for two weeks, at which point you can make full payment on it.

The dealer agrees but insists that he will have to charge you $5,000 for the option to buy the car in two weeks for the set price of $100,000. You agree to the terms and give him a nonrefundable deposit of $5,000 (known as the *premium* in options-speak), which gives you the right, but not the obligation, to come back in two weeks and purchase the car of your dreams. The dealer, on the other hand, is obligated to sell you the car if you choose to exercise your option to do so. In this situation, you're the *holder* of the option and the dealer is its *underwriter*.

Consider two different scenarios that unfold during the two-week period. The first one is that, a few days after you purchase the option to buy the vehicle, the car manufacturer announces that it will stop making vehicles of this kind — the car is now a limited edition and becomes a collector's car. Congratulations! The value of the car has now doubled overnight! Because you and the dealer entered into an options agreement, the dealer is obligated to sell you the car at $100,000 even though the car now costs $200,000 — if you choose to exercise your rights as the option holder. You come back to see the dealer, and you buy the car at the agreed-upon price of $100,000. You can now either drive your new car or sell it at current market price for a cool $95,000 profit ($200,000 – $100,000 – $5,000 = $95,000)!

The second scenario isn't as rosy as the first. A few days after you sign the options agreement, the car manufacturer announces that there's a defect with the car's CD player. The car works fine, so the manufacturer doesn't need to recall it, but the built-in CD player is defective and not usable. Because of this development, the value of the car drops to $80,000 (drivers like listening to their CDs, after all). As the holder of the option, you aren't obligated to purchase the car. Remember, you have the right — but not the obligation — to follow through on the contractual agreements of the contract. If you choose not to purchase the car, you will have incurred the $5,000 loss of the premium you paid for the option.

In a nutshell, that example is what trading options is all about. You can now apply this concept to profit in the capital markets in general and the commodities market in particular. For example, if you expect the price of the June copper futures contract on the CME to increase, you can buy an option on the CME that gives you the right to purchase the June copper futures contract for a specific price. You pay a premium for this option and, if you don't exercise your option before the expiration date, the only thing you lose is the premium.

Understanding trader talk

When talking about options, you need to know certain terms:

- **Premium:** The price you actually pay for the option. If you don't exercise your option, the only money you lose is the premium you paid for the contract in the first place.

- **Expiration date:** The date at which the option expires. After the expiration date, the contract is no longer valid.

- **Strike price:** The predetermined price at which the underlying asset is purchased or sold.

- **At-the-money:** When the strike price is equal to the market price, the option is known as being at-the-money.

- ✔ **In-the-money:** In a call option, when the asset's market price is above the strike price, it's in-the-money. In the land of puts, an option is in-the-money when the market price is below the strike price.

- ✔ **Out-of-the-money:** When the market price is below the strike price in a call option, that option is a money-loser: It's out-of-the-money. When the market price is greater than the strike price in a put option, it's out-of-the-money.

- ✔ **Open interest:** The total number of options or futures contracts that are still open on any given trading session. Open interest is an important measure of market interest.

Selecting option characteristics

Every option has different characteristics, depending on how you want to exercise the option and what action you want to conduct when it's exercised. Put simply, you can use options that allow you to either buy or sell an underlying security. You can further specify at which point you want to exercise the options agreement. This section lays out these characteristics for you.

Call options: Calling all investors

If you expect rising prices, you can buy a *call option* that gives you the right — but not the obligation — to *purchase* a specific amount of a security at a specific price at a specific point in the future.

When you buy a call option, you're being bullish and are expecting prices to increase — call options are similar to having a long position. When you *sell* a call option, you expect prices to fall. If the prices fall and never reach the strike price, you get to keep the premium. If prices increase and the holder exercises her option, you're obligated to sell her the underlying asset at the agreed-upon price.

Put options: Putting everything on the line

A *put option* is the exact opposite of a call option because it gives you the right, but not the obligation, to *sell* a security at some point in the future for a predetermined price. When you think the price of a security is going down, you want to use a put option to try to take advantage of this price movement.

Buying a put option is one way of shorting a security. If prices do decrease, you can purchase the security at the agreed-upon (lower) price and then turn back and sell it on the open market, pocketing the difference. On the other hand, if prices increase, you can choose to let the option expire. In this case, you lose only the premium you paid for the option.

When you *sell* a put option, you believe that prices are going to increase. If you're correct and prices increase, the holder won't exercise the option, which means you get to collect the premium. So when you sell a put option, you're actually being bullish.

Here are the possible combinations of buying and selling put and call options, accompanied by their corresponding market sentiment:

- ✓ Buying a call: Bullish
- ✓ Selling a call: Bearish
- ✓ Buying a put: Bearish
- ✓ Selling a put: Bullish

Looking at American options

When you buy an American option, you have the right to exercise that option at any time during the life of the option — from the start of the option until the expiration date. Most options traded in the United States are American options. You get a lot more flexibility out of them because you have the freedom to exercise them at any point

Taking the European alternative

The European option allows you to exercise the option only at expiration. This is a fairly rigid kind of option. The only possible advantage of a European option over an American option is that you may be able to pay a smaller premium for this option. However, because of its rigidity, I highly recommend using American options in your trading strategies.

Part III
The Power House: How to Make Money in Energy

The 5th Wave   By Rich Tennant

"This is the lowest I've seen oil in a long time."

In this part . . .

Energy is the largest commodities asset class and presents some solid investment opportunities. I help you navigate the ins and outs of the energy markets and show you ways to profit in this sector, from trading crude oil futures contracts to investing in diversified electric utilities.

Chapter 10

It's a Crude, Crude World: Investing in Crude Oil

. . . .

In This Chapter

▶ Taking a look at key metrics

▶ Getting a grip on the market fundamentals

▶ Profiting from the high price of crude

. . . .

Crude oil is undoubtedly the king of commodities, in both its production value and its importance to the global economy. Crude oil is the most-traded nonfinancial commodity in the world today, and it supplies 40 percent of the world's total energy needs — more than any other single commodity. Since the first edition of *Commodities For Dummies* was published in 2006, the importance of crude oil has only increased. Despite many calls to shift energy consumption toward more renewable energy sources, the crude reality is that petroleum products are still the dominant resource worldwide. In fact, to this day, more barrels of crude oil are traded daily (87 million barrels by 2010 figures) than any other commodity. Crude oil's importance also stems from the fact that it's the base product for a number of indispensable goods, including gasoline, jet fuel, and plastics.

Oil is truly the lifeblood of the global economy. Without it, the modern world would come to a screeching halt. Drivers wouldn't be able to drive their cars, ships would have no fuel to transport goods around the world, and airplanes would be grounded indefinitely.

Because of its preeminent role in the global economy, crude oil makes for a great investment. In this chapter, I show you how to make money investing in what is arguably the world's greatest natural resource. However, the oil industry is a multidimensional, complex business with many players that often have conflicting interests. Proceeding with a bit of caution and making sure that you understand the market fundamentals is essential for success.

In the following sections, I give you an overview of the global oil industry and the many links in the oil supply chain. I analyze consumption and production figures, introduce you to the major players (both countries and companies), and show you the best ways to execute a sound investment strategy.

Seeing the Crude Realities

Having a good understanding of the global consumption and production patterns is important if you're considering investing in the oil industry. Knowing how much oil is produced in the world, which countries are producing it, and which consumers are accepting the shipments allows you to develop an investment strategy that benefits from the oil market fundamentals.

I'm sometimes amazed at some of the misconceptions regarding the oil industry. For example, I was once speaking with students about energy independence and was shocked when a majority of them claimed that the United States got more than 50 percent of its oil from the Persian Gulf and Saudi Arabia, in particular; in fact, nothing could be further from the truth.

The United States is the third-largest producer of crude oil in the world. Take a look at Table 10-2, and you'll quickly see that the United States produces more than 7 million barrels a day (this includes oil products), behind only Saudi Arabia and Russia. In fact, the United States didn't become a net importer of oil until 1993; until that point, the United States produced more than 50 percent of the oil it consumed domestically.

According to 2010 figures, the United States imports about 65 percent of its oil. If energy (oil) independence is measured by the percentage of oil a country imports, then the United States is more energy-independent than both Germany (which imports 80 percent of its oil) and Japan (which imports more than 90 percent).

A crude oil history lesson

The Arab Oil Embargo of 1973 underscored the importance of crude oil to the global economy. During that year, the Arab members of the Organization of Petroleum Exporting Countries (OPEC) placed an embargo on crude oil shipments to Western countries. Within a matter of weeks, the price of crude oil skyrocketed by 400 percent, and a number of industrialized nations were thrown into recessions, experiencing high inflation and high unemployment for a number of years thereafter. The oil price shocks of the 1970s and their debilitating effects on the global economy underscored crude oil's indispensability.

Mad Max is mad about oil

Remember the 1980s movie *Mad Max*, which launched Mel Gibson's career? Released only a few years after the Arab Oil Embargo of 1973, the movie is actually a depiction of a world without oil. It portrays a society plunged into civil disorder, chaos, and unrest as a result of a fuel shortage. The citizens resort to violence and mayhem to steal any fuel they can get their hands on.

This high-octane drama demonstrates the extent to which societies were affected by the oil shocks of the 1970s and underscores the importance of oil as an essential element of modern life.

The biggest oil exporter to the United States isn't a Middle Eastern country, but our northern neighbor. That's right, Canada is the largest exporter of crude oil to the United States! Persian Gulf oil makes up about 20 percent of imported oil to the U.S.

My point here is that a lot of misinformation about this topic persists, and you need to be armed with the correct figures to be a successful investor. In the following sections, I introduce you to all the market participants (traders, major oil companies, and producing/consuming countries) and the metrics they monitor, such as global reserve estimates, daily production rates, daily consumption rates, daily export figures, and daily import figures. I present you with the most up-to-date information regarding oil production and consumption patterns. Because these patterns are likely to change in the future because of supply and demand, I also tell you where you can go to get the latest information on the oil markets. Having the facts makes you a better investor.

No need for a reservation: Examining global reserve estimates

As an investor, knowing which countries have large crude oil deposits is an important part of your investment strategy. As demand for crude oil increases, countries that have large deposits of this natural resource stand to benefit tremendously. One way to benefit from this trend is to invest in indigenous countries and companies with large reserves of crude oil. (I go through this strategy in detail in the section "Get your passport ready: Investing overseas," later in this chapter.)

Oil & Gas Journal estimates that global proven crude oil reserves as of 2009 are 1,342 billion barrels (1.34 trillion barrels). Table 10-1 lists the countries with the largest proven crude oil reserves, according to 2010 data. These figures may change as new oil fields are discovered, as new technologies facilitate the extraction of additional oil from existing fields, and as a result of natural depletion.

Table 10-1	Largest Oil Reserves by Country, 2010	
Rank	**Country**	**Proven Reserves (Billion Barrels)**
1	Saudi Arabia	261
2	Iran	150
3	Iraq	143
4	Kuwait	104
5	United Arab Emirates	99
6	Venezuela	98
7	Russia	60
8	Libya	41
9	Nigeria	36
10	United States	21

Source: Oil & Gas Journal

Although Canada isn't on this list, it has proven reserves of 4.7 billion barrels of *conventional* crude oil, which is crude that's easily recoverable and accounted for. In addition to conventional crude, Canada is rich in unconventional crude oil located in oil sands. Oil from oil sands is much more difficult to extract and, as a result, generally isn't included in the calculation of official and conventional reserve estimates. However, if Canada's oil sands were included, Canada would be catapulted to the number two spot, with a grand total of 178 billion barrels.

Having large deposits of crude doesn't mean that a country has exploited and developed all its oil fields. For example, although Iraq has the third-largest oil deposits in the world, it's not even among the top ten producing countries, because of poor and underdeveloped infrastructure. There's a big difference between proven reserves and actual production, as you can see by comparing Tables 10-1 and 10-2.

Brazil offshore

One of the most noteworthy events to grip the petroleum industry over the last several years has been the prolific discoveries of oil in offshore Brazil. Since 2007, the steady stream of important discoveries coming out of Brazil has seemed endless. First, the Tupi oil field that was discovered off the southeastern coast, not far from Rio de Janeiro, added between 6 billion and 8 billion barrels to the country's petroleum reserves. Most of this oil is located in what is known as "pre-salt regions," which are more difficult to access but still fully recoverable.

A few months after Brazil's state-owned oil company, Petrobras, discovered the Tupi oil field, privately held oil company OGX announced another large discovery in more shallow waters of the Campos Basin. OGX's discovery of approximately 3.7 billion barrels helped catapult its main shareholder, Eike Batista, into the ranks of the world's billionaires. These discoveries and other activities in the Brazilian commodities space make Batista now the seventh-richest person in the world, according to *Forbes* magazine.

Not long after these two major discoveries, Petrobras announced an even larger discovery: the Libra field, which may hold at least 10 billion to 15 billion barrels of recoverable oil in an offshore field. These major discoveries mean that Brazil has the fastest-growing reserves in the world, faster than Angola, Venezuela, and Australia. According to BP, Brazil's reserves have the capacity to grow at least 700 percent due to the oil in its pre-salt offshore region. It's therefore critical to keep an eye on Brazil and other discoveries that may shift the global petroleum calculus.

The calculation of proven, recoverable deposits of crude oil isn't an exact science. For example, *Oil & Gas Journal* figures are different from those of the Energy Information Administration (EIA), whose figures, in turn, are different from those of the International Energy Agency (IEA). I recommend taking a big-picture approach to global reserve estimates and consulting all the major sources for these statistics. To keep up on updated figures and statistics on the oil industry, check out the following organizations and their Web sites:

- **BP Statistical Review (BP):** www.bp.com
- **Energy Information Administration (EIA):** www.eia.doe.gov
- **International Energy Agency (IEA):** www.iea.org
- *Oil & Gas Journal:* www.ogj.com

Staying busy and productive: Looking at production figures

Identifying the countries with large reserves is important, but it's only a starting point as you begin investing in the oil markets. To determine which countries are exploiting these reserves adequately, I recommend looking at another important metric: actual production. Having large reserves is meaningless if a country isn't tapping those reserves to produce oil. Table 10-2 lays out the top ten producers of crude oil.

Table 10-2	Largest Producers of Crude Oil, 2009	
Rank	*Country*	*Daily Production (Million Barrels)*
1	Saudi Arabia	10.8
2	Russia	9.8
3	United States	8.5
4	Iran	4.2
5	China	4.0
6	Canada	3.4
7	Mexico	3.2
8	United Arab Emirates	3.0
9	Kuwait	2.8
10	Venezuela	2.6

Source: United States Department of Energy

A number of factors influence how much crude a country is able to pump out of the ground daily, including geopolitical stability and the application of technologically advanced crude-recovery techniques. Also remember that daily production may vary throughout the year because of disruptions resulting either from geopolitical events such as embargos, sanctions, and sabotage that put a stop to daily production or from other external factors, like weather. For example, consider Hurricane Katrina and its devastating effect on U.S. oil supply in summer 2005, as well as the BP Gulf oil spill in 2010.

You need to keep a close eye on global daily supply because any disruption in the production supply chain can have a strong impact on the current price of crude oil. Because there's a tight supply-and-demand equation, any disruption in supply can send prices for crude skyrocketing.

Traders in the commodity exchanges follow the daily crude oil production numbers closely. Benchmark crude oil contracts such as both the *West Texas Intermediate* (WTI), traded on the Chicago Mercantile Exchange (CME), and the North Sea Brent, traded on the Intercontinental Exchange (ICE) in London, are affected by supply numbers. As a result, the market closely watches any geopolitical event or natural disaster that may reduce production. (Check out Chapter 9 for more on the crude oil futures contracts.)

If you're an active oil trader with a futures account, following these daily production numbers — which are available through the Energy Information Administration (EIA) Web site, at www.eia.doe.gov — is crucial. The futures markets are particularly sensitive to daily crude oil production numbers, and any event that takes crude off the market can have a sudden impact on crude futures contracts. If you're a long-term investor in the markets, monitoring this number is also important because production figures can have an effect on the general stock market performance as well. For example, if rebels seize a pipeline in Nigeria and 300,000 barrels of Nigerian crude are taken off the market, this will result in higher crude prices, which will have an impact on U.S. stocks (they generally fall). Thus, your stock portfolio holdings may be at risk because of daily crude oil production disruptions. Therefore, monitoring this statistic regularly is important for both short-term traders and long-term investors.

It's a demanding field: Checking out demand figures

The United States tops the list of oil consumers and has been the single largest consumer of crude oil for the last 25 years. Although a lot of folks pay attention to the demand increase from China and India, most of the demand for crude oil (and the resulting price pressures) still comes from the United States. Traders around the world closely watch supply, but demand figures are equally important because they indicate a steady and sustained increase in crude demand for the mid- to long term. This is likely to maintain increased pressure on crude prices. I list the top ten consumers of crude oil in the world in Table 10-3.

Table 10-3	Largest Consumers of Crude Oil, 2009	
Rank	*Country*	*Daily Consumption (Million Barrels)*
1	United States	19.5
2	China	7.8
3	Japan	4.8
4	India	3.0
5	Russia	2.9
6	Germany	2.6
7	Brazil	2.5
8	Saudi Arabia	2.4
9	Canada	2.3
10	South Korea	2.2

Source: United States Department of Energy

As of 2010, global consumption stood at approximately 86 million barrels per day. The United States and China are currently the biggest consumers of crude oil in the world, and this trend will continue throughout the 21st century, with global consumption expected to increase to 120 million barrels a day by 2025. An important development to keep track of is that although global consumption figures might remain within a tight trading band, the consumer profile is likely to change. Specifically, you can expect oil consumption in OECD and developed countries to remain stagnant — and, in some cases, experience a decrease — and consumption in emerging market nations to increase. For example, the trend is for countries like China, India, Russia, and Saudi Arabia to continue to increase domestic consumption as their economies remain in a rapid growth trajectory. Countries that are fairly mature, such as Germany and Canada, won't experience growth nearly as fast as the emerging market economies.

Figure 10-1 shows the expected global consumption through 2025, as well as the expected growth from the two largest consumers, the United States and China.

Figure 10-1: Expected daily global consumption of crude oil, 2001–2025.

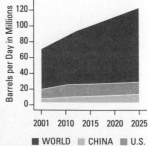

Always design an investment strategy that will profit from long-term trends. This steady increase in global demand for crude oil is a good reason to be bullish on oil prices.

Going in and out: Eyeing imports and exports

When planning your investments in the oil market, another pair of numbers to keep close tabs on is export and import figures. Exports are different from production: A country can produce a lot of oil and consume most, if not all, of it — as the United States does. On the other end of the spectrum, a country can produce plenty of oil and export most of it, as is the case in the United Arab Emirates.

Identifying the top exporting countries allows you to zero in on the countries that are actually generating revenues from selling crude oil to other countries. Countries that are net exporters of crude stand to benefit tremendously from the oil boom, and you can get in on the action by investing domestically in these countries; I outline a strategy in the later section "Get your passport ready: Investing overseas." In Table 10-4, I list the top oil-exporting countries in 2009.

Table 10-4	Top Ten Oil Exporters, 2009	
Rank	*Country*	*Daily Oil Exports (Million Barrels)*
1	Saudi Arabia	8.1
2	Russia	7.1
3	United Arab Emirates	2.5
4	Iran	2.3
5	Norway	2.3
6	Kuwait	2.2
7	Nigeria	2.1
8	Venezuela	1.9
9	Algeria	1.8
10	Angola	1.7

Source: United States Department of Energy

What is OPEC and how does it affect the oil markets?

The *Organization of Petroleum Exporting Countries* (OPEC) is made up of countries that are involved in the production and export of crude oil products around the world. Currently, OPEC has 11 member countries: Algeria, Indonesia, Iran, Iraq, Kuwait, Libya, Nigeria, Qatar, Saudi Arabia, the United Arab Emirates (UAE), and Venezuela. Because OPEC's members collectively hold about 65 percent of total crude oil reserves and produce 40 percent of the world's oil, they have considerable influence on the markets.

OPEC's members meet regularly at its headquarters in Vienna, Austria, to establish the course of action for its members. Because its members are key players in the global oil markets, any decision OPEC takes can significantly affect the price of oil on a global scale. One mechanism OPEC uses to achieve this influence is its quota system, in which individual members must follow pre-established production quotas.

OPEC quotas are an important statistic to regularly monitor because they dictate the level of oil production for some of the world's most important oil producers. But even more important than the self-imposed quotas is the actual oil production from each member country, because that may differ from the quotas: Some countries, enticed by the high price of crude, are sometimes tempted to increase their production because this means more petrodollars in their coffers. Ironically, the production quota is partly responsible for the increased prices, meaning that prices decrease as production increases. You can keep track of regular developments from OPEC that may affect oil markets through the OPEC Web site, at www.opec.org. Although OPEC's influence on the markets has diminished since the 1973 Arab Oil Embargo, it still wields considerable influence over the oil markets.

Traders pay a lot of attention to exports, but imports, which represent the other side of equation, are equally important. Countries that are main importers of crude oil are primarily advanced, industrialized societies like Germany and the United States. These countries are rich enough that they can absorb crude oil price increases, but as a general rule, the importers face a lot of pressure during any price increases. This pressure sometimes translates into lower stock market performances in the importing countries, which means you need to be careful if you're exposed to the domestic stock markets of these oil importers. I list the top crude oil–importing countries of 2009 in Table 10-5.

Table 10-5	Top Ten Oil Importers, 2009	
Rank	**Country**	**Daily Oil Imports (Million Barrels)**
1	United States	1,012.2
2	Japan	4.9
3	China	3.7

Rank	Country	Daily Oil Imports (Million Barrels)
4	Germany	2.3
5	South Korea	2.2
6	India	1.9
7	France	1.8
8	Spain	1.5
9	Italy	1.5
10	Taiwan	1.0

Source: United States Department of Energy

Going Up the Crude Chain

Crude oil by itself isn't very useful; it derives its value from its products. Only after it's processed and refined into consumable products such as gasoline, propane, and jet fuel does it become so valuable.

Crude oil was formed over millions of years from the remains of dead animals and other organisms whose bodies decayed in the earth. Because of a number of geological factors such as sedimentation, these remains were eventually transformed into crude oil deposits. Therefore, crude oil is literally a *fossil fuel* — a fuel derived from fossils. As a matter of fact, the word *petroleum* comes from the Latin words *petra,* which means "rock," and *oleum,* which means "oil." So the word *petroleum* literally means "oil from the rocks."

Take a look at Figure 10-2 to see some of the products an average barrel of crude oil yields.

A barrel holds 42 gallons of crude oil or crude oil equivalents. (That's about 159 liters.) *Barrel* is abbreviated as *bbl, barrels* as *bbls.*

Not all crudes are created equal. If you invest in crude oil, you need to realize right off the bat that crude oil comes in different qualities with different characteristics. You'd be surprised by how different that "black stuff" can be from region to region. Generally, crude oil is classified into two broad categories: light and sweet, and heavy and sour. Other classifications are used, but these are the two major ones.

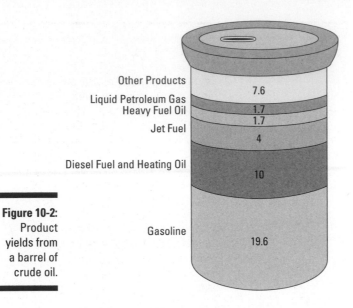

Other Products — 7.6

Liquid Petroleum Gas — 1.7
Heavy Fuel Oil — 1.7

Jet Fuel — 4

Diesel Fuel and Heating Oil — 10

Gasoline — 19.6

Figure 10-2:
Product
yields from
a barrel of
crude oil.

The two criteria most widely used to determine the quality of crude oil are density and sulfur content.

- ✓ **Density** usually refers to how much a crude oil yields in terms of products, such as heating oil and jet fuel. For instance, a crude oil with lower density, known as a *light crude,* tends to yield higher levels of products. On the other hand, a crude oil with high density, commonly referred to as a *heavy crude,* has lower product yields.

  The density of a crude oil, also known as the *gravity,* is measured by a scale devised by the American Petroleum Institute (API). The higher the API number, expressed in degrees, the lower the density of the crude oil. Therefore, a crude oil with a density of 43 degrees API will yield more desirable crude oil products than a crude oil with a density of 35 degrees API. Heavy crude (which is found in Venezuela and Canada) has an API degree of 20 or below.

- ✓ **Sulfur content** is another key determinant of crude oil quality. Sulfur is a corrosive material that decreases the purity of a crude oil. Therefore, a crude oil with high sulfur content, which is known as *sour,* is much less desirable than a crude oil with low sulfur content, known as *sweet* crude.

What's the deal with peak oil?

Is the world really running out of oil? The concept of *peak oil* has generated much attention in recent years. A plethora of books have been written about whether the world is running out of oil, and proponents (and opponents) of this theory have hit the airwaves en masse. This topic is a serious one, but unfortunately, folks tend to get carried away and start spinning tales of global gloom and doom. It's important to remain level-headed when talking about this issue. Basically, two schools of thought have arisen.

The first school argues that the world has already reached peak production and that demand is going to quickly suck out what's remaining of crude oil in the world. The other side argues that the world still has abundant crude oil supplies and that, through technological developments and other means, crude oil that wasn't previously extractable will be brought to market. Both arguments have some merit. First, crude oil is a finite resource and, by definition, is available only in limited quantities. However, people have been saying that the world is going to run out of oil since the first commercially viable oil well was discovered in Titusville, Pennsylvania, back in 1859. One hundred and fifty years later, the world still hasn't run out of oil. Does this mean that the world will never run out of oil? Of course not. But it does indicate that these calls have been made before and are likely to continue well into the future.

Many experts agree that completely running out of oil in the near future is an unlikely event. I prefer to put it this way: The world isn't about to run out of oil — the world is about to run out of cheap, high-quality, and readily available oil. The light, sweet crude oil that refiners prefer because of its high products yield (discussed in the section "Going Up the Crude Chain" and in Chapter 13) is running low. However, the world still has plenty of crude that's of a heavier quality. Just look at Canada's oil sands. This heavy crude isn't preferred because of its low quality, but there's plenty of it to go around for a long time. In addition, technological advances (such as horizontal drilling) are enabling previously unextractable oil to now be extracted. Therefore, the oil fields are yielding more crude than ever, both in terms of percentage and on an absolute basis.

As an investor, you need to focus on the fundamentals of the market. Whether the world is running out of oil is a hot debate that garners a lot of attention, but panic isn't an investment strategy. Even if the world truly is running out of oil, you still need to look at the market fundamentals and develop an investment strategy that's going to take advantage of these fundamentals.

If history is a guide, humans can be extremely resourceful in sustaining themselves. If crude does run out, we'll find alternative sources of energy (which I look at in Chapter 13). Because energy is necessary to human life, you can be sure that people will develop alternatives. A move is already underway toward investing in alternative energy sources, such as wind and solar energy, as well as other, more abundant fossil fuels such as coal. This trend likely will continue in the coming years. As an investor, you need to go where the value is.

How is this criteria important to you as an investor? First, if you want to invest in the oil industry, you need to know what kind of oil you're going to get for your money. If you're going to invest in an oil company, you need to be able to determine which type of crude it's processing. You can find this information in the company's annual or quarterly reports. A company involved in producing light, sweet crude will generate more revenue from this premium crude than one involved in processing heavy, sour crude. This distinction doesn't mean that you shouldn't invest in companies with exposure to heavy, sour crude; you just have to factor the type into your investment strategy.

Table 10-6 lists some important crude oils and their characteristics.

Table 10-6	Crude Oil Grades	
Crude Oil Type	*Density (API)*	*Sulfur Content*
North West Shelf (Australia)	60.0	0.01
Arab Super Light (Saudi Arabia)	50.0	0.06
Bonny Light (Nigeria)	35.4	0.14
Duri (Indonesia)	21.5	0.14

As you can see, you can choose from a wide variety of crude oil products as investments. If you're interested in investing in a specific country, you need to find out what kind of crude oil it produces. Ideally, you want a crude oil with low sulfur content and a high API number as a density benchmark.

Making Big Bucks with Big Oil

The price of crude oil skyrocketed during the first decade of the 21st century, as you can see in Figure 10-3. If this period is any indication of what's in store for oil, you definitely want to develop a winning game plan to take advantage of this trend. That said, crude remains a volatile commodity that's subject to external market forces. Specifically, the Global Financial Crisis of 2008 and its aftermath resulted in a price collapse of global crude oil markets during that time period.

The period leading up to 2008 witnessed an overheating global economy, with excess liquidity, historically low interest rates, and increasing global trade. These forces (along with several others) pushed oil prices to their record highs, approaching $150 per barrel. However as the financial crisis struck Wall Street, Europe, and the rest of the world markets, oil prices experienced an asset price deflation similar to what most other assets were experiencing worldwide. Therefore, it's advisable to be mindful of economic forces operating outside internal market-specific considerations when trading oil markets. In other words, you must view spare capacity, production volumes, and other metrics inherent to the petroleum markets within the context of global market forces.

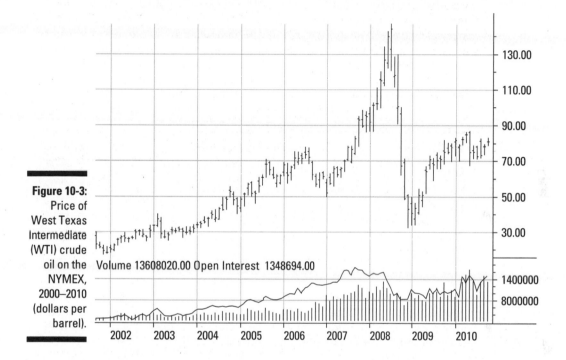

Figure 10-3:
Price of West Texas Intermediate (WTI) crude oil on the NYMEX, 2000–2010 (dollars per barrel).

I talk about how to invest directly in West Texas Intermediate crude oil and other oil futures contracts in Chapter 9.

A lot of people are making a lot of money from the price fluctuations of crude and gasoline. Why shouldn't you be one of them? In this section, I show you how to actually profit from the prices at the pump!

Oil companies: Lubricated and firing on all cylinders

Oil companies get a bad rap. Whatever you may think of them, they make for a great investment. Oil companies are responsible for bringing precious energy products to consumers, and for this service they're compensated — handsomely. Oil companies are for-profit companies that are run for the benefit of their shareholders. Instead of complaining about oil companies, why not become a shareholder of one (or more)?

In this section, I talk about the integrated oil companies, sometimes known as "big oil," "the majors," or "integrated oil companies." These are the oil companies that are involved in all the phases of the oil-production process, from exploring for oil to refining it and then transporting it to consumers. ExxonMobil, Chevron Texaco, and BP are all "big oil" companies.

Big oil companies aren't the only players in the oil business. Many other companies are involved in specific aspects of the transformational process of crude oil. For example, some companies, like Valero, are primarily involved in refining; others, such as General Maritime, own fleets of tankers that transport crude oil and products. I discuss how to invest in these companies — the refiners, transporters, and explorers — in Chapter 14.

Flying solo: Looking at individual oil companies

The major oil companies have been posting record profits in recent years. In 2005, ExxonMobil announced the largest annual corporate profit in history as it earned a staggering $36.1 billion on revenues of $371 billion! To put it in perspective, Saudi Arabia's 2005 GDP was $338 billion. Exxon continued its record string of earnings, posting net income of $40.1 billion in 2007 and $45 billion in 2008. It went through a rough patch in 2009 with the Global Financial Crisis but still managed to earn more than $19 billion for the year. Another big oil company, ConocoPhillips (NYSE: COP), raked in $13.53 billion in profits for 2005, up 66 percent from the previous year. In 2009, ConocoPhillips posted net income of $4.8 billion. Meanwhile, Chevron Corp. posted $10.4 billion in net income for 2009.

These announcements are a result of the increased global demand for crude oil and its products, as well as the technological and managerial efficiency practiced by the majors. As global demand continues and supplies remain limited, I expect big oil companies to keep generating solid revenues and profits. As the Global Financial Crisis amply demonstrated, earnings and revenues don't move in a straight line; you need to be able to tactically position your portfolio to profit from short-term market disruptions. In Table 10-7, I list some of the companies you may want to include in your portfolio.

Table 10-7	Major Integrated Oil Companies, 2009		
Oil Company	*Ticker*	*Revenues*	*Earnings*
ExxonMobil	XOM	$301 billion	$19 billion
BP	BP	$239 billion	$16 billion
PetroChina	PTR	$70 billion	$18 billion
Chevron	CVX	$167 billion	$10 billion
ConocoPhillips	COP	$152 billion	$5 billion

Oil Company	Ticker	Revenues	Earnings
Eni	E	$95 billion	$5 billion
Petrobras	PBR	$91 billion	$15 billion
Repsol	REP	$55 billion	$1.5 billion

This table is only a brief snapshot of some of the major integrated oil companies you can choose to add to your portfolio. For a more comprehensive list, check out Yahoo! Finance's section on integrated oil companies, at `biz.yahoo.com/ic/120.html`.

Most of these traditional oil companies have now moved into other areas in the energy sphere. These companies not only process crude oil into different products, but they also have vast petrochemicals businesses, as well as growing projects that involve natural gas and, increasingly, alternative energy sources. (To reflect this shift, for example, BP has changed its name from British Petroleum to Beyond Petroleum.) The bottom line is that investing in these oil companies gives you exposure to other sorts of products in the energy industry as well.

Although revenues and earnings are important metrics to look at before investing in these companies, you also need to perform a thorough due diligence that considers other important factors to determine a company's health. I introduce some of these key metrics in Chapter 14, to help you select the most suitable energy companies for your portfolio.

Slippery slopes

Although energy companies involved in the petroleum and hydrocarbon business provide indispensable services to the global economy, the nature of the work involved carries large amounts of risk. One such risk is environmental risk, as the world clearly saw during BP's oil spill in the Gulf of Mexico in 2010. What started out as routine offshore drilling ended up as one of the costliest and most serious environmental disasters of the last decade. Thousands of wildlife species and hundreds of miles of coastline were affected. In addition to the environmental costs associated with such events — which are extremely high — the financial costs to the community, the company, shareholders, and investors are significant.

As an investor, it's extremely difficult to fully hedge against such types of events. To mitigate any risk factors when such events occur, it's critical that you monitor your commodity investments as frequently as possible; in fact, I recommend that you follow the markets and developments in your portfolio holdings at least daily. Doing so ensures that you're in a position of rapid tactical response to limit and protect your downside as an investor.

John D. Rockefeller: Father of the modern oil industry

Most of today's most important oil companies are offspring of the Standard Oil Company, which John D. Rockefeller started in the late 19th century. Perhaps no other company has had as much of an impact on an industry as Standard Oil has on the oil industry. Standard Oil was one of the first truly global companies that was involved in all aspects of the oil supply chain, from extraction and production to transportation, distribution, and marketing. The company got so big that the Department of Justice ordered its breakup. The resulting companies are still today's dominant energy companies. Standard Oil of New Jersey became Exxon, and Standard Oil of New York became Mobil — the two companies eventually merged and are now ExxonMobil; Standard of California became Chevron, and Standard of Ohio is now known as Marathon Oil. Even though the company was forced to break up, the influence of Rockefeller's Standard Oil Company is still felt in the industry today.

Oil company ETFs: Strength in numbers

If you can't decide which oil company you want to invest in, you have several other options that allow you to buy the market, so to speak. One option is to buy *exchange-traded funds* (ETFs) that track the performance of a group of integrated oil companies. I discuss ETFs in depth in Chapter 5, but here are a few oil company ETFs to consider:

- ✔ **Energy Select Sector SPDR (AMEX: XLE):** The XLE ETF is the largest energy ETF in the market. It's part of the S&P's family of *Standard & Poor's Depository Receipts* (SPDR), commonly referred to as *spiders,* and tracks the performance of a basket of oil company stocks. Some of the stocks it tracks include the majors ExxonMobil and Chevron; however, it also tracks oil services companies such as Halliburton and Schlumberger (which I discuss in Chapter 14). You get a nice mix of integrated oil companies and other independent firms by investing in the XLE.

- ✔ **iShares Goldman Sachs Natural Resources Sector (AMEX: IGE):** The IGE ETF mirrors the performance of the Goldman Sachs Natural Resources Sector index, which tracks the performance of companies like ConocoPhillips, Chevron, and BP, as well as refiners such as Valero and Suncor. (I talk about refiners in Chapter 14.) Although most of this ETF is invested in integrated oil companies, it also enables you to play a broad spectrum of energy companies.

- ✔ **iShares S&P Global Energy Sector (AMEX: IXC):** This ETF mirrors the performance of the Standard & Poor's Global Energy Sector index. Buying this ETF gives you exposure to companies such as ExxonMobil, Chevron, ConocoPhillips, and Royal Dutch Shell. Launched at the end of 2001, the ETF has 35 percent aggregate returns for a three-year period.

Get your passport ready: Investing overseas

Another great way to capitalize on oil profits is to invest in an emerging market fund that invests in countries that both sit on large deposits of crude oil and have the infrastructure in place to export crude oil.

A country may have large deposits of crude oil, but it isn't necessarily able to produce and export crude oil for a profit. Iraq is a good example. Even though it sits on the third-largest reserves of crude oil in the world (see Table 10-1), Iraq isn't even one of the top ten exporters of crude because its infrastructure and security environment isn't secure enough.

Countries that export crude oil have seen their current account surpluses reach record highs. (*Current account* measures a country's balance of payments as they relate to trade.) These windfall profits are having a tremendous effect on the economies of such countries. The stock markets of some of these countries, particularly the Persian Gulf countries (known as the *Gulf Cooperation Council,* or GCC), have had a remarkable run during the first decade of this century, averaging double-digit compounded annual returns. As their economies have grown from their hydrocarbon wealth, these countries have established sovereign wealth funds (SWFs) to diversify their earnings and holdings away from petroleum products.

Many Persian Gulf countries have large capital resources that they're deploying across global capital markets and asset purchases. Abu Dhabi, the city-state with the largest oil reserves in the United Arab Emirates, has established the Abu Dhabi Investment Authority (ADIA), the Abu Dhabi Investment Council (ADIC), and the International Petroleum Investment Corporation (IPIC) to invest its hydrocarbon receipts. This move has resulted in a broad and significant diversification of Abu Dhabi's economy away from petroleum and into other strategic sectors, such as technology and aerospace. The local stock markets are a great way to get exposure to these economies, and you can also follow private equity opportunities as an investor.

The current account surplus is an important measure of how much a country is benefiting from the current oil boom. For example, Saudi Arabia's current account surplus reached a record-setting $150 billion in 2005, thanks largely to its oil exports. OPEC countries (see the sidebar "What is OPEC and how does it affect the oil markets?") are expected to generate a whopping $500 billion current account surplus in 2006 because of the high price of oil.

For the uninitiated, investing directly in emerging markets can be a risky proposition and requires a lot of research. Some countries have different regulatory rules than the United States, and you need to know those rules before you get involved in a foreign venture.

One way to play emerging markets while avoiding direct risks is to invest in emerging markets funds located in the United States. These funds hire professionals who are familiar with the business environment in target countries and can navigate these foreign investment seas. These funds enable you to take advantage of booms in foreign countries, while remaining within the safe regulatory and investing environment of the United States.

A couple emerging markets funds give you indirect exposure to the booming oil-exporting countries:

✔ Evergreen Emerging Markets Growth I (EMGYX)

✔ Fidelity Emerging Markets (FEMKX)

For more information on how to choose the right mutual fund manager, turn to Chapter 7.

If you're interested in finding out more about the global oil industry, I highly recommend Daniel Yergin's masterpiece on the subject, *The Prize: The Epic Quest for Oil, Money and Power* (Free Press).

Chapter 11

Welcome to Gas Vegas, Baby! Trading Natural Gas

*I*f crude oil is the king of commodities, natural gas is sometimes said to be the queen. Although crude oil accounts for about 40 percent of total energy consumed in the United States (the biggest energy market in the world), approximately 25 percent of energy consumption comes from natural gas. Natural gas is therefore an important source of energy both in the United States and around the world, and it can offer tremendous moneymaking opportunities.

Similar to crude oil (see Chapter 10) and coal (see Chapter 13), natural gas is a *nonrenewable fossil fuel* found in large deposits within the earth. As a matter of fact, natural gas is sometimes found not too far away from crude oil deposits. Crude oil is the liquid fossil fuel, coal is the solid one, and natural gas is the gaseous fossil fuel.

People are sometimes confused by the term *natural gas* because they think (incorrectly) that it refers to the *gas* (gasoline) they use to fill their tanks. Although natural gas is sometimes used as a transportation fuel, the gasoline you buy at the gas station and natural gas have nothing to do with each other. The gasoline your car consumes is a product of crude oil, whereas natural gas is an entirely different member of the fossil fuel family, used primarily for heating, cooling, and cooking purposes.

Because of its importance as a source of energy, natural gas makes for a good investment. It's an important commodity with many applications. In this chapter, I present you with all the information you need to develop an investment strategy in the natural gas segment of energy. Because it's important to get all the facts up front about this commodity, I first provide you with hands-on information about the applicability of natural gas — how it's used and how you can profit from these uses. Then I give you a snapshot of the global natural gas market so you know who's producing it and who's consuming it. Identifying these patterns is a necessary part of developing a sound investment strategy. Finally, I show you how to actually start investing in and trading nat gas, as traders sometimes call it. Natural gas may not get the same kind of attention as crude oil, but it still makes for a great investment!

What's the Use? Looking at Natural Gas Applications

Because it's one of the cleanest-burning fossil fuels, natural gas has become increasingly popular as an energy source. In the United States alone, natural gas accounts for nearly a quarter of total energy consumption, as Figure 11-1 shows.

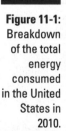

Figure 11-1: Breakdown of the total energy consumed in the United States in 2010.

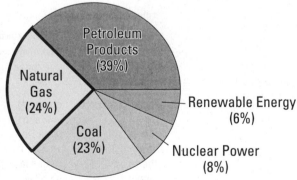

Source: U.S. Department of Energy

As you can see from Figure 11-1, natural gas is second only to petroleum when it comes to generating energy in the United States.

So who uses all this natural gas? The primary consumers of this commodity are the industrial sector, commercial interests, residential elements, transportation, and electricity generation. I list the consumption ratio of these sectors in Figure 11-2.

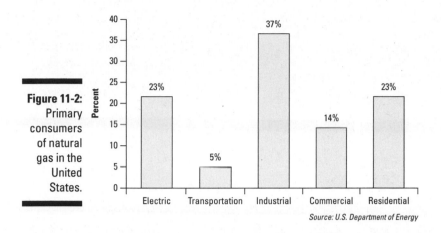

Figure 11-2:
Primary
consumers
of natural
gas in the
United
States.

Source: U.S. Department of Energy

How do you measure natural gas?

Measuring natural gas can be confusing because multiple measurement methods exist. These measurements basically boil down to how much physical natural gas there is and how much energy the natural gas generates.

Whereas crude oil is measured in barrels (each barrel contains 42 gallons of oil), natural gas is measured in cubic feet. Recall from chemistry class that a cubic foot is a measure of volume for a square prism with six sides, each 1 foot in length. (The technical name for this shape is a *regular hexahedron,* but you can simply think of it as the shape of a sugar cube!) Because natural gas is in a gaseous state, it's easier to measure it in cubic feet. Sometimes natural gas is converted into liquid form, known as liquefied natural gas (LNG), which I cover in the section "Liquefied Natural Gas: Getting Liquid Without Getting Wet." LNG is also measured in cubic feet.

The abbreviation for cubic feet is *cf* (both letters are lower case). Therefore, 10 cubic feet is abbreviated as 10 cf. To have practical applications, cubic feet must be able to measure large amounts of volume. Consider the abbreviations for measuring larger volume amounts of cubic feet:

- ✔ 100 cubic feet: 1 Ccf
- ✔ 1,000 cubic feet: 1 Mcf
- ✔ 1 million cubic feet: 1 Mmcf
- ✔ 1 billion cubic feet: 1 Bcf
- ✔ 1 trillion cubic feet: 1 Tcf

Note that *cf* is always in lower case, and the first letter of the abbreviation is always capitalized. Many futures contracts based on natural gas are measured in cubic feet.

Natural gas can also be measured by the amount of energy it generates. This energy content is captured by a unit of measurement known as the *British thermal unit,* or *Btu.* One Btu measures the amount of heat necessary to increase the temperature of 1 pound of water by 1°F. To put it in perspective, 1 cf is the equivalent of 1,027 Btu. British thermal units, sometimes called *therms,* may appear on your gas bill to express the amount of natural gas your household consumed during a particular period of time.

For investment purposes, however, natural gas is generally quantified by using cubic feet.

Calling all captains of industry: Industrial uses of natural gas

The industrial sector is the largest consumer of natural gas, accounting for almost 40 percent of total consumption. Although industrial uses of natural gas have always played a major role in the sector, their significance has increased during the last several years and will continue to do so. As you can see in Figure 11-3, the industrial sector has always accounted for a large part of natural gas use, and because this trend will continue, it's a good area to consider investing in. (Actually, demand for natural gas products as a whole will increase throughout the first quarter of the 21st century, for reasons I discuss in the next section; see Figure 11-8.)

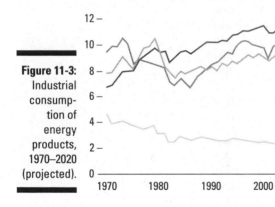

Figure 11-3: Industrial consumption of energy products, 1970–2020 (projected).

Source: Energy Information Administration

Increased industrial demand should put upward price pressures on natural gas. One way to profit from this demand is by being long natural gas futures (for more on going long on futures, flip to the section "Natural selection: Trading nat gas futures").

As an investor, looking at long-term trends helps you develop an investment strategy that takes advantage of the market fundamentals.

So what specific parts of the industrial sector use natural gas? Natural gas is a truly versatile form of energy because it has many applications in industry. Consider a few industrial applications of natural gas products:

- Feedstock for fertilizers
- Food processing

✔ Glass melting

✔ Industrial boiler fueling

✔ Metal smelting

✔ Waste incineration

The chemical composition of natural gas consists primarily of *methane,* a hydrocarbon molecule. It also includes other hydrocarbons, such as *butane, ethane,* and *propane* — all gases that have important industrial uses.

When the industrial sector is firing on all cylinders, so to speak, demand for natural gas tends to increase. Keep an eye out for increased activity from the industrial sector because this is a bullish sign for natural gas. One indicator you can use to gauge the economic output from the industrial sector is the *Producer Price Index* (PPI). The PPI measures the average change in prices producers get for their products, expressed as a percent change. The PPI, compiled by the Bureau of Labor Statistics (BLS), is a good measure of the health in the industrial sector. You can get the latest PPI reports at www.bls.gov/ppi.

If you can't stand the heat, get out of the kitchen! Natural gas in your home

Residential use accounts for almost a quarter of total natural gas consumption (refer to Figure 11-2). A large portion of homes in the United States, as well as other countries, use natural gas for both their cooking and heating needs — the two largest applications of natural gas in the home.

About 70 percent of households in the United States have natural gas ovens in the kitchen. The use of natural gas for cooking purposes has steadily increased as technological developments have allowed for an efficient and safe use of natural gas. How does this affect you as an investor? As long as folks need to cook, you can bet that natural gas will be there to fill this important need. This essential usage ensures that demand from the residential sector for natural gas will remain strong — a bullish sign for nat gas.

More than 50 percent of homes in the United States use natural gas for heating purposes. One way to benefit from this particular application is to identify peak periods of natural gas consumption. Specifically, demand for natural gas for heating increases in the Northern Hemisphere during the winter seasons. Therefore, one way to profit in the natural gas markets is to calibrate your strategy to this cyclical, weather-related trend. In other words, all things constant, natural gas prices should go up during the winters as folks seek to stay warm.

TIP

Although my aim in this book is to help you make money by *investing* in commodities such as natural gas, I'm going to take the liberty of showing you how to *save* money by using natural gas in your home. Natural gas is one of the cheapest energy forms, as measured by dollars per unit of energy generated. Look at Figure 11-4, and you'll quickly realize that you get more energy from natural gas per dollar (as measured in British thermal units, the standard energy measurement unit) than from almost any other source. Using natural gas may save you some money during the winters — which you can then use to bulk up your commodities investments!

Figure 11-4:
Residential cost of energy per British thermal unit, measured in dollars.

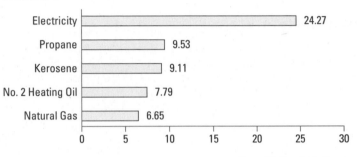

Source: U.S. Department of Energy

Going commercial: Natural gas's commercial uses

About 40 percent of the energy consumed by commercial users, such as hospitals and schools, comes from natural gas, accounting for about 15 percent of total natural gas consumption. Figure 11-5 lists the uses of natural gas by the commercial sector.

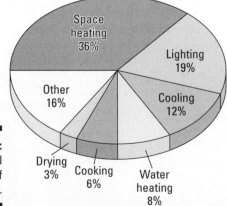

Figure 11-5:
Commercial uses of natural gas.

Source: Energy Information Administration

Because commercial users include establishments such as schools, hospitals, restaurants, movie theaters, malls, and office buildings, demand for natural gas from these key drivers of the economy rises during times of increasing economic activity. This trend means that, all things equal, you need to be bullish on natural gas during times of economic growth. (For more on how to gauge economic activity, turn to Chapter 3.)

One place to look for important economic clues that affect demand for natural gas is the Energy Information Administration (EIA), a division of the U.S. Department of Energy (DOE). The EIA provides a wealth of information regarding consumption trends of key energy products, such as natural gas, from various economic sectors. For information on the commercial usage of natural gas, visit www.eia.doe.gov/oiaf/aeo/aeoref_tab.html.

Truly electrifying! Generating electricity with natural gas

Natural gas is quickly becoming a popular alternative for generating electricity, with just less than 25 percent of natural gas usage going toward generating electricity. Actually, natural gas is used to produce approximately 10 percent of electricity generation in the United States. As you can see from Figure 11-6, that figure will increase dramatically in the coming years.

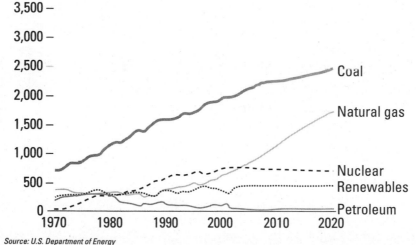

Figure 11-6: Sources of electricity generation, 1970–2020 (projected), measured in billion kilowatt-hours.

Source: U.S. Department of Energy

The long-term trend is that more natural gas will be required to generate electricity. This increased demand from a critical sector will keep upward pressures on natural gas prices over the long term. Keep this in mind as you consider investing in this commodity.

Getting from here to there: Natural gas and transportation

It's not a widely known fact, but natural gas is used in a number of vehicles (approximately three million worldwide) as a source of fuel. These vehicles, known simply as *natural gas vehicles* (NGV), run on a grade of natural gas called *compressed natural gas* (CNG). This usage accounts for only about 5 percent of total natural gas consumption, but demand for NGV may increase as a viable (cheaper) alternative to gasoline (a crude oil derivative).

Since the first edition of this book, NGVs have become much more prevalent. As of 2010, more than 11 million NGVs are in circulation worldwide. The most dominant countries using NGVs are Pakistan, Argentina, Brazil, and Iran. Expect to see more of these vehicles on the road as countries continue their shift toward cleaner sources of transportation fuels.

Keep a close eye on technological developments of natural gas in the transportation sector. If natural gas grabbed a slice of the transportation market, which now accounts for almost two-thirds of crude oil consumption, prices for natural gas could increase dramatically. For the latest on NGV, consult the *International Association of Natural Gas Vehicles,* at www.iangv.org.

Liquefied Natural Gas: Getting Liquid Without Getting Wet

Liquefied natural gas, or LNG, is a recent development in the field. LNG is exactly what it says it is: natural gas in a liquid form. The reason for this development is quite simple: As demand for natural gas increases, you need to be able to transport this precious commodity across vast distances (for example, across continents and through oceans). Transporting it is difficult to do when it's in a gaseous state. Enter LNG, which is nothing but natural gas in a liquid state to make it easy to transport.

Transforming natural gas from its gaseous state into a liquid state is a complex process. The natural gas must first be cooled to a temperature of –260°F to transform it to its liquid state. An additional advantage of LNG is that it takes up considerably less space — about 600 times less — which means that you can transport a lot more of it farther and more economically. When the natural gas is in a liquid state, it's usually transported in specially designed tankers to consumer markets. (I present some of the companies that transport energy products around the world in Chapter 14.) Before it's actually delivered to consumers, it goes through a regasification process.

In the United States, most natural gas is transported through pipelines in a gaseous state. The natural gas pipeline system in the United States is one of the most extensive in the world — 300 million miles of pipeline — and it connects major natural gas–producing regions (such as the Gulf of Mexico) to large natural gas consumers (such as the East Coast). Although the pipeline remains the dominant method of transporting natural gas, LNG is quickly establishing itself as a viable source of natural gas, particularly as domestic production declines and imports increase. Some of the major operators of these pipelines that transport both natural gas and LNG are entities known as *master limited partnerships* (MLPs). The good news is that you can profit from moving natural gas across the United States by investing in MLPs, which I cover in Chapter 7.

In 2005, the United States received only about 1 percent of its total natural gas (170 Bcf) through LNG. By 2010, that figure had shifted dramatically upward, coming in at 452 Bcf. The top six exporters of LNG to the United States include Trinidad and Tobago, Egypt, Algeria, Nigeria, Norway, and Qatar. This trend is now well established and is set to increase in the coming years.

Investing in Natural Gas

The future for natural gas looks bright. The total natural gas consumption on a global scale in 2005 was approximately 100 trillion cubic feet (100 Tcf). In 2010, that figure increased to 120 Tcf. By 2020, that figure is estimated to increase by more than 50 percent, to a total of 156 Tcf, as you can see in Figure 11-7.

Knowing that demand for natural gas will remain steady until 2025 is an important piece of information for you as an investor. Perhaps even more important is figuring out which countries and companies will be meeting this demand. Determining who's going to be supplying this natural gas will help you devise an investment strategy to profit from this increased natural gas demand. Table 11-1 lists the countries with the largest reserves of natural gas in the world.

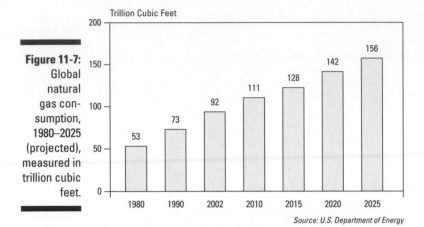

Figure 11-7:
Global
natural
gas con-
sumption,
1980–2025
(projected),
measured in
trillion cubic
feet.

Trillion Cubic Feet

Source: U.S. Department of Energy

Table 11-1   Top Ten Natural Gas Reserves by Country, 2009

Rank	Country	Proven Reserves (Tcf)	Percent of World Total
1	Russia	1,680	27.8%
2	Iran	1,050	15.9%
3	Qatar	910	15.1%
4	Saudi Arabia	235	3.9%
5	United Arab Emirates	212	3.5%
6	Nigeria	190	3.1%
7	United States	189	3.1%
8	Algeria	161	2.7%
9	Venezuela	151	2.5%
10	Iraq	110	1.8%

Global natural gas reserves are estimated at 6,040 Tcf, which is the equivalent of approximately 6 quadrillion cubic feet (quadrillion, not zillion, is the next figure above trillion). You can get exposure to this huge natural gas market in a couple ways: by trading futures contracts or by investing in companies that are involved in the production and development of natural gas fields in some of the countries listed in Table 11-1. I discuss the pros and cons of each invest-ment method in the following sections.

Natural selection: Trading nat gas futures

The most direct method of investing in natural gas is to trade futures contracts on one of the designated commodities exchanges (see Chapter 8). The Chicago Mercantile Exchange (CME), the exchange for energy products, gives you the option to buy and sell natural gas futures and options.

To trade futures, you need to have a futures account with a designated broker, known as the *futures commission merchant* (FCM). After you open a futures account, you can start trading these derivative products. For more on futures and options, turn to Chapter 9. To find out how to open a futures account, turn to Chapter 8.

The natural gas futures contract is the second-most popular energy contract on the CME, right behind crude oil. It's traded under the ticker symbol NG, and it trades in increments of 10,000 Mmbtu. You can trade it during all the calendar months, to periods up to 72 months after the current month. (I cover tradability in Chapter 6.)

The CME offers a mini version of this contract for individual hedgers and speculators. Check out the nat gas section of the CME Web site for more on this contract: www.cmegroup.com/trading/energy/natural-gas/natural-gas.html.

Trading natural gas futures contracts and options isn't for the fainthearted. Even by commodities standards, natural gas is a notoriously volatile commodity, subject to wild price fluctuations. If you're not an aggressive investor willing to withstand the financial equivalent of a wild roller-coaster ride, nat gas futures may not be for you. To give you a picture of the prices, Figure 11-8 shows a historical overview of the price action of the CME natural gas contract.

Nat gas companies: The natural choice

Investing in companies that process natural gas is a positive investment choice because it offers you exposure to this market through the expertise and experience of industry professionals, without the volatility of the futures market. Some natural gas companies are involved in the production of natural gas fields; others are responsible for delivering natural gas directly to consumers.

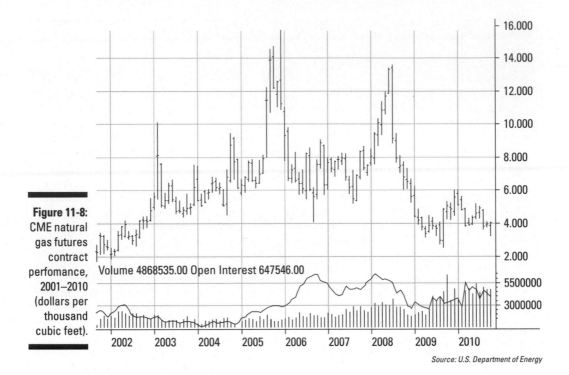

Figure 11-8:
CME natural gas futures contract perfomance, 2001–2010 (dollars per thousand cubic feet).

Volume 4868535.00 Open Interest 647546.00

Source: U.S. Department of Energy

I list companies that are *fully integrated* natural gas companies, which means they're involved in all the production, development, transportation, and distribution phases of natural gas. Investing in these companies gives you a solid foothold in this industry. Here's your hit list:

- **Allegheny Energy (NYSE: AYE):** Provides natural gas–based electricity to consumers in the eastern United States, primarily in Pennsylvania, Virginia, and Maryland. This S&P 500 company is a good option if you want regional exposure to natural gas production.

- **Alliant Energy (NYSE: LNT):** Provides consumers with natural gas and electricity derived from natural gas throughout the United States. This company is a good choice if you want exposure to the North American nat gas market.

- **Nicor Inc. (NYSE: GAS):** Nicor's operations are primarily centered in Illinois, where it provides natural gas to more than two million consumers. This company is another good regional investment.

For a complete listing of companies involved in natural gas production and distribution, look at the American Gas Association Web site: www.aga.org.

Qatari Natural Gas

Qatar is a fascinating country in many respects. Surrounded by Saudi Arabia, the United Arab Emirates, and Iran, this Persian Gulf country is one of the largest producers of LNG in the world. It also has the third-largest proven reserve of natural gas globally, behind only Russia and Iran. Unlike many of its natural gas counterparts, which have populations in the tens of millions, Qatar has a population of about one million. The abundance of natural gas reserves, a booming economy, and a strategic location give this country one of the highest GDP rates in the world, about three times as high as the GDP per capita of the United States.

Strategic geographic location, abundance of natural resources (specifically, natural gas and oil), a highly educated workforce, and no income taxes (that's right — no corporate or personal income taxes in Qatar) make this country one of the most appealing places to invest and work. You can get direct exposure by investing in the Qatari stock market, which has several companies involved in the Qatari natural gas and power industries. For more information, visit www.dsm.com.qa.

Chapter 12

Keeping It Natural: Investing in Renewable Energy

In This Chapter

▶ Examining the dynamics of the renewable energy industry

▶ Profiting from solar power

▶ Considering wind energy

▶ Looking at biofuels

*T*wo problems plague traditional sources of energy, such as oil, natural gas, and coal: their increasing monetary cost and their increasing opposition from environmentalists concerned about the hazards of burning these fuels. It's not hard to see that renewable sources of energy, such as solar and wind power, will attract more attention in the near future. Since the first edition of this book was published, renewable energy as an industry has received a tremendous amount of media, social, and political coverage. The number of experts in this field has mushroomed, as has the number of companies involved. Many factors account for this increased attention, least of all the calls for countries to reduce their fossil fuel consumption in light of the global environmental impact of burning such fuels.

Currently, renewable sources of energy make up about 7 percent of total energy use in the world (see Figure 12-1 for the breakdown). This figure pales compared to the 87 percent share of fossil fuels, but it has the potential to grow as nonrenewable energy sources are depleted. The field of renewable energy is getting a lot of attention, and there's certainly potential to make some money in this field. In this chapter, I give you an overview of this dynamic industry and focus on specific fields — including solar energy, wind power, and biofuels — to help you develop an investment strategy rooted in the market fundamentals.

Always Brand Spanking New: Getting to Know Renewable Energy

Perhaps the most vocal and high-profile figure in the environmentalist movement is Al Gore, former vice president of the United States. Already a major proponent of environmental issues as vice president, Gore continued his campaigning for environmental causes when his term ended in 2000. He continued to raise concerns about man-made environmental issues in general and the hazardous consequences of global warming in particular. His presentations on the topic culminated in the critically acclaimed documentary *An Inconvenient Truth.*

In the documentary, Gore makes a presentation that directly ties man-made activities such as burning fossil fuels to changes in the earth's temperature, emphasizing the resulting negative impacts these actions have on the planet. Detrimental effects include increased weather pattern disruptions, resulting in increased temperatures in already warm climates, and fiercer and harsher winters in cold regions. The film also includes warnings about melting polar ice caps and the increased likelihood of floods, earthquakes, and volcanic eruptions due to global warming. Although the documentary (and the broader environmentalist movement) has come under fire for inaccuracies, it has nevertheless caught the attention of people worldwide, including investors.

I can't comment extensively on the validity of the scientific approach of the global warming movement, but I can say that it has raised some serious issues and attracted the attention of investors, corporations, and individuals around the world. To the extent that it has spurred advances in the renewable energy space and opened up new investment opportunities for investors, it's worth examining it from a portfolio investment perspective.

In practical terms, *renewable energy* refers to sources of energy that are essentially always present, always available, and always renewable. The sun and wind are traditional sources of renewable energy because the sun always shines and the wind always blows, day in and day out. Harnessing these renewable sources of energy is beneficial for a couple reasons. First, they're always there. Second, they don't emit any greenhouse gases, which decreases pollution output.

The benefits of renewable energy are obvious, but one of the big obstacles to implementing a large-scale, global industry is less obvious: cost. For instance, the cost of harnessing the power of the sun to generate electricity is extremely high and requires massive commitments of capital expenditures. The solar industry currently needs heavy government subsidies to be able to generate enough profits to remain competitive; the same applies to wind energy and other types of renewable energy, such as ethanol.

Global warming

Scientifically speaking, global warming is the increase in the earth's temperature in surface and near-surface air and oceans due to increased greenhouse gas emissions from man-made activities such as the burning of fossil fuels. According to the Intergovernmental Panel on Climate Change (IPCC), a United Nations intergovernmental body, global warming is a scientific fact that can be proven using empirical scientific methods. In 2007, the IPCC received the Nobel Peace Prize for its work on global warming; Al Gore was a co-recipient.

This group has come under fire by many in the energy and fossil fuel industry who challenge the assumptions behind the scientific approach used to reach these conclusions. According to this camp, increased temperatures have been part of the earth since prehistoric times and have little to do with man-made activities. These two camps are bitterly divided, which has decreased the likelihood of reaching a compromise on the scientific approach. You're entitled to your own opinions on the validity of these claims and counterclaims, but it's indisputable that the renewable energy industry is here to stay — and presents some terrific investment opportunities.

In Figure 12-1, I list the different types of renewable energy sources available and the percentage of consumption they're accountable for. As you can see in the figure, renewable energy as a whole represents only a small fraction of the total energy landscape in the United States, which is also attributable to the broader global footprint. Getting exposure to some of these sectors from an individual portfolio perspective is difficult. For example, unless you own or operate geothermal plants, you have few direct methods for getting this kind of exposure. For this reason, I focus only on renewable energy sources for which there are tradable, liquid, and transparent instruments — specifically, solar, wind, and biomass.

Total= 101.605 Quadrillion   Total= 6.830 Quadrillion Btu

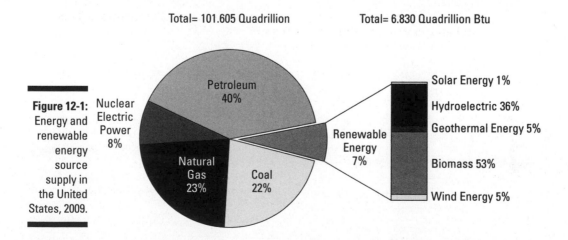

Figure 12-1: Energy and renewable energy source supply in the United States, 2009.

Although it's currently more challenging to get direct exposure to different renewable energy submarkets (such as geothermal), this will undoubtedly change in the future as more instruments are made available and as the market gains more breadth and credibility. In addition, you can adopt a creative approach to getting this kind of exposure; for example, if you want to get exposure to hydroelectric power generation, you can examine the electric utilities universe for companies that have hydroelectric power assets (flip to Chapter 13 for more on electric utilities). This strategy may not give you that direct investment route, but you can still manage to generate indirect exposure in your portfolio.

If you're interested in keeping up-to-date on the latest developments in the renewable energy space, I recommend that you check out the Department of Energy's Energy Efficiency and Renewable Energy (EERE) initiative, at www. eere.energy.gov. For the United Nations' official intergovernmental policy view on global warming and greenhouse gases, consult the Intergovernmental Panel on Climate Change (IPCC), at www.ipcc.ch.

Sunny Delight: Investing in Solar Energy

Solar power currently accounts for only 1 percent of total renewable energy sources, but it's one of the fastest-growing areas in the space. Governments around the world are in the process of announcing massive infrastructure spending programs dedicated to harnessing the sun's power and turning it into electricity and other forms of energy.

India and China have been at the forefront of this trend, with $30 billion in projects announced in the 20 years ahead. Even countries that you may not associate with renewable energy are taking the lead on this matter; Saudi Arabia, the world's largest oil producer, and the United Arab Emirates have both dedicated large budgets to the development of solar power. Even the Kingdom of Morocco has jumped on the bandwagon, with 3,000 megawatts projected by 2020 to come from solar plants located in the Sahara Desert.

Masdar City

Ironically, the government of Abu Dhabi sits on more than 100 billion barrels of oil, yet it's one of the avant-gardes of the renewable energy drive. In 2010, Abu Dhabi unveiled the first carbon-neutral and carbon-free city, Masdar City, located a few kilometers from this Arabian Gulf Emirate. Masdar City generates all its energy through solar panels; this $22 billion project aims to become the first sustainable urban development on earth and is closely watched by industry insiders. If successful, it will be the first city that generates zero greenhouse emissions. This could be a turning point for the entire renewable energy industry.

Broadly speaking, solar power is the process by which energy from the sun is harnessed and channeled into a usable energy form, generally heat or electricity. Two different processes can transform solar power:

- **Solar photovoltaic energy:** Don't be intimidated by this high-sounding name — it simply describes the method by which energy from the sun is captured and transformed into electricity.

- **Solar thermal energy:** This method transforms the sun's energy into heat, which may be used for a number of different purposes, such as interior space heating or water heating. If you've ever seen flat-panel solar collectors mounted on homes or buildings, they're used for solar thermal energy purposes.

Many companies are trying to turn these two methods of transforming solar energy into a commercially viable enterprise, but they face some challenges. One of the biggest impediments to the commercial success of solar power is the sun itself! Specifically, the sun isn't a resource that you can control. For one thing, you can't manipulate the weather, so you're at the mercy of rain, fog, clouds, the earth's rotation, and other natural external factors that block the sun. For this reason, solar power accounted for a little less than 0.06 percent of total energy consumed in the United States during 2005.

Currently, the equity markets give you a direct way to get exposure to the solar industry. Following are some of the top names in the industry to choose from:

- **First Solar, Inc. (NASDAQ: FSLR):** FSLR was one of the first solar companies to go public. It's involved in the manufacture and sales of photovoltaic solar panels to end users, including governments, corporate entities, and private individuals. Its two main revenue generators come from the components sector (selling parts for specific solar projects) and the systems segment (installation of solar farms). With net profit margins in excess of 22 percent (2010 figures), this company offers solid exposure to the photovoltaic market segment (see Figure 12-2 for recent equity performance).

- **Suntech Power Holdings (NYSE: STP):** Suntech is a world leader in the development, design, and implementation of solar photovoltaic systems and products. In addition to providing construction services, the company offers engineering and maintenance services to its clients around the world. It has a global footprint, with operations in Germany, the United States, Australia, South Africa, Japan, and South Korea. For a truly diversified global exposure to the solar industry, be sure to consider Suntech.

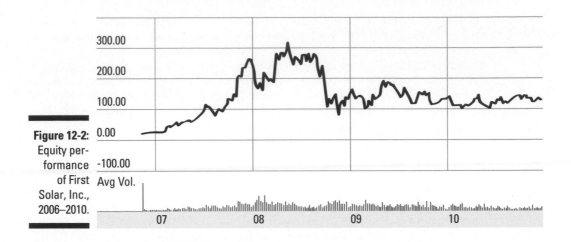

Figure 12-2:
Equity performance of First Solar, Inc., 2006–2010.

Fast and Furious: Trading in Wind Energy

Wind energy is another renewable resource that's getting increasing attention from investors. Energy is generated by huge wind machines (similar to traditional windmills), which are placed side by side in *wind farms*.

The challenge to wind energy is that it's dependant on the wind, a very unpredictable natural phenomenon. Wind has traditionally held a small part in the energy generation spectrum, but it's increasing as it becomes a cost-effective solution. Currently, few publicly traded companies deal specifically in wind power.

That said, many industrial companies are beginning to implement large-scale investments in wind energy production. If you're looking for some indirect exposure to wind, you can always consider an investment in General Electric (NYSE: GE). Although GE is known for its large industrial footprint, it's becoming one of the leaders in the wind space and is the global leader in manufacturing and sales of wind turbines across dozens of markets.

With rising energy prices, wind energy may get more focus. If you're interested in investing in wind power and want to stay on top of emerging trends, check out the American Wind Energy Association, at www.awea.org. The site maintains a database of private companies involved in wind energy that may go public one day.

Betting on Biomass

Biomass is currently the biggest component of the renewable energy industry, accounting for 53 percent of total production estimates (refer to Figure 12-1). Scientifically speaking, biomass energy is produced by processing common wastes and transforming them into renewable energy through a biochemical conversion process.

Some common feedstock is used in this process:

- Corn
- Ethanol
- Eucalyptus
- Forestry crop residues
- Industrial residues
- Municipal solid wastes
- Palm oil
- Sugarcane
- Vegetable oil

As you can see, the raw material inputs are varied and come from a wide array of sources, which offers benefits and competitive advantages to the industry. Specifically, because such a large number of inputs are available, the process can be replicated across different markets, landscapes, and geographies. For example, agriculturally rich countries such as Brazil can process large amounts of agricultural wastes (such as ethanol and sugarcane waste) to generate energy; on the other hand, countries with large industrial apparatuses, such as Russia, can also take advantage of the biomass process by using industrial residues and municipal wastes as primary inputs. The process is thus versatile and scalable, which accounts for its ubiquity in the energy spectrum.

For now, investors have no direct plays into the biomass and biofuels market; in the current industry structure, only privately held companies, municipalities, and other governmental institutions run biomass plants and operations.

What's up with ethanol?

Ethanol is an alcohol fuel used in transportation that can be made from corn, sugar, wheat, and other agricultural products. Because of its origins, ethanol is a renewable source of energy. In Brazil, the world's largest producer of ethanol fuel, ethanol is the primary automotive fuel. The United States has seen an increase in the use of ethanol as a transportation fuel, and that trend is likely to increase. One company involved in producing ethanol that I recommend is Pacific Ethanol (NASDAQ: PEIX). If you're interested in getting exposure to ethanol, PEIX is a good way to go.

However, a company located in Brazil is a world leader in biomass generation: *CPFL Energia* (CPFL). CPFL generates, distributes, and sells electricity to the Brazilian domestic market. It derives a significant portion of its revenues from biomass generation, specifically the transformation of sugarcane waste into electricity. The company trades on the Sao Paulo Stock Exchange (the *BOVESPA*) but recently listed its shares on the New York Stock Exchange under the ticker CPL, via an American Depository Receipt (ADR). See Figure 12-3.

As a result, you can now get exposure to an exciting market that was nonexistent only a few years ago. I expect more companies involved in the biomass space to go public in the coming years, giving you a broader range of options to choose from. In the meantime, I encourage you to monitor CPFL.

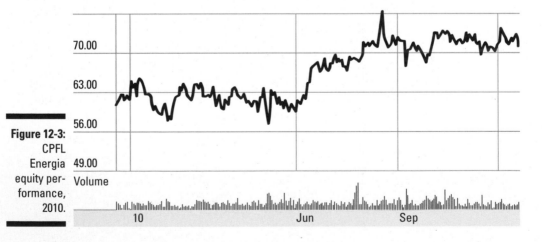

Figure 12-3:
CPFL
Energia
equity per-
formance,
2010.

Chapter 13

Fuel for Thought: Looking at Alternative Energy Sources

*T*he world's demand for energy is in an upward trend and is likely to remain elevated for decades to come. Currently, fossil fuels meet almost 90 percent of the world's total energy needs: crude oil (39 percent), natural gas (24 percent), and coal (24 percent). For a number of reasons — environmental, political, geopolitical — there's a strong push to move away from fossil fuels as the main sources of energy and toward alternative energy sources such as nuclear, wind, and solar. As a result, these alternative sources can give you some solid moneymaking opportunities.

In this chapter, I go through the global energy scene and identify some of the major trends affecting it. I also introduce you to alternative energy sources and show you how to profit from this segment of the energy market. Specifically, I provide you with investment opportunities in the following areas: coal, nuclear power, and electricity.

Digging Up New Energy Sources

As the global population increases and emerging countries industrialize (see Chapter 2), the demand for energy products will rise throughout the first quarter of the 21st century. The Energy Information Administration (EIA) anticipates that global demand for energy products will increase by more than 70 percent between 2003 and 2030. You can take a look at this expected increase in Figure 13-1.

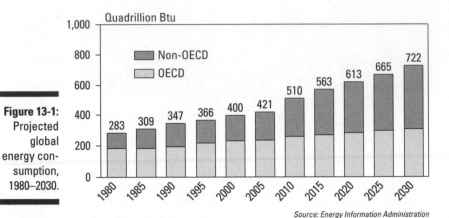

Source: Energy Information Administration

Figure 13-1:
Projected
global
energy con-
sumption,
1980–2030.

In 2009, fossil fuels (oil, natural gas, and coal) accounted for 85 percent of total energy consumption. Crude oil alone was responsible for almost 40 percent of global energy use. However, as the price of these traditional energy sources increases (driven by both strong demand and limited supply), the calls for new sources of energy are increasing as well. For example, in 2005, many members of Congress pushed for an alternative energy initiative to promote the use of solar, wind, and other renewable energy sources.

Despite numerous calls, however, the energy landscape is unlikely to change anytime soon, which means that fossil fuels will remain the dominant source of global energy for years to come. Alternative energies may generate a lot of attention, but how much actual progress will be made is still up in the air. Keep this in mind as you're looking at investing in these alternatives.

For example, take a look at Figure 13-2. You can see that the energy picture until 2030 will remain fairly static on a percentage basis; fossil fuels will continue to be the dominant fuel for the global economy, and alternatives will keep playing an important but less significant role.

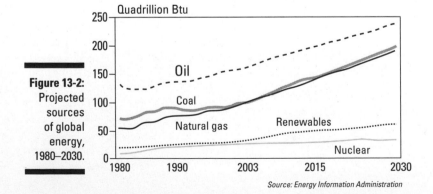

Figure 13-2:
Projected
sources
of global
energy,
1980–2030.

Source: Energy Information Administration

Despite the dominance of fossil fuels, particularly crude oil, the alternative space is a dynamic area and a fertile ground for investment opportunities.

Reexamining King Coal: Not As Scary As You Think

Before the beginning of the 20th century, coal was truly the king of commodities. Coal was the dominant source of energy during the tumultuous Industrial Revolution. People still often associate the Industrial Revolution with images of coal mines. The beginning of the end of coal as the dominant energy source can be traced to a fateful day in 1912 when Winston Churchill, the First Lord of the Admiralty in the British Navy, ordered the conversion of all coal ships to oil. That move resulted in the rise of oil as the dominant global energy source, at the expense of coal.

Although Churchill's decision to switch the British Navy from coal to oil effectively dethroned coal as the fossil fuel of choice, coal still enjoys an elevated position in global energy markets. For example, in 2009 in the United States (the world's most important energy market), coal accounted for 23 percent of total fossil fuel consumption. Therefore, coal is still an important source of energy and can provide some good moneymaking opportunities. In this section, I show you how to make money in coal.

Coal hard facts

Coal is used primarily for electricity generation (steam coal) and steel manufacturing (metallurgical coal). Besides its practical uses in these two important areas, coal is an increasingly popular fossil fuel because of its large reserves. Specifically, companies in the United States have long touted the benefits of moving toward a more coal-based economy because the United States has the largest coal reserves in the world. I list in Table 13-1 the countries with the largest coal reserves.

Coal is measured in short tons. One *short ton* is the equivalent of 2,000 lbs. In terms of energy, one short ton of *anthracite,* the coal of highest quality (see the later section "Paint it black"), contains approximately 25 million Btu of energy.

Table 13-1	Coal Reserves by Country, 2006		
Rank	Country	Reserves (Million Short Tons)	Percent of World Total
1	United States	246,643	27.13%
2	Russia	157,010	17.27%
3	China	114,500	12.60%
4	India	92,445	10.17%
5	Australia	78,500	8.64%
6	South Africa	48,750	5.36%
7	Ukraine	34,153	3.76%
8	Kazakhstan	31,279	3.44%
9	Poland	14,000	1.54%
10	Brazil	10,113	1.11%

Source: World Energy Council

If you're going to invest in companies that process coal, I recommend selecting a company with heavy exposure in one of the countries listed in Table 13-1. Specifically, because the United States, Russia, and China collectively hold more than 55 percent of the world's total coal reserves, investing in a coal company with large operations in any of these countries gives you exposure to this important segment of the market. I introduce some of these coal companies in the section "It's a coal investment."

Just because a country has large deposits of a natural resource, however, doesn't mean that it exploits them to full capacity. As such, there's a significant gap between countries with large coal reserves and those that produce the most coal annually. To give you a better idea of this market characteristic, I list in Table 13-2 the top coal-producing countries.

Table 13-2	Hard Coal Production by Country, 2009	
Rank	Country	Production (Million Short Tons)
1	China	2,971
2	United States	919
3	India	526
4	Australia	335
5	Indonesia	263

Rank	Country	Production (Million Short Tons)
6	South Africa	248
7	Russia	229
8	Kazakhstan	96
9	Poland	78
10	Colombia	73

Demand for coal is expected to increase during the first quarter of the 21st century, as you can see in Figure 13-3. Most of this growth will come from the emerging market economies, particularly the economies of China and India, which will account for approximately 75 percent of the demand increase for coal. (China is currently the largest consumer of coal in the world, ahead of the United States, India, and Japan.)

Figure 13-3:
Projected global coal consumption, 1970–2025.

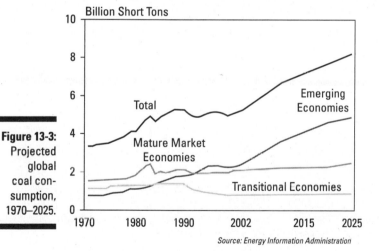

Source: Energy Information Administration

Demand for coal has resulted in strong price movements in the commodity itself. Before the 2008 Global Financial Crisis, prices for coal experienced a major uptrend, going from $50 per short ton in 2006 to almost $200 per short ton in 2008 (see Figure 13-4). The financial crisis resulted in a severe quasi-crash scenario for coal prices, as was the case for several other important commodities. This correction was necessary because the rally was overdone on the way up; coal prices seem to have stabilized in the $100 range, but expect much more activity surrounding this commodity in the future.

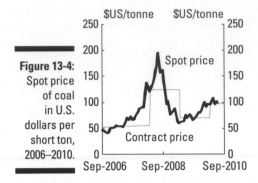

Figure 13-4:
Spot price
of coal
in U.S.
dollars per
short ton,
2006–2010.

Paint it black

As with other fossil fuels, coal comes in different qualities. Specifically, coal comes in four categories, classified by its carbon, sulfur, and ash content, as well as by the level of energy it releases.

Here are the four major categories of coal:

✔ **Lignite:** Lignite contains the least amount of carbon and the most sulfur and ash of all coal types, so it's considered the least valuable. Sometimes called brown coal, it's primarily used in generating electricity.

✔ **Sub-bituminous:** This type of coal contains a little more carbon than lignite and thus is considered to be of a higher quality. It also has lower levels of sulfur and ash than lignite. It's used mostly to heat water in electricity-generating steam turbines.

✔ **Bituminous:** Because bituminous coal burns well and creates a lot of energy, it's of high value. The most common type of coal found in the United States, it's used to generate electricity and, in the steel industry, create high-quality steel.

✔ **Anthracite:** By far the most valuable type of coal, anthracite contains the highest levels of carbon and the least amount of sulfur and ash; it also provides the most energy on a per-unit basis. Because of its high value, anthracite is used for residential and commercial space heating.

Before you invest in companies involved in the coal business, find out which type of coal they produce. This information will help you better understand the company's business and profit margins. You can find this information in a company's annual and quarterly reports.

It's a coal investment

You can get access to the coal markets either by trading coal futures directly or by investing in coal companies.

Coal futures contract

As with other members of the fossil fuel family, coal has an underlying futures contract that trades on a commodity exchange — in this case, the Chicago Mercantile Exchange (CME). This coal contract gives commercial users (such as coal producers, electric companies, and steel manufacturers) the opportunity to hedge against market risk and offers speculators a chance to profit from this market risk. (For more on the CME and other commodity exchanges, turn to Chapter 8. Review Chapter 9 for more on futures contract specifications.)

The coal futures contract on the CME tracks the price of the *Central Appalachian* type of coal. Central Appalachian coal, known as CAPP, is a high-quality coal with low sulfur and ash content. The CAPP futures contract (which traders sometimes affectionately call "the big sandy" because it's produced in the area between West Virginia and Kentucky where the Ohio River flows) is the premium benchmark for coal prices in the United States.

The contract trades under the ticker symbol QL and is tradable during all the calendar months of the current year, in addition to all calendar months in the subsequent three years. Additional information on this futures contract is available on the CME Web site, at www.cmegroup.com.

Although the coal futures contract does offer you exposure to coal, be warned that the market for this contract is fairly illiquid, meaning that the trading volume is low. Most of the traders involved in this market represent large commercial interests that transact with each other. A few speculators trade the coal futures markets, but they don't represent a significant portion of the market. You may not be able to get involved directly in this market without large capital reserves to compete with the commercial interests.

Coal company

One of the best ways to invest in coal is to invest in a company that mines it. The following three companies are the best, in my opinion:

  ✔ **Arch Coal (NYSE: ACI):** Arch Coal is smaller in size than its main competitors, Peabody and Consol, but I like it because the coal it produces is of very high quality. It operates more than 30 mines in the continental U.S. and controls more than 3 billion short tons of reserves.

It has operations in the largest coal-producing regions in the United States, including in the Appalachians, the Powder River Basin (on the Montana/Wyoming border), and the Western Bituminous region (on the Colorado/Utah border).

✓ **Consol Energy (NYSE: CNX):** With headquarters in Pittsburgh, Consol Energy has significant operations in the coal mines of Pennsylvania and nearby coal-rich states of West Virginia and Kentucky. As of 2009, it controlled 8 billion short tons of coal reserves, with operations in more than 17 mines across the United States. CNX is well positioned to take advantage of the booming domestic coal market.

✓ **Peabody Energy (NYSE: BTU):** Peabody Energy is the largest coal company, with approximately 15 billion short tons of coal reserves. The coal it produces is responsible for generating approximately 10 percent of the electricity in the United States. With 2009 revenues exceeding $5 billion, Peabody Energy is the largest coal company out there today; it's the ExxonMobil of coal companies. I like the company because of its size and because it has mining operations in the United States but also in Australia and Venezuela, two important coal markets. You can examine the price performance of this stock in Figure 13-5.

Figure 13-5: Equity performance of Peabody Energy, 2006–2010.

If you want to invest in coal companies with more international exposure to markets in Russia, China, and other coal-rich countries, I recommend that you consult the World Coal Institute, at www.worldcoal.org.

Investing in Nuclear Power: Going Nuclear without Going Ballistic

When most people think of nuclear power, they tend to think of nuclear weapons and mushroom clouds. However, nuclear power has an important civilian role, too. Civilian and commercial nuclear power is an integral part of the global energy supply chain and is a valuable energy source for residential, commercial, and industrial consumers worldwide. In fact, nuclear power generates more than 20 percent of the electricity in the United States. In countries like France, nuclear power generates more than 75 percent of electricity!

Nuclear power currently accounts for about 5 percent of total global energy consumption (refer to Figure 13-1), and it's expected to remain at these stable levels until 2030. But if the price of fossil fuels rises (oil, natural gas, and coal) dramatically enough to start affecting demand (creating what is called *demand destruction*), nuclear power may play an important role in picking up the slack.

One way you can profit from increased interest in nuclear power is to invest in uranium, the most widely used fuel in nuclear power plants. However, you're not likely to hear about this opportunity from your local financial media because uranium is a pretty obscure investment area. But sometimes as an investor, you need to be able to think creatively and look at opportunities that other investors haven't considered. Investing in uranium to benefit from the increased demand in nuclear power is not a well-known or well-advertised investment play, but it can be profitable nevertheless.

Splitting atoms

The primary use of civilian nuclear power is in generating electricity. Electricity is generated by heating water to very high temperatures to create steam that powers the turbines in a steam turbine. In a nuclear power plant, the water is heated through a process known as nuclear fission, in which atoms are split to release large amounts of energy. (This process is the opposite of nuclear fusion, in which atoms are fused.)

You may be surprised to find that the period of 2000–2008 saw a major bull market in uranium, with prices moving from $20 per pound to almost $140 per pound. The Global Financial Crisis brought some sense back into the market, as this commodity attracted many players of a speculative nature (see Figure 13-6). Prices post-2008 went back to above precrisis levels, to a more reasonable $50 per pound, and this presents a potential opportunity for the discriminating investor.

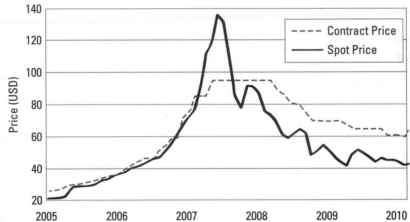

Figure 13-6:
Spot price of uranium, 2005–2010.

Uranium equities

Because uranium isn't a widely tradable commodity, the best way to profit from this trend is to invest in companies that specialize in the mining, processing, and distribution of uranium for civilian nuclear purposes. I like these companies in this sector:

- **Cameco Corporation (NYSE: CCJ):** Cameco is the marquee name in the uranium mining space. The company operates four uranium mines in the United States and Canada. The company mines uranium and is also involved in refining and converting the uranium into fuel that's sold to nuclear power plants to generate electricity (see Figure 13-7).

- **Strathmore Corporation (Toronto: STM):** Whereas UEX is involved in the exploration of uranium ore, Strathmore — another Canadian company — specializes in the mining of uranium. The company, which trades on the Toronto Stock Exchange, operates in the Athabasca region in Canada, as well as in the U.S.

- **UEX Corporation (Toronto: UEX):** UEX is a Canada-based mining company that specializes in the exploration and mining of uranium in the Athabasca basin. The Athabasca basin in Canada is an important region in global uranium mining that accounts for about 30 percent of total world production. The company is currently still in exploration phases, but it could become a real moneymaker if it comes across large deposits of uranium. The company trades on the Toronto Stock Exchange.

Figure 13-7:
Equity per-
formance
of Cameco
Corporation,
2006–2010.

Uranium ETF

In addition to getting direct equity exposure, you can invest in uranium companies with the convenience of an exchange-traded fund (ETF). In 2010, ETF provider Global X Funds out of New York launched the first-ever uranium-based ETF, the Global X Uranium ETF (NYSE: URA).

URA tracks a basket of the most actively traded uranium stocks, as measured by the Solactive Global Uranium Index, its underlying benchmark. As such, URA gives you exposure to some of the most high-profile names in the industry, including Cameco, Uranium One, Paladin Resources, Denison Mines, and Kalahari Minerals. If you're looking for broad-based exposure to the uranium equity markets, URA is a good choice for your investment objectives. For more information on URA, visit www.globalxfunds.com. Chapter 5 tells you how you can incorporate ETFs into your trading strategy.

Uranium futures

If you have a good grip on futures trading and are looking for a new instrument to add to your portfolio, I'm happy to report that you can now invest directly in uranium itself. The Chicago Mercantile Exchange (CME) now offers the UxC (CME: UX), the first contract of its kind that gives you direct exposure to this precious resource. For more information on this contract, visit www.cmegroup.com.

Trading futures contracts involves a higher degree of risk due to the use of margin, volatility, and other factors. Make sure that you trade futures contracts only if you already have plenty of experience. For more on trading these instruments, turn to Chapter 9.

For more information on nuclear power, the Energy Information Administration (EIA) has an excellent Web site with all sorts of practical information on this industry, at `www.eia.doe.gov/fuelnuclear.html`. The Ux Consulting Company is a great resource for everything regarding uranium and nuclear power. Its Web site is located at `www.uxc.com`.

You've Been Zapped! Trading Electricity

Benjamin Franklin may not have imagined what his kite experiment would mean for the world, but his experimentation paved the way for developments in electricity, which is now a necessity of modern life. Electricity is also a tradable commodity. In this section, I show you how to make money by investing in electricity.

Brushing up on current affairs

Have you ever wondered where the electricity that allows you to watch TV, use your air conditioner, or power your computer comes from? Getting electricity to residential, commercial, and industrial consumers is a lengthy process. The electricity is first created in a generator at a power plant and is then sent through transmission lines at very high voltages to a substation near consumers. The substation is equipped with a generator that transforms the high-voltage electricity into a low-voltage form, which is then sent to consumers via distribution lines. So how can you profit from it? It's quite simple.

Most of the electricity in the United States is generated through steam turbines. The water used to generate steam is heated to very high temperatures using traditional energy sources such as coal, natural gas, and nuclear power, as well as other renewable sources (such as wind and solar). Look at Figure 13-8 for a breakdown of how electricity was generated in the United States in 2008.

Electricity is measured in watts, with 1 kilowatt equal to 1,000 watts and a megawatt equal to 1 million watts. In the power industry, watts are expressed in terms of hours of operation, where 1 kilowatt-hour (1 kWh) is 1,000 watts working for a period of 1 hour. Your electricity bill is measured in kilowatt-hours, and 1 kWh is the equivalent of 3,412 Btu. To put it in perspective, the United States consumed a grand total of 3,669 billion kWh of electricity in 2003.

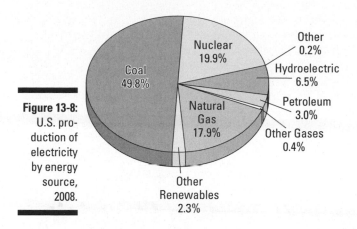

Figure 13-8:
U.S. production of electricity by energy source, 2008.

Investing in the power industry

As you can see from Figure 13-8, investing in coal as well as nuclear power is one way to invest in electricity. But you can invest directly in the power industry in several other ways as well. I discuss these investment procedures in the following sections.

Charged and ready to go

The most direct way of investing in electricity is . . . to buy it! The Chicago Mercantile Exchange (CME) offers a futures contract that tracks the price of electricity as administered by PJM Interconnection. PJM is a *Regional Transmission Organization* (RTO) that oversees the largest electric grid system in the world and services more than 50 million customers in the United States. It's responsible for generating more than 700 million megawatt-hours of electricity across 55,000 miles of transmission lines. Because of its dominance in the U.S. electricity market, the PJM electricity futures contract on the CME/NYMEX provides you with a widely recognizable and tradable electricity benchmark. For more information on the CME/NYMEX and other commodity exchanges, flip to Chapter 8.

The PJM contract gives you the option of trading both *on-peak* and *off-peak* electricity hours. On-peak times are defined as Monday through Friday between 7 a.m. and 11 p.m., the times when the most electricity is consumed in the United States. Off-peak hours go from midnight to 7 a.m. local time Monday through Friday and include Saturday and Sunday as well. On-peak hours are usually more liquid because that's when most of the electricity is consumed.

The PJM contract is traded in units of 40 mWh (megawatt-hours) under the ticker symbol JM. For more information on this specific contract, check out the CME/NYMEX Web site, www.nymex.com/jm_desc.aspx. To find out more about futures contracts in general, turn to Chapter 9.

Although most of the market participants in the electricity futures market are local and regional power providers and suppliers, the futures contract lends itself to being traded by individual speculators as well. In recent years, as interest in commodities as an asset class has increased, the number of speculative participants in the electricity market has grown as well.

Power to the people

You probably get a letter from them every month, but you may have never given too much thought about the investment opportunities they present. I'm talking, of course, about electric utilities. *Utilities* are the companies responsible for providing electricity to millions of folks in the United States and around the world.

I like utilities for a number of reasons, particularly for their very high dividend payout. The industry has an average 5 percent dividend yield, one of the highest of any industry. However, remember when you're investing for dividend income that dividends are subject to market fluctuations. I list in Table 13-3 some utilities to consider, along with their dividend yield.

Table 13-3	Publicly Traded Utilities, 2010 Dividend Yields	
Utility	*Ticker*	*Dividend Yield*
Great Plains Energy	NYSE: GXP	4.60%
Consolidated Edison	NYSE: ED	4.80%
Duke Energy Corp.	NYSE: DUK	5.50%
Dominion Resources	NYSE: D	4.30%
PG&E Corp.	NYSE: PCG	3.80%
Entergy Corp.	NYSE: ETR	4.70%

Dividends are a taxable source of income. Because of recent tax relief legislation, taxes on income generated through dividends are capped at 15 percent. However, Congress is considering an overhaul of the dividend tax in 2008 that may result in an increase in the dividends tax rate. Keep a close eye on these dividend tax issues, because they'll have a direct impact on your utility investments.

In addition to juicy dividend yields, utilities offer you solid capital appreciation opportunities. Consider these companies when implementing your utility trading strategy.

- **Consolidated Edison (NYSE: ED):** If you live or have ever lived in New York, you're familiar with ConEd. ConEd is the main utility for New York State and New York City; its main line of business is regulated electric, gas, and steam delivery to wholesale and retail customers. ED provides electricity to more than 3.5 million clients and has a coverage of more than 650 square miles. This company is a good option if you're looking for exposure to the robust East Coast (especially New York) utility market. (See Figure 13-9.)

- **Duke Energy Corp. (NYSE: DUK):** Duke Energy is one of the main players in the U.S. utility market. With a staggering 35,000 MW electricity-generating capacity, it has a footprint that spans the East Coast and the Midwest, and it has a portfolio in Latin America as well. In addition, Duke Energy owns and operates a natural gas–distribution business in Ohio and Kentucky, with an additional portfolio of renewable energy assets. With net profit margins of 16 percent (2010 figures), I recommend this company for broad-based utility exposure in the Americas.

Figure 13-9: Equity performance of Consolidated Edison, 2006–2010.

Chapter 14

Totally Energized: Investing in Energy Companies

In This Chapter

▶ Profiting from discoveries

▶ Examining refineries

▶ Investing in transportation and shipping

*O*ne way to play the energy markets is to invest in the companies involved in the production, transformation, and distribution of the world's most important energy commodities. In this chapter, I look at specialized energy and oil companies that are critical links in the global crude oil supply chain. This chain is long and convoluted, and these industries move in cycles, so identifying who does what allows you to develop a targeted investment strategy.

I show you in the following sections how to profit from the first step of the oil industry (exploration and production), through the transformational process (refining), and finally through the delivery system (transportation). Each of the companies operating in these segments of the market offers unique moneymaking investment opportunities. (See Chapter 10 for the goods on the large integrated oil companies — often referred to as "the majors" — that allow you to buy the market, so to speak, because they're involved in all facets of the global energy industry.)

Bull's-Eye! Profiting from Oil Exploration and Production

The oil industry starts in one place: at the oil field. The birth of the modern oil industry began with "Colonel" Edwin Drake's discovery of the first commercially viable oil field in Titusville, Pennsylvania, in 1859. (Drake wasn't really a colonel. He simply called himself that in order to get permits from the local authorities to drill for oil!) Ever since that day, individuals, companies, and countries have relentlessly pursued the discovery of oil fields and oil wells.

Among industry insiders, exploring for oil and gas is affectionately called *wild-catting*. Most wildcatting expeditions end up without any oil discoveries. When wildcatters drill a hole in the ground and no oil comes out, it's known as a *dry hole,* the unfortunate opposite of a *gusher,* a well that literally gushes oil.

The exploration and discovery of oil is a lucrative segment in the oil business. So how you can you strike it rich by discovering oil? Fortunately, you don't have to roll up your sleeves and go prospecting for oil in the Texas heartland. You can invest in companies that specialize in the exploration and production of oil fields, known in the business as *E&P.*

Oil wells are found in two places: on land and at sea. In recent years, offshore drilling has generated a lot of interest among investors, and a flurry of activity has been taking place in this sector as oil on land becomes scarcer. In this section, I introduce you to some of the companies involved in this exciting segment of the market.

Going offshore

The offshore drilling business is a technology-heavy industry, and you want to be familiar with some of the associated terminology, to make the most out of your investments.

Because offshore drilling activity may take place in unforgiving locations, companies have to deploy specific vessels for specific drilling projects. These vessels are among the most technologically advanced structures created by man. Some vessels are designed to withstand harsh winds and high waves. Others are more suited for shallow-water exploratory projects and need to move from location to location quickly.

Going upstream

The oil business is effectively divided into three phases. The first phase involves extracting the oil from the ground (or the sea). This is known in the industry as the *upstream* segment of the market. Next, the oil needs to be refined into consumable products such as gasoline and jet fuel. The companies involved in the refining process are known as *midstream* companies. Finally, the specific products must be delivered to consumers, either via pipeline or by ships (sometimes by other means, but these are the two dominant methods). This last phase is known as the *downstream* portion of the market.

Here are the names of some of these vessels you can expect to come across as you start investing in offshore drilling companies:

- **Drilling barge:** The drilling barge is one of the most nimble vessels in the market. It's a floating device usually towed by tugboat to target drilling locations. The drilling barge is primarily used inland, in still, shallow waters such as rivers, lakes, and swamps.

- **Jack-up rig:** The jack-up rig is a hybrid vessel that's part floating barge, part drilling platform. The jack-up rig is towed to the desired location, usually in open, shallow waters where its three "legs" are lowered and "jacked" down to the seafloor. When the legs are secured, the drilling platform is elevated to the desired levels to enable safe drilling.

- **Submersible rig:** The submersible rig is similar to the jack-up rig, in that it's primarily used for shallow-water drilling activity and is secured to the seabed.

- **Semi-submersible rig:** Sometimes referred to as a *semi,* this structure is a feat of modern technological development. It's similar to a submersible, except that it has the capacity to drill in deep waters under harsh and unforgiving weather conditions. The drilling platform is elevated and sits atop a floating structure that's semi-submerged in the water (hence the name) and secured by large anchors that can weigh up to 10 tons each.

- **Drill ship:** The drill ship is essentially a ship with a drilling platform. It's perhaps the most versatile drilling vessel because it can be easily dispatched to remote offshore locations, including drilling in very deep waters.

- **Offshore oil platform:** When one of the previous vessels discovers a commercially viable offshore oil field, a company may decide to build a permanent platform to exploit this discovery. Enter the offshore oil platform. These structures are a sight to behold and are truly man-made floating cities. They house personnel, include living quarters, and are often even equipped with heliports. They're ideally suited to harsh, deepwater conditions.

You can get information on an offshore drilling company's fleet in its annual report. Companies usually lease these vessels to customers, which may include independent oil and gas companies, national oil companies, and the major integrated oil companies, for a premium. A company also includes this type of financial information regarding its fleet in the annual report. (See more on annual reports and other important forms in the sidebar "In the public eye: Looking at a company's public disclosure forms.")

In the public eye: Looking at a company's public disclosure forms

The *Securities and Exchange Commission* (SEC) requires publicly traded companies in the United States to file annual and quarterly reports. The quarterly report, known as *Form 10Q,* contains information about the company's financial operations during each of the first three fiscal quarters in a given year. (A company doesn't need to file a quarterly report at the end of the fiscal year, because that's when the annual report is released.) *Form 10K,* which is the annual report, contains a much more comprehensive overview of a company's financial operations. It's released at the end of the fourth quarter of the fiscal year and includes information on the company's structure, shareholders, business activities, assets, and liabilities.

An additional disclosure form you may want to look at is *Form 8K.* A company is required to file Form 8K with the SEC if it undertakes structural changes, such as a merger or acquisition, bankruptcy, or election of new board members. Form 8K may contain important information regarding the company's future plans. So where can you check out a company's annual report or Form 8K? Perhaps the best resource for this type of information is EDGAR (www.edgar-online.com). It includes the most comprehensive SEC filings I've ever come across. You may need a subscription to access it.

Some of the leading companies in the offshore drilling business include the following:

- ✔ **Diamond Offshore Drilling (NYSE: DO):** With 50 offshore rigs, Diamond Offshore is one of the dominant players in the offshore drilling industry. Headquartered in Houston, Texas, DO has a wide global footprint, with deepwater drilling operations in Brazil, Scotland, Australia, and the Gulf of Mexico. The company has particular expertise in ultra deepwater drilling, with significant operations in Brazil through Petrobras, the state-owned oil company.

  As easily accessible oil becomes scarcer, I expect national oil companies and the majors to make more use of DO's deepwater expertise.

- ✔ **Noble Corporation (NYSE: NE):** Founded in 1921 in Texas, Noble is one of the oldest drilling contractors in the world. It has a fleet of more than 60 vessels and operations stretching from Brazil to the North Sea, and it has an edge in implementing technologically oriented solutions to meet customer demands.

  Noble Corporation has a subsidiary, Noble Technology Services Division, that's a sort of technological think tank dedicated to generating technical solutions for customers.

✔ **Transocean Inc. (NYSE: RIG):** Transocean, whose company motto is "We're never out of our depth," is the ExxonMobil of the offshore drillers. It's the largest company in terms of market capitalization and the size and scope of its operations. The company has more than 90 offshore drilling units at its disposal and is an expert in operating under harsh and extreme weather conditions. It has offshore operations in the U.S. Gulf of Mexico, Brazil, South Africa, the Mediterranean Sea, the North Sea, Australia, and Southeast Asia. In 2007, Transocean agreed to merge its operations with the operations of GlobalSanteFe, the second-largest offshore driller at the time. The combined entity saw the addition of 60 vessels and an expanded global footprint, to include the Middle East and Canada. If you're looking for the largest and most diversified company in the group, Transocean is it.

If you want to dig deeper into this sector, you can check out the Web site www.rigzone.com, which includes up-to-date information on the offshore industry and the oil industry as a whole.

Staying on dry land

A large part of E&P activity takes place on dry land. Actually, the first commercially viable oil wells were discovered on land. Most industry insiders agree that most onshore oil wells have been discovered, but you can still benefit by investing in companies that are involved in the exploitation and production of onshore oil fields.

You may consider investing in a couple companies in this segment of the *drilling* market:

✔ **Nabors Industries (NYSE: NBR):** Nabors is one of the largest land-drilling contractors in the world. It has a division that can perform heavy-duty and horizontal drilling activities.

✔ **Patterson-UTI Energy Inc. (NASDAQ: PTEN):** Patterson-UTI is an onshore oil field drilling contractor that has extensive operations in North America. It operates in a number of segments, including drilling new wells and servicing and maintaining existing oil wells. It's part of the *S&P 400 MidCap* stocks.

Servicing the oil fields

Another area I recommend taking a close look at is companies that focus on oil field maintenance and services. The oil field services sector is dominated by technology-oriented and labor-intensive companies that seek to maximize an oil field's output by using sophisticated technological techniques, such as horizontal drilling and 3-D mapping and imaging.

The major integrated oil companies or national oil companies generally hire oil field services companies for general oil field and oil well maintenance and extraction solutions. For example, Saudi Aramco, the largest oil company in the world in terms of proven reserves, may turn to an oil field services company for the maintenance of a particular oil field. The services company may get involved in actually extracting crude from the oil well, providing data and statistics on current and past usage and on potential future output, using technologically oriented techniques to extract hard-to-recover oil, and performing other specific and general oil field–management services.

The added value of the oil field services companies is that they can improve oil recovery rates on existing fields and recover previously untapped oil pockets in old fields. As fewer oil fields are discovered, the world's major oil companies are looking for ways to maximize existing oil fields. Therefore, the role of the oil field services companies will become increasingly important in the future.

Perhaps the most well-known oil field services company is Halliburton (NYSE: HAL). A lot of people are familiar with the name because it's a high-profile Defense Department contractor that Vice President Dick Cheney once headed. Because of the nature of its political contracts, Halliburton is often a lightning rod for criticism. I recommend going beyond some of this criticism and directly analyzing the company's balance sheet, income statement, and other metrics to get a more accurate sense of the company's scope of operations. Although some of its work is political in nature (government contracts), that work represents only a fraction of its operational activities. More important, although Halliburton is the most notorious of the oil field services companies, it's certainly not representative of the other companies in the field. Many of the other players in this space focus exclusively on oil field maintenance and services, and aren't involved in work of a political nature.

These companies make up your hit list, if you're looking to invest in the oil field services space:

- ✔ **Baker Hughes, Inc. (NYSE: BHI):** As with most oil field services companies, Baker Hughes is headquartered in Houston, Texas. The company operates both in the United States and internationally, with operations stretching from the Persian Gulf to West Africa. Baker Hughes provides technologically oriented solutions to its customers to maximize oil field output efficiency. Baker Hughes isn't the biggest company in the group, but it's certainly a nimble competitor.

- ✔ **Halliburton Co. (NYSE: HAL):** This company, based in Houston, Texas, makes a lot of headlines (sometimes not very positive ones) because of the political nature of its work with the U.S. government and military.

Besides its governmental contracts — which make up only a fraction of its revenues — the company is a leader in oil and gas field maintenance. It helps customers extract as much energy from existing wells as possible, while maintaining low costs. This makes Halliburton a knowledgeable company in the petroleum services sector.

✔ **Schlumberger Ltd. (NYSE: SLB):** Schlumberger may not be a household name, but it's well known and well regarded in the oil industry. The company is one of the most technologically savvy services companies out there and can provide solutions regarding all aspects of oil field–management services, from exploration and extraction to maintenance and abandonment. It provides evaluations to help customers identify the short-term and long-term viability of an oil field and specializes in maximizing oil field output through technologically advanced solutions.

For more information on the oil field services sector and all the companies involved in it, I recommend checking out the Yahoo! Finance Web site, at `biz.yahoo.com/ic/124.html`.

Oh My, You're So Refined! Investing in Refineries

Crude oil by itself doesn't have many useful applications — it needs to be refined into consumable products such as gasoline and jet fuel. Refineries are a critical link in the crude oil supply chain because, after crude oil is discovered, that oil needs to be transformed into products before it's sent to consumers.

This list details some of the products refineries derive from refining crude oil:

✔ Asphalt

✔ Automotive lubricating oil

✔ Diesel fuel

✔ Gasoline

✔ Heating oil (commercial and residential)

✔ Jet fuel (military and commercial aviation)

✔ Kerosene

✔ Petrochemicals

✔ Propane

Given the importance of these derivative products, you can imagine that you can make a lot of money investing in refineries. But before I give you a few company options, you need to look at three criteria when considering investing in companies that operate refineries:

- ✔ **Refinery throughput:** The capacity for refining crude oil over a given period of time, usually expressed in barrels

- ✔ **Refinery production:** Actual production of crude oil products, such as gasoline and heating oil

- ✔ **Refinery utilization:** The difference between production capacity, the throughput, and what's actually produced

You can find this information in a company's annual or quarterly reports. Figure 14-1 presents an example of a refinery's earnings.

	2006 Bpd	2006 %	2005 Bpd	2005 %
Refinery Throughput:				
Sour crude	62,720	88.9	41,096	86.6
Sweet crude	3,191	4.5	2,829	6.0
Blendstocks	4,618	6.6	3,522	7.4
Total Refinery Throughput	**70,529**	**100.0**	**47,447**	**100.0**
Refinery Production:				
Gasoline	32,846	47.2	21,562	45.8
Diesel/jet	23,701	34.1	15,232	32.4
Asphalt	6,444	9.3	4,297	9.1
Petrochemicals	4,266	6.0	3,617	7.7
Other	2,346	3.4	2,352	5.0
Total Refinery Production (17)	**69,603**	**100.0**	**47,060**	**100.0**
Refinery Utilization (18)		**94.2%**		**88.9%**

Figure 14-1: Example of a refinery's throughput and yield data for the two months ending March 31, 2006, and March 31, 2005.

The largest refinery in the United States is located in Baytown, Texas, and is operated by ExxonMobil. It has a refining capacity of 557,000 barrels per day. Most major integrated oil companies have a large refining capacity. These include some of the majors, like ExxonMobil and BP. One way to get exposure to the refining space is to invest in these major companies. I discuss the majors, their scope of activity, and how to invest in them in Chapter 10.

Another, more direct, way to profit from refining activity is to invest in independent refineries. The marquee name in this area is a company called The Valero Energy Corporation (NYSE: VLO). Valero is the largest independent refining company in North America. It has a throughput capacity of 3.3 million barrels per day and operates the largest number of refineries in North America.

I like Valero because, if you want to play the refinery card, it gives you one of the most direct ways to do so. The major integrated companies are a good play, but they're so big that you don't get the same kind of direct exposure you do from Valero.

Although Valero is the goliath in the refinery space, a number of smaller companies can offer you a lot of value. Take a look at a couple of these companies:

- **Sunoco Inc. (NYSE: SUN):** Sunoco is the second-largest refiner in terms of total refinery throughput. It refines approximately 1 million barrels of crude oil a day into refined products, which it distributes primarily in the eastern United States.

  Sunoco, with headquarters in Philadelphia, operates refineries in Pennsylvania, Ohio, and New Jersey, and has a wide distribution network across the East Coast.

- **Tesoro Corp. (NYSE: TSO):** Tesoro, headquartered in San Antonio, Texas, is one of the leading refiners in the midcontinental and western United States. Its refineries transform crude oil into gasoline that's distributed through a network of about 500 retail outlets in the western United States. This option is a good regional play.

  It operates refineries in Utah, California, Washington, Alaska, and even Hawaii.

Refiners operate in an extremely cyclical industry, which poses an inherent investment risk that favors only the most savvy operators. An additional risk involves the very business model that refiners rely on. Independent refiners must purchase the raw material — crude oil — at market prices and must resell the finished product — gasoline, heating oil, and so on — at market prices. However, many majors also operate internal refineries that compete aggressively with the independents; whereas the independents must purchase the raw material at market prices, however, internal refineries often get oil at subsidized prices. This market dynamic makes it extremely difficult for independents to compete on an equal footing with the majors. Keep this in mind as you're analyzing independent refiners.

The Energy Information Administration compiles data on all U.S. refineries at www.eia.doe.gov/neic/rankings/refineries.htm.

Becoming an Oil Shipping Magnate

Commodities such as oil and gas would be useless if there was no way of transporting them to consumers. In fact, transporting commodities to consumers is probably as important as finding and processing them in the first place. Fortunately, as an investor, this need provides you with fertile ground to make money in the transportation of commodities.

This statistic can put things in perspective for you: Two out of every three barrels of oil that are transported are moved around in ships. The remaining one-third is transported via pipelines. (For more on how to invest in pipeline infrastructure, consider master limited partnerships, which I discuss in Chapter 7.) Therefore, the shipping industry plays a crucial role in the integrated oil business.

Perhaps no one person embodies the shipping industry like Aristotle Onassis, the Greek shipping magnate. Onassis built one of the largest fortunes in the world by shipping oil and other commodities around the world. Although I don't promise to make you as rich as Onassis, I'm confident that investing in the seaborne transportation business can give your portfolio a big boost.

In this section, I give you tools to help you invest in the oil-shipping business. I introduce you to the types of vessels that make up a modern oil tanker fleet, point out some of the major companies involved in the business, and offer you advice on pinpointing the right entry and exit points.

Swimming in oil: Transportation supply and demand

One of the most common questions I get asked about the oil-shipping industry is the following: What's the relationship between the price of crude oil and oil tanker profit margins? As with many good questions, this one has no straight answer. It depends on a lot of factors.

Tanker spot rates — the bread and butter of the shipping industry — are determined by supply and demand. The supply side, in this case, consists of how many ships are available to transport crude and products to the desired destinations around the world. On the demand side is how much crude oil and products need to be shipped from point A to point B. In the global shipping business, these factors are the two you need to watch closely.

For example, recently tanker spot rates have experienced some supply-side pressure. Because of a series of environmental incidents, in 1997 the International Maritime Organization (the global regulatory body of the shipping industry; www.imo.org) ordered the phasing out of all single-hull ships, to help prevent further oil spills.

Single-hull ships have just one layer of protection. *Double-hull ships* provide more protection against oil leaks because they have two layers, one exterior and one interior.

Because of this regulation, the number of ships in the open sea transporting oil and products has decreased. A supply-side crunch arose, contributing to the increase in tanker spot rates during 2002–2004, the largest run-up in tanker spot rates in recent memory. (See Figure 14-2, later in the chapter.) The program to phase out all single-hull ships from open waters is scheduled to end before 2010.

Shipping companies are planning to replace these single-hull ships with double-hull ships, but as with almost anything that has to do with the commodities business, constructing these ships takes time. Therefore, the supply-side pressure on tanker spot rates will remain until these newly designed double-hull ships are brought onboard.

On the demand side of the equation, demand for crude oil and products worldwide remains robust. In 2010, the world consumed on average 87 million barrels of oil *a day,* and that number is growing.

Another important demand factor that many industry onlookers sometimes overlook is *oil import dependency.* Crude oil demand is critical, but if oil could be produced and consumed without the need to transport it across long distances on seaborne voyages, the oil-shipping industry would be out of business. The lifeblood of the global oil tanker business is the international flow of oil across countries and continents, or the dependence on oil imports. One key metric to help you gauge the level of activity in this area is global import and export data, which the Energy Information Administration's energy statistics division monitors. Its Web site is www.eia.doe.gov/oil_gas/petroleum/info_glance/petroleum.html.

As long as the supply of ships remains tight and the demand for crude oil seaborne transportation remains high, tanker spot rates will stay elevated. Now, to the extent that crude oil prices affect the demand of crude oil worldwide, crude oil prices will have an effect on tanker spot rates. Specifically, if crude oil prices go so high that folks are no longer willing to buy crude, thus causing demand destruction, the demand for shipping crude oil worldwide will also decrease (this is the notion of *elasticity,* which I cover in Chapter 2), causing tanker spot rates to go down as well. However, this rate drop is an indirect effect of rising oil prices, which is why the relationship between crude oil prices and tanker spot rates isn't easily quantifiable. Too many variables are at play.

At the end of the day, as long as there's a demand for crude to be transported from producers to consumers, you can rest assured that oil shippers will remain in business.

Crude oil ships ahoy!

One factor you need to consider as you're planning investments in the oil-shipping industry is the ships themselves. Before you invest in a tanker stock, closely examine the fleet of vessels it operates.

To help you with this examination, I list some of the types of vessels used in the global crude oil-shipping industry:

- **Ultra Large Crude Carrier (ULCC):** This type of vessel, known in the industry as the ULCC, is the largest vessel in the market. It's used for long-haul voyages. It offers economies of scale because it can carry large amounts of oil across long distances.

- **Very Large Crude Carrier (VLCC):** The VLCC is the vessel of choice for long-distance seaborne voyages. It's ideally suited for intercontinental maritime transportation; its areas of operation include the Persian Gulf to East Asia and West Africa to the United States, among other routes.

- **Suezmax:** This vessel is named thus because its design and size allows it to transit through the Suez Canal, in Egypt. The Suezmax is among the vessels used to transport oil from the Persian Gulf to Europe, as well as to other destinations. It's ideally suited for medium-haul voyages.

- **Aframax:** The Aframax, whose first four letters are an acronym for Average Freight Rate Assessment, is considered the "workhorse" in the tanker fleet. Because of its smaller size, it's ideally suited for short-haul voyages and has the ability to transport crude and products to most ports around the world.

- **Panamax:** Like the Suezmax, the Panamax gets its name from its ability to transit through a canal — in this case, the Panama Canal. This vessel is sometimes used for short-haul voyages between the ports in the Caribbean, Europe, and the United States.

Besides their catchy names, these vessels are identified by how much crude oil and products they can transport on sea. The unit of measurement used to capture this capacity is known as the *Dead Weight Ton,* or DWT. DWT measures the weight of the vessel, including all cargo it's carrying. Most ships are constructed in such a way that 1 DWT is the equivalent of 6.7 barrels of oil.

I list in Table 14-1 the DWT capacity of the vessels described previously, along with their equivalent in barrels of oil.

Table 14-1	Vessel Capacity in DWT and Oil Equivalents	
Vessel Type	*Dead Weight Tons*	*Oil Equivalent (Barrels)*
ULCC	320,000 and up	2+ million
VLCC	200,000–320,000	2 million
Suezmax	120,000–200,000	1 million
Aframax	80,000–120,000	600,000
Panamax	50,000–80,000	300,000

Masters of the sea: Petroleum shipping companies

The companies responsible for transporting crude oil and petroleum products are an essential link in the global energy supply chain. This group is a diverse bunch, and each company provides a necessary and important service to this crucial industry. Some companies concentrate their operations regionally, such as in the Gulf of Mexico or the Persian Gulf. Others have extensive transportation capabilities with operations in all four corners of the globe. Some operate a small group of VLCC vessels, whereas others operate a large number of smaller vessels. Still others specialize in shipping only crude oil, and others focus primarily on petroleum products such as gasoline.

With so many options to choose from, trying to identify which company to invest in can be confusing. In this section, I list all the major publicly traded oil-shipping companies, and I go through their operations and scope of activities so you can decide which one is right for your investment needs.

- **Frontline Ltd. (NYSE: FRO):** Founded in 1948, Frontline is one of the oldest shipping companies in the world. It also operates one of the world's largest fleets of VLCC vessels, with more than 44 VLCCs. Frontline also owns more than 35 Suezmax vessels (1 million barrel capacity), making it one of the largest tanker companies in the world in terms of transportation capacity. Cumulatively, Frontline has the capacity of 18 million DWT. With operations in the Persian Gulf, Europe, the United States, and Asia, Frontline runs a very tight ship indeed!

In addition to its tanker fleet, Frontline offers shareholders one of the highest dividend payouts I've ever seen: an eye-popping $6 per share. At current market prices, that's a yield of more than 18 percent! (See Table 14-2 for more on dividend yields.)

✔ **General Maritime Corp. (NYSE: GMR):** General Maritime focuses on the small and midsize segment of the tanker market. It operates a fleet of Suezmax and Aframax vessels, with operations primarily focused in the Atlantic basin. General Maritime links producers and consumers from Western Africa, the North Sea, the Caribbean, the United States, and Europe. If you're looking for exposure to the trans-Atlantic oil seaborne trade, GMR is a good bet.

The fact that GMR offers a $5 dividend per share also makes this an attractive tanker stock.

✔ **Overseas Shipholding Group, Inc. (NYSE: OSG):** Unlike many of its competitors, which are incorporated in offshore locations such as Bermuda and the Bahamas, OSG is headquartered in New York City. Although it has an international presence, it's the only company with a large presence in the American shipping market. Its U.S. vessels are mainly engaged in transporting crude oil from Alaska to the continental United States, and products from the Gulf of Mexico to the East Coast.

Additionally, OSG has one of the highest profit margins in the industry: a whopping 45 percent profit margin (2006 figures). If you're interested in the domestic crude oil transportation market, take the plunge with OSG.

✔ **Teekay Shipping Corp. (NYSE: TK):** Teekay Shipping is one of the world's largest seaborne transporters of crude oil and crude oil products. It operates a fleet of more than 130 vessels, including one VLCC (2 million barrel capacity) that transports crude from the Persian Gulf and West Africa to Europe, the United States, and Asia; about 15 Suezmax vessels (1 million barrel capacity) that connect producers in North Africa (Algeria) and West Africa to consumers in Europe and the United States; and more than 40 Aframax vessels (0.6 million barrel capacity) that operate in the North Sea, the Black Sea, the Mediterranean Sea, and the Caribbean.

In addition to conventional tankers, Teekay operates a fleet of offshore tankers that are constructed to transport crude from offshore locations to onshore facilities. If you're interest in a truly global and diversified oil-shipping company, you can't go wrong with Teekay Shipping.

I give you here a snapshot of global tanker activities. If you do decide to invest in the global oil-shipping business, I recommend digging deeper into a target company's operations. You can find most of the information you need in a company's annual report (Form 10K) or quarterly report (Form 10Q). You can obtain additional information through third parties, such as analyst reports.

One of the best-kept secrets in this industry is the high dividend payout these companies issue. I'm a huge fan of dividends because they provide you with certainty in an uncertain investment world. And oil tanker stocks offer some of the highest dividend payouts out there. Table 14-2 gives you a group of shipping company stocks that offer some remarkable dividend payouts.

Table 14-2	Oil Tanker Stocks, 2010 Dividend Yields	
Company	*Ticker*	*Dividend Yield*
Frontline	NYSE: FRO	10.9%
Knightsbridge Tankers	NASDAQ: NVLCCF	9%
Nordic American Tankers	NYSE: NAT	9%

Calculating dividend payouts can be tricky because a company isn't obligated to give back money to shareholders in the form of dividends. Some companies pay out high dividends one year but not the next; for others, paying dividends may be only a one-time event. One way to determine future dividend payouts is to examine the company's dividend payout history. Any good stock screener should have this information handy. I find that the Yahoo! Finance Web site does the job: www.finance.yahoo.com.

Swimming with sharks: Avoiding industry risk

As with most aspects of commodities, tanker spot rates and fixed rates, which provide the bulk of a shipping company's revenue stream, are highly cyclical. It's not extraordinary for shipping rates to fluctuate by 60 or 70 percent on a daily basis. Take a look at the tanker spot rate volatility in Figure 14-2.

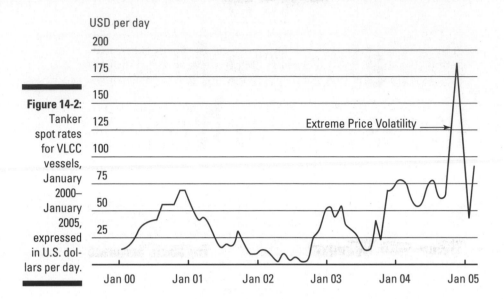

USD per day

Figure 14-2:
Tanker
spot rates
for VLCC
vessels,
January
2000–
January
2005,
expressed
in U.S. dol-
lars per day.

So how do you protect yourself from these extreme price volatilities? One way to hedge your positions is to invest in one of the large oil tanker stocks I mention in the preceding section. These companies have been in the business a long time and have substantial experience managing these wild price swings.

Another factor to consider is global economic growth. The oil-shipping industry depends on a strong global economy with a healthy appetite for crude oil and crude oil products. If the global economy is thrown into a recession, you can expect the tanker stocks to take a hit. With everything else equal, if the world demand for oil products slows down, I recommend getting out of these tanker stocks.

If you're a more adventurous investor, you always have the option to short the stock of companies you know aren't going to do well. You can short a company's stock through various means, such as buying a put option or even selling a call option. I discuss short selling in Chapter 9.

To find out more about the oil-shipping industry, I recommend checking out Martin Stopford's excellent book on the subject, *Maritime Economics* (Routledge).

Part IV

Pedal to the Metal: Investing in Metals

The 5th Wave   By Rich Tennant

©RICHTENNANT

"Remember, I'm heavily invested in metals, so buy all the aluminum jewelry you want."

In this part . . .

People have always been fascinated by precious metals such as gold. In this part, I cover not only precious metals such as gold, silver, and platinum, but also important base and industrial metals like copper, aluminum, zinc, and steel. I give you an in-depth look at these markets and introduce you to some of the world's best mining companies, to help you profit in that market as well.

Chapter 15

All That Glitters: Investing in Gold, Silver, and Platinum

. . . .

In This Chapter

▶ Getting access to gold investments

▶ Making money in silver

▶ Exploring investments in platinum

. . . .

Metallurgy and civilization go hand in hand. Man's ability to control metals enabled him to develop modern society and civilization. As a matter of fact, human prehistory is classified by using a three-age system based on man's ability to control metals: the Stone Age, the Bronze Age, and the Iron Age. Societies that have mastered the use of metals in weaponry and tool making have been able to thrive and survive. Societies without this ability have faced extinction.

Similarly, investors who have been able to master the fundamentals of the metals markets have been handsomely rewarded. In this chapter, I introduce you to the fascinating world of precious metals, which includes gold, silver, and platinum. These metals can play a role in your portfolio because of their precious metal status, their ability to act as a store of value, and their potential to provide a hedge against inflation. In this chapter, you discover all you need to know to incorporate precious metals into your portfolio.

As a general rule, metals are classified into two broad categories: *precious metals* and *base metals*. This classification is based on a metal's resistance to corrosion and oxidation: Precious metals have a high resistance to corrosion, whereas base metals (which I cover in Chapter 16) have a lower tolerance.

Investing in companies that mine precious metals — or any other commodity, for that matter — doesn't give you direct exposure to the price fluctuations of that commodity. You need to be familiar with the fluctuations and patterns of the equity markets to profit from this investment methodology. You also need to consider any external factors that impact the performance of the company, such as management effectiveness, total debt levels, areas of operation, and other metrics that are specific to companies. That said, investing in the equity markets still gives you access to the commodities markets.

Going for the Gold

Perhaps no other metal — or commodity — in the world has the cachet and prestige of gold. For centuries, gold has been coveted and valued for its unique metallurgical characteristics. It was such a desirable commodity that it developed monetary applications, and a number of currencies were based on the value of gold. In 1944, for example, 44 of the world's richest countries (including the United States) decided to peg their currencies to the yellow metal, in what is known as the Bretton Woods Agreement. Although President Nixon removed the dollar from the gold standard in 1971, many countries still use gold as a global currency benchmark.

In addition, gold has a number of applications in industry and jewelry that have resulted in increased demand for this precious metal. Check out the price of gold between 2000 and 2010 in Figure 15-1.

Figure 15-1: Historical price levels of gold on the CME/COMEX, 2000–2010 (dollars per troy ounce).

The golden boy from the gold rush

The California Gold Rush was a defining moment in the history of the United States. When word spread that gold had been discovered in the San Francisco area, many young men rushed out West with a burning desire to strike it rich. A number of success stories emerged from this era. However, one of the greatest *untold* stories of the California Gold Rush is the story of Samuel Brannan, who was California's first millionaire. Brannan was the third man to find out that gold had been discovered in California. Not surprisingly, the first two people who knew about the gold — John Sutter and James Marshall — wanted to keep the discovery a secret. Brannan had other plans.

Instead of keeping quiet about the discovery, Brannan quickly got out the word that gold had

been discovered in California. What's remarkable is that Brannan made a fortune without digging a single hole or prospecting for a single nugget of gold. How did he make his money? By selling shovels to all the people who were interested in digging for the gold! Before he spread the world about the California gold, Brannan quietly bought almost all the shovels in Northern California. When the prospectors flooded in, the price of shovels went through the roof, and Brannan was the only man in town to sell them. He reaped untold fortunes selling shovels during the Gold Rush.

One of the lessons of Brannan's story is that you don't have to actually dig for gold to profit from it. You need to keep your mind open to creative investment ideas that will allow you to profit creatively from the commodities boom.

When I wrote the first edition of *Commodities For Dummies* in 2006, I strongly urged investors to invest in gold for the long term. Back when I first made this recommendation, gold was trading in the range of $500 per ounce; the current gold price at the end of 2010 was $1,450 per ounce. Investors who acted on my recommendation would now be up approximately 300 percent at a time of increased volatility and reduced returns in the global market indexes.

My outlook for gold during the next five years remains positive. Overall, I believe demand for gold will continue to increase, especially as a store of value, driven in part by the weakening paper currency environment that's a result of expansionary monetary policy in the Organization for Economic Cooperation and Development (OECD) countries. As paper currencies come under increased pressure, expect demand for gold to increase. Of course, no investment goes up in a straight line, so expect a bumpy ride and some periods of big pullbacks along the way. For more on my views on gold and the world economy, visit www.commodities-investors.com.

Getting to know the gold standard

The increased demand for gold is linked to a number of reasons. To profit from this increased demand, you need to be familiar with the fundamentals of the gold market. I go through these market fundamentals in this section.

First, you need to know what gold is used for. You may not be surprised to hear that jewelry accounts for a large portion of gold demand. However, did you know that dentistry also represents a significant portion of the gold market? Take a look at some of the uses of gold:

- **Dentistry:** Because gold resists corrosion, it has wide application in dentistry. It's alloyed with other metals, such as silver, copper, and platinum, to create dental fixtures.

- **Electronics:** Because of its ability to efficiently conduct electricity, gold is a popular metal in electronics. It's used as a semiconductor in circuit boards and integrated boards in everything from cellphones and TVs to missiles.

- **Jewelry:** Since man first discovered it thousands of years ago, gold has been used as an ornament and in jewelry. The ancient Egyptian King Tutankhamen was so enamored with gold that he was buried in a gold coffin. Today jewelry is the most important consumer use of gold in the world, accounting for more than 70 percent of total consumption.

- **Monetary:** Many central banks hold reserves of gold. In addition, gold is one of the only commodities that's held in its physical form for investment purposes by the investing public (see the "Let's get physical" section, later in this chapter). Another monetary use of gold, aside from central bank reserves and investor portfolios, is the use of gold in coinage. In countries such as Canada and South Africa, some gold coins are actually legal tender.

Many countries and banks hold reserve assets of gold. I list in Table 15-1 the top ten holders of gold around the world.

Table 15-1	World Gold Holdings in Tons, 2010
Country/Entity	*Reserves (Tons)*
USA	8,135
Germany	3,401
International Monetary Fund	2,846
Italy	2,450
France	2,435
China	1,050
Switzerland	1,040
Japan	765
Netherlands	612
India	557

Source: World Gold Council

What makes gold valuable

Why is gold such an important metal? These traits can help you understand where gold derives its value:

- ✔ **Ductility:** Gold is a very ductile metal. In metallurgy, *ductility* measures how much a metal can be drawn out into a wire. For example, 1 ounce of gold can be converted into more than 50 miles of gold wire! This gold wire can then be applied in electronics and used as an electric conductor.

- ✔ **Malleability:** Pure gold (24 karat) is a very malleable metal and is prized by craftsmen around the world who shape it into jewelry and other objects of beauty. One ounce of gold can be transformed into more than 96 square feet of gold sheet!

- ✔ **Quasi-indestructibility:** Gold has high resistance levels and doesn't easily corrode. Corrosive agents such as oxygen and heat have almost no effect on gold, which can retain its luster over long periods of time (think thousands of years). The only chemical that can affect gold is cyanide, which dissolves gold.

- ✔ **Rarity:** Gold is one of the rarest natural resources on earth. Most people don't realize this, but only about 150,000 tons of gold have ever been produced since humans first began mining gold more than 6,000 years ago. To give you an idea of how little that is, all the gold in the world wouldn't even fill up four Olympic-size swimming pools! And because most gold is recycled and never destroyed, a majority of gold is still in use today. About 15 percent of gold is recycled every year.

How to measure gold

Gold, like most metals, is measured and weighed in *troy ounces*. One troy ounce is the equivalent of 31.10 grams. (Despite the common misperception, the troy ounce does not take its name from the mythic ancient Greek city of Troy. It's named after the French town of Troyes, which was an important center of trade and commerce with a thriving precious metals market during the Middle Ages.) When you buy gold for investment purposes, such as through an exchange-traded fund (ETF) or gold certificates, troy ounces is the measurement of choice.

When you want to refer to large quantities of gold, such as the amount of gold a bank holds in reserves or the amount of gold produced in a mine, the unit of measurement you use is *metric tons*. One metric ton is equal to 32,150 troy ounces.

If you've bought gold jewelry, you may have come across the following measurement: karats. *Karats* (sometimes spelled *carats*) measure the purity of gold. The purest form of gold is 24-karat gold (24K). Everything below that number denotes that the gold is alloyed, or mixed, with another metal.

Table 15-2 shows what the different numbers of karats translate to in terms of gold's purity.

Table 15-2	Purity of Gold, Measured in Karats
Karats	Purity (Percentage)
24K	100%
22K	91.67%
18K	75%
14K	58.3%
10K	41.67%
9K	37.5%

If you buy physical gold for either adornment (jewelry) or investment (gold coins/bars), you want to get the purest form of gold, 24K. If you can't get 24K gold, aim to get the purest form of gold you can get your hands on. Remember that the purer the gold, the higher its value. Pure gold (24K) is always a yellow color. However, you've probably encountered white gold or even red gold — these other colors are created by alloying gold with metals such as nickel or palladium for a white color or with copper to create *red gold*. By definition, white and red gold aren't pure gold.

Whereas purity measures how precious gold is in a percentage basis, *fineness* measures gold's purity expressed as a whole number. Fortunately, fineness and purity are so similar that gold with 91.67 percent purity has a fineness of 0.9167.

Good as gold: Finding ways to invest in gold

In this section, I introduce you to the different ways you can invest in gold: physical gold, gold ETFs, gold-mining companies, and gold futures contracts.

Let's get physical

Gold is unlike any other commodity because it's one of the few commodities that can be physically stored to have its value preserved or increased over periods of time. One investment method unique to gold is to actually buy it — hard, physical gold. You can purchase gold bars, bullion, and coins and store them in a safe location as an investment. Perhaps no other commodity offers you this unique opportunity. (Storing physical coal or uranium for investment purposes just doesn't work, believe me!) In some countries, folks actually buy gold jewelry for the dual purpose of adornment and investment. You can get your hands on these different forms of gold:

✔ **Gold bars:** Gold bars have an undeniable allure. In pop culture, for example, gold is usually depicted as large gold bars. Think of the movies *Goldfinger* and *Die Hard 3,* for instance. Much more than great movie props, gold bars are a great investment. Whereas gold coins are more suited for smaller purchases, gold bars are ideal if you're interested in purchasing larger quantities of gold. Despite popular depictions, gold bars come in all shapes and sizes. They can be as small as 1 gram or as large as 400 troy ounces. Despite the size, most gold bars are high quality, with a fineness of 0.999 and above (24 karats). For a comprehensive listing of gold bars, I recommend *The Industry Catalogue of Gold Bars Worldwide,* which you can find at `www.grendon.com.au/goldbars cat.htm`. Perhaps the only drawback of gold bars is their size, which makes them harder (and more expensive) to store.

Gold *bullion* is nothing more than large gold bars.

✔ **Gold certificates:** Gold certificates are a hybrid instrument that allows you to own physical gold without actually taking possession of it. As the name implies, gold certificates certify that you own a certain amount of gold, which is usually stored in a safe location by the authority that issues the gold certificates. Owning gold certificates is my favorite way of owning physical gold because they're safe and easy to store. When you own gold bars or coins, safety is always a concern — someone could literally steal your gold. Storage is another concern, particularly if you have large quantities of the stuff, because it can end up costing you a lot to store your gold (such as in a bank vault or personal safe). The gold standard of gold certificates is the Perth Mint Certificate Program (PMCP).

The Perth Mint, Australia's oldest and most important mint, administers the PMCP. At one point, the Perth Mint had as much gold as Fort Knox. The PMCP is the only certificate program guaranteed by a government — in this case, the government of Western Australia. The PMCP issues you a certificate and stores your gold in a secure government vault. You may retrieve or sell your gold at any point. For more on this program, check out the Perth Mint's Web site, at `www.perthmint.com.au`.

✔ **Gold coins:** One of the easiest ways to invest in physical gold is to buy gold coins. I like gold coins because they give you a lot of bang for your buck. Unlike large gold bars, gold coins allow you to purchase the yellow metal in smaller quantities and units. This flexibility offers two advantages: First, you don't have to put up as much money to buy a gold coin, compared to buying a gold bar. Second, if you want to sell part of your gold holdings, you can easily sell five gold coins and keep five — that's not possible when you have only one gold bar. Another reason I like gold coins is that you can easily and safely store them; they're more discrete than having large gold bullion. The third reason I like gold coins is that they're issued by a federal government and instantly recognized as such; in some countries (Canada and South Africa), they're even considered legal tender. I list the most popular types of gold coins, by country of issuance, here:

- **Gold eagle:** The U.S. government issues the gold eagle coin; it has the full backing of Congress and the U.S. Mint. It comes in various sizes, including 1 ounce, ½ ounce, ¼ ounce, and ⅒ ounce. At 22K, the gold eagle coin is a high-quality coin that you can actually use to fund an IRA account.

- **Gold Krugerrand:** The gold Krugerrand is issued by the South African government and is one of the oldest gold coins issued in the world. It has a fineness of 0.916.

- **Gold maple leaf:** You guessed it — the Canadian government backs the gold maple leaf. It's issued by the Royal Canadian Mint and, at 24K, is the purest gold coin on the market.

If you want to purchase gold coins, bars, or even certificates, you need to go through a gold dealer. One gold dealer I recommend is Kitco (`www.kitco.com`). Before you do business with any gold dealer, though, find out as much information about the business (and business history) as possible. You can check out different gold dealers by going through the Better Business Bureau, at `www.bbb.org`.

Gold ETFs

Exchange-traded funds that offer exposure to commodities are a popular investment gateway for folks who don't want to mess around with futures contracts, as I explain in Chapter 5. Signaling gold's importance, one of the first commodity ETFs to hit the market is, you guessed it, a gold ETF. Currently, you can choose from two gold ETFs:

- **iShares COMEX Gold Trust (AMEX: IAU):** The iShares gold ETF holds a little more than 1.3 million ounces of gold in its vaults. The per-unit price of the ETF seeks to reflect the current market price in the spot market of the ETF gold.

- **StreetTracks Gold Shares (NYSE: GLD):** The StreetTracks gold ETF is the largest gold ETF on the market today. Launched in late 2004, it holds about 12 million ounces of physical gold in secured locations. The price per ETF unit is calculated based on the average of the bid/ask spread in the gold spot market. This fund is a good way to get exposure to physical gold without actually owning it.

Find out about the fees and expenses associated with each of the ETFs mentioned. These ETFs have to pay a number of entities to actually hold physical gold, so inquire about any storage fees. These fees are in addition to the general fund expenses, such as registration and administration fees. Carefully consider all expenses and fees, because they have a direct impact on your bottom line. (For more on ETFs, turn to Chapter 5.)

Because both the StreetTracks and iShares ETFs track the price of gold on the spot market, their performance is remarkably similar — at times, it's actually identical. Therefore, if you can't decide between the two, I recommend StreetTracks because it holds more physical gold and, more important, offers you more liquidity than the iShares ETF.

Stocks in gold companies

Another way to get exposure to gold is to invest in gold-mining companies. A number of companies specialize in mining, processing, and distributing this precious metal. I recommend these companies:

- ✔ **AngloGold Ashanti Ltd. (NYSE: AU):** AngloGold, which is listed in five different stock exchanges around the world, is a truly global gold company. Based in South Africa, it operates more than 20 mines and has significant operations in Africa and South America, particularly in South Africa, Namibia, Tanzania, Ghana, Mali, Brazil, Argentina, and Peru, which all have major gold deposits. It has additional operations in Australia and North America. AngloGold is a wholly owned subsidiary of Anglo-American, the global mining giant (which I cover in Chapter 18).

- ✔ **Barrick Gold Corporation (NYSE: ABX):** Barrick is a Canadian company with headquarters in Toronto. It's a premier player in the gold-mining industry and has operations in Argentina, Australia, Canada, Chile, Papua New Guinea, Peru, South Africa, Tanzania, and the United States. It also has a foothold in the potentially lucrative Central Asian market, where it has joint operations in Mongolia, Russia, and Turkey. Another reason I like Barrick is that it has one of the lowest production costs per ounce of gold in the industry.

- ✔ **New Gold, Inc. (AMEX: NGD):** New Gold is a junior gold-mining company headquartered in Vancouver, British Columbia. It was founded in 2005 and currently operates three highly profitable mines in California, Mexico, and Australia; the cash costs per ounce for each of these mines are in the industry lows, translating into high margins. In addition, NGD is in the process of exploiting two additional mines, one in Canada and the other in Chile, two mining-friendly jurisdictions. The management team's successful track record in making acquisitions and operating mines makes this an indispensable investment for anyone looking for exposure to gold markets.

- ✔ **Newmont Mining Corporation (NYSE: NEM):** Newmont, headquartered in Colorado, is one of the largest gold-mining companies in the world. It has operations in Australia, Bolivia, Canada, Indonesia, Peru, the United States (Nevada and California), and Uzbekistan. It's actually the largest gold producer in South America. Additionally, it has exploration programs in Ghana that may be very promising for the company. If you're looking for a truly global and diversified gold producer with real growth potential, you can't go wrong with Newmont.

A number of other mining companies have gold-mining operations that are part of a general mining program that includes other metals, such as silver and copper. I selected these companies because their sphere of operations revolves almost exclusively around gold mining.

The performance of these companies isn't directly proportional to the spot or future price of gold. These companies don't give you the direct exposure to gold that gold certificates or bars do, for example. Also, by investing in these stocks, you're exposing yourself to regulatory, managerial, and operational factors.

Gold contracts

Gold futures contracts give you a direct way to invest in gold through the futures markets. You can choose from two gold futures contracts that are widely traded in the United States (see Chapter 9 for the goods on futures contracts):

- **CME/CBOT Mini-Gold (CBOT: YG):** Launched in 2004, this gold contract, trading in the CBOT section of the Chicago Mercantile Exchange (CME), is a relative newcomer to the North American gold futures market. However, it's a popular contract because you can trade it online through the CME's electronic trading platform. In addition, at a contract size of 33.2 troy ounces, the mini is popular with investors and traders who prefer to trade this smaller-size contract than the larger 100-ounce contract.

- **CME/CBOT E-Micro Gold (CBOT: MGC):** Launched in 2010, this gold contract trades on the COMEX section of the Chicago Mercantile Exchange (CME). The contract is relatively new, and popularity has been growing each month with its electronic execution traded on the CME Globex platform. At a contract size of 10 troy ounces, the E-Micro is popular with investors and traders who prefer to trade a smaller size contract than the Mini-Gold 33.2 troy ounce.

- **CME/COMEX Gold (COMEX: GC):** The COMEX gold futures contract was the first such contract to hit the market in the United States (back in the 1970s). It's traded on the COMEX division of the CME, and it's the most liquid gold contract in the world. It's used primarily by large commercial consumers and producers, such as jewelry manufacturers and mining companies, for price-hedging purposes. However, you can also purchase the contract for investment purposes. Each contract represents 100 troy ounces of gold.

When investing in the futures markets, always trade in the most liquid markets. *Liquidity* is an indication of the number of contracts traded on a regular basis. The higher the liquidity, the more likely you are to find a buyer or seller to close out or open a position. You can get information on the volume and open interest of contracts traded in the futures markets through the Commodity Futures Trading Commission (CFTC) Web site, at www.cftc.gov.

Get the Tableware Ready: Investing in Silver

Silverware and jewelry aren't the only uses for silver. As a matter of fact, silverware is only a small portion of the silver market. A large portion of this precious metal goes toward industrial uses, such as conducting electricity; creating bearings; and welding, soldering, and brazing (the process by which metals are permanently joined together). Because of its numerous practical applications and its status as a precious metal, investing in silver can bolster your portfolio. In this section, I introduce you to the ins and outs of the silver market and then show you how to actually include silver in your portfolio.

Checking out the big picture on the silver screen

Silver has a number of uses that make it an attractive investment. This list details the most important ones, which account for more than 95 percent of total demand for silver:

- **Industrial:** The industrial sector is the single largest consumer of silver products, accounting for almost 50 percent of total silver consumption in 2010. Silver has a number of applications in the industrial sector, including creating control switches for electrical appliances and connecting electronic circuit boards. Because it's a good electrical conductor, silver will keep playing an important role in the industrial sector.

- **Jewelry and silverware:** Many people believe (incorrectly) that the largest consumer of silver is the jewelry industry. Although silver does play a large role in creating jewelry and silverware, demand from this sector accounted for 25 percent of total silver consumption in 2010.

- **Photography:** The photographic industry is also a major consumer of silver, accounting for about 20 percent of total consumption in 2006. In photography, silver is compounded with halogens to form *silver halide,* which is used in photographic film. Digital cameras, which don't use silver halide, are becoming more popular than traditional cameras. As a result, photography demand for silver went from 20 percent in 2006 to less than 10 percent in 2010.

Monitor the commercial activity in each of these market segments and look for signs of strength or weakness, because a demand increase or decrease in one of these markets, such as photography, will have a direct impact on the price of silver.

Knowing where the silver comes from is always important to an investor, so I list the top producers of silver in the world in Table 15-3.

Table 15-3	Top Silver Producers, 2009
Country	*Production (Millions of Ounces)*
Peru	124
Mexico	105
China	89
Australia	52
Bolivia	42
Russia	42
Chile	41
Poland	40
United States	39
Kazakhstan	20

If you're interested in finding out more about silver and its investment possibilities, the Silver Institute, a trade association for silver producers and consumers, maintains a comprehensive database on the silver market. Its Web site is www.silverinstitute.org.

Getting a sliver of silver in your portfolio

Silver can play an important role in your portfolio. Because of its precious metal status, you can use it as a hedge against inflation and to preserve part of your portfolio's value. In addition, because it has important industrial applications, you can use it for capital appreciation opportunities. Whether for capital preservation or appreciation, I believe any portfolio has room for some exposure to silver. In this section, I introduce you to the different ways you can invest in silver.

Buying physical silver

One of the unique characteristics of silver is that you can invest in it by actually buying the stuff, as you can buy gold coins and bars for investment purposes. Most dealers that sell gold generally offer silver coins and bars as well.

- **100-ounce silver bar:** If you're interested in something substantial, you can buy a 100-ounce silver bar. Before buying it, check the bar to make sure that it's pure silver (you want 99 percent purity or above).

- **Silver maple coins:** These coins, which are a product of the Royal Canadian Mint, are the standard for silver coins around the world. Each coin represents 1 ounce of silver and has a purity of 99.99 percent, making it the most pure silver coin on the market.

The term *sterling silver* refers to a specific silver alloy that contains 92.5 percent silver and 7.5 percent copper (other base metals are occasionally used as well). Pure silver is sometimes alloyed with another metal, such as copper, to make it stronger and more durable. Just remember that if you're considering silver jewelry as an investment, sterling silver won't give you as much value in the long term as pure silver.

Buying the silver ETF

One of the most convenient ways of investing in silver is to go through an exchange-traded fund (ETF). Until recently, no ETFs tracked silver. However, Barclays Global Investors (a subsidiary of the investment bank) launched an ETF through its iShares program in April 2006 to track the price of silver. The iShares Silver Trust (AMEX: SLV) holds silver bullion in a vault and seeks to mirror the spot price of that silver based on current market prices. This new silver ETF is a testament to the increased demand by investors to include silver in their portfolios.

Looking at silver-mining companies

Another alternative investment route is to go through companies that mine silver. Although some of the larger mining companies (which I cover in Chapter 18) have silver-mining operations, you can get more direct exposure to the silver markets by investing in companies that specialize in mining this precious metal. These companies may not be household names, but they're a potentially good investment nevertheless. This list details a couple companies that focus exclusively on mining silver:

- **Pan American Silver Corporation (NASDAQ: PAAS):** Pan American Silver, based in Vancouver, has extensive operations in the Americas. It operates six mines in some of the most prominent locations in the world, including Bolivia, Mexico, and Peru. If you're interested in a well-managed company to get exposure to Latin American silver mines, you won't go wrong with Pan American Silver.

✔ **Silver Wheaton Corp. (NYSE: SLW):** Silver Wheaton is one of the only mining companies that generates all its revenues from silver-mining activity. Whereas other mining companies may have smaller interests in other metals, Silver Wheaton focuses exclusively on developing and mining silver. It has operations in geographically diverse areas that stretch from Mexico to Sweden. If you're looking for a geographically diverse company to give you direct access to silver-mining activities, Silver Wheaton is your best bet.

Checking out silver futures contracts

Similar to gold futures, silver futures contracts give you the most direct access to the silver market. Following are the most liquid silver futures contracts:

✔ **CBOT Mini-Silver (CBOT: YI):** The Mini-Silver contract that trades on the CBOT division of the CME represents a stake in 1,000 troy ounces of silver with a purity of 99.9 percent. This contract is available for electronic trading.

✔ **COMEX Silver (COMEX: SI):** The COMEX silver contract is the standard futures contract for silver. It's traded on the COMEX division of the CME and represents 5,000 troy ounces of silver per contract.

To give you an idea of the performance of the CME/COMEX silver futures contract, I list its price in Figure 15-2. For more on futures, check out Chapter 9.

Figure 15-2: Historical price levels of silver on the CME/COMEX, 2002–2010 (dollars per troy ounce).

Volume 1753133.00 Open Interest 113391.00

Bling Bling: Investing in Platinum

Platinum, sometimes referred to as "the rich man's gold," is one of the rarest and most precious metals in the world. Perhaps no other metal or commodity carries the same cachet as platinum, and for good reason: It's by far the rarest metal in the world. If you put all the platinum that has ever been mined into an Olympic-size swimming pool, that platinum wouldn't even cover your ankles! Whereas precious and base metals such as gold and copper have been exploited for thousands of years, man's interest in platinum developed only in the 17th century, when the Conquistadors discovered large amounts of the metal in South America. Platinum was soon discovered to have superior characteristics to most metals: It's more resistant to corrosion, doesn't oxidize in the air, and has stable chemical properties. Because of these characteristics, platinum is a highly desirable metal and can play an important role in your portfolio.

Platinum is also the name of the group of metals that includes platinum, palladium, osmium, ruthenium, rhodium, and iridium. In this section, I talk about the metal, not the group of metals, although I cover palladium in Chapter 17.

Gathering platinum facts and figures

Deposits of platinum ore are extremely scarce and, more important, are geographically concentrated in a few regions around the globe, primarily in South Africa, Russia, and North America. South Africa has the largest deposits of platinum in the world and, by some accounts, may contain up to 90 percent of the world's total reserve estimates. Russia is also a large player in the production of platinum, currently accounting for 20 percent of total global production (2010 figures). North America also contains some commercially viable platinum mines, located mostly in Montana.

So who uses platinum? Platinum has several uses, but these are the most important:

- **Catalytic converters:** You may be surprised to find out not only that platinum is used in catalytic converters in transportation vehicles, but also that this accounts for more than 45 percent of total platinum demand. Platinum's unique characteristics make it a suitable metal in the production of these pollution-reducing devices. As environmental fuel standards become more stringent, expect the demand from this sector to increase.

- **Industrial:** Because it's a great conductor of heat and electricity, platinum has wide applications in industry. It's used in creating everything from personal computer hard drives to fiber-optic cables. Despite its relative value, platinum will continue to be used for industrial purposes.

✔ **Jewelry:** At one point, jewelry accounted for more than 50 percent of total demand for platinum. Although that number has decreased, the jewelry industry is still a major purchaser of platinum metals for use in highly prized jewelry.

A change in demand from one of these industries will affect the price of platinum. The International Platinum Association maintains an updated database of the uses of platinum. Check out its Web site for more information on platinum supply and demand, at www.platinuminfo.net.

Going platinum

Platinum's unique characteristics as a highly sought-after precious metal with industrial applications make it an ideal investment. Fortunately, you can invest in platinum in a number of ways. I list a couple of these methods in the following sections.

Platinum futures contract

The most direct way of investing in platinum is to go through the futures markets. The Chicago Mercantile Exchange (CME) offers a platinum futures contract. Due to platinum's uses in industry and a store of value, it has experienced increased demand from investors; however, platinum is also a highly sensitive trading instrument and tends to react drastically to any price shocks, as was the case during the Global Financial Crisis of 2008. Platinum can be subject to wide price swings, so it's not for the buy-and-hold investor; taking advantage of this opportunity requires quick and tactical trading strategies. Check out the price of platinum in Figure 15-3.

The CME platinum futures contract represents 50 troy ounces of platinum and is available for trading electronically. It trades under the ticker symbol PL.

Platinum-mining companies

Check out a couple companies that give you direct exposure to platinum-mining activities:

✔ **Anglo-American PLC (NASDAQ: AAUK):** Anglo-American is a diversified mining company that has activities in gold, silver, platinum, and other precious metals. I recommend Anglo-American because it has significant interests in South African platinum mines, the largest mines in the world. If you're looking for an indirect exposure to South Africa's platinum mining industry, Anglo-American does the trick.

✔ **Stillwater Mining Company (NYSE: SWC):** Stillwater Mining is headquartered in Billings, Montana, and owns the rights to the Stillwater mining complex in Montana, which contains one of the largest commercially viable platinum mines in North America. This option is a good play on North American platinum-mining activities.

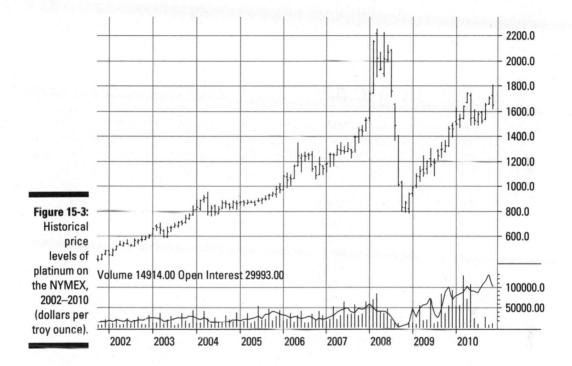

Figure 15-3: Historical price levels of platinum on the NYMEX, 2002–2010 (dollars per troy ounce).

Chapter 16

Metals That Prove Their Mettle: Steel, Aluminum, and Copper

Steel, aluminum, and copper may not be as glamorous as their precious metals counterparts — gold, silver, and platinum, covered in Chapter 15 — but they're perhaps even more precious to the global economy. Gold, silver, and platinum do have industrial applications, but their primary value is derived from their ability to act as stores of value, in addition to their use in jewelry. Steel, aluminum, and copper are the most important *industrial* components of the metals complex, used to build everything from railcars to bridges. You may be surprised to hear that steel is the most widely used metal in the world — more than 1.2 billion tons of it were produced in 2009. Steel is closely followed by aluminum, which is closely followed by copper in terms of total global output. So steel, aluminum, and copper — in that order — rank at the top of the metals complex, based on total output.

Without these metals, which are literally the building blocks of modern societies, life as you and I know it wouldn't exist. Buildings couldn't be built without steel, cars wouldn't be as lightweight and efficient without aluminum, and you probably wouldn't be able to get any electricity in your home without copper, which is the electrical conductor of choice. Due in part to rapid industrialization in China (which happens to be the largest steel producer), India, and other leading developing countries, demand for these three building block metals is strong and will remain robust for the medium to long term. The future looks bright for these metals. In this chapter, I help you develop a game plan for investing in these powerhouse metals.

Building a Portfolio That's As Strong As Steel

The development of steel, alongside iron, changed the course of human history. In fact, the last stage of prehistoric times, the *Iron Age,* is named thus because humans mastered the iron- and steel-making processes. This development allowed societies to build tools and weapons, which speeded advancements in construction and technology. Steel was responsible for another revolution in the 19th century: the Industrial Revolution. Today, in a high-tech world dominated by software and technological gadgets, this age-old metal is still as reliable as ever. In fact, steel is making a resurgence as advanced developing countries — China, India, and Brazil — barrel down a path toward rapid industrialization not unlike the one the West experienced in the 19th century (see Chapter 2). *Steel,* which is iron alloyed with other compounds (usually carbon), is still the most widely produced metal in the world.

Steel is measured in *metric tons,* sometimes abbreviated as MT. For *global* production and consumption figures, *million metric tons* (MMT) is used.

Steely facts

Before I introduce the best ways to invest in steel, take a look at the dynamics of the broader steel industry. China dominates steel production, with generous subsidies in place for its steel manufacturers. China now produces three times more steel than Japan, the second-largest producer. For a long time, the United States was the number one producer of steel, but its dominance eroded largely because of competition from Asia (especially China and Japan) and partly for internal reasons (such as the high costs of running a steel mill in the United States). The United States is still an important player in the steel industry; other countries worth mentioning include Russia, Germany, and South Korea. In Table 16-1, I list the top steel producers in the world in 2009. To put things in perspective, total global steel production in 2009 stood at 1,220 MMT.

Table 16-1	Top Steel-Producing Countries, 2009
Country	*Production (Million Metric Tons)*
China	567 MMT
Japan	88 MMT
United States	60 MMT

Country	Production (Million Metric Tons)
Russia	59 MMT
India	56 MMT
South Korea	48 MMT
Germany	32 MMT
Ukraine	29 MMT
Brazil	27 MMT

Source: International Iron and Steel Institute

If you're interested in exploring additional statistical information relating to steel production and manufacturing, I recommend checking out the following resources:

- ✔ **Association for Iron and Steel Technology:** www.aist.org
- ✔ **International Iron and Steel Institute:** www.worldsteel.org
- ✔ **Iron and Steel Statistics Bureau:** www.issb.co.uk

Investing in steel companies

Although futures contracts are available for everything from crude oil to coffee, there's no underlying futures contract for steel. However, a number of exchanges have expressed interest in developing a steel futures contract, so keep an eye out for such a development.

For now, the best way to get exposure to steel is to invest in companies that produce steel, specifically globally integrated steel companies. The companies I list in Table 16-2 are global leaders in the steel industry.

Table 16-2	Top Steel-Producing Companies, 2009
Company	**Production (Million Metric Tons)**
ArcelorMittal (worldwide)	78
Baosteel (China)	31
POSCO (South Korea)	30
Nippon Steel (Japan)	27
JFE Group (Japan)	27
Jiangsu Shagang (China)	21

(continued)

Table 16-2 *(continued)*

Company	Production (Million Metric Tons)
Tata Steel (India)	20
Ansteel (China)	20
Severstal (Russia)	17
Evraz (Russia)	15

Source: International Iron and Steel Institute

The companies in Table 16-2 are the world leaders in the industry. However, not all are available for investment. Some of them are private, and others trade on foreign exchanges that don't issue *American Depository Receipts* (ADRs). (Turn to Chapter 18 for more on ADRs, which essentially allow you to invest in foreign companies through U.S. stock exchanges.) The following list represents good investments that not only are the best-run companies, but also display the greatest potential for future market dominance:

- **Arcelor-Mittal (NYSE: MT):** Arcelor-Mittal resulted when the Indian company Mittal acquired the European Arcelor in 2006, in one of the biggest consolidation plays the industry has ever seen. Combining the number one and number two steel producers has created a dominant leader with output, almost double that of its nearest competitor. If you're looking for broad exposure to the steel industry, you can't go wrong with Arcelor-Mittal.

- **Gerdau (NYSE: GGB):** Gerdau is a Brazilian vertically integrated steel producer with operations across several countries. Gerdau is a dominant player in the long steel category, with mills in Brazil, Argentina, Mexico, Colombia, and the United States. It brought in a net income of more than $800 million in 2009, so you can remain confident that this company will generate long-term value for its shareholders.

- **Nucor Corp. (NYSE: NUE):** The American steel industry remains a robust competitor on the global stage, despite the dominance of Asian (particularly Chinese) companies. Nucor operates almost exclusively in the United States; if you're interested in getting exposure to the American steel market, consider investing in it. Nucor is also one of the only companies to operate *minimills* domestically, which many argue are more cost efficient than the traditional blast furnaces.

- **U.S. Steel (NYSE: X):** U.S. Steel, which was formed as a result of the consolidation of Andrew Carnegie's steel holdings in the early 20th century, is one of the oldest and largest steel companies in the world. By itself, U.S. Steel represents the whole history of the modern steel industry. At one point, it was the largest producer of steel in the world. Although it has scaled down its operations, it's still a significant player in the industry today. U.S. Steel is involved in all aspects of the steel-making process, from iron ore mining and processing to the marketing of finished products.

Andrew Carnegie: Man of steel

Perhaps no single individual has had as much of an impact on the modern, global steel industry as Andrew Carnegie, the self-made industrialist. Carnegie single-handedly established the steel industry in Pittsburgh, Pennsylvania, which dominated the steel industry for decades. He established the Carnegie Steel Corporation, which eventually became U.S. Steel, in the 1890s and played a decisive role in the industrialization of the young nation. His steel was used in everything from bridges to railroads. Another contribution to the steel industry, which is perhaps less known, is Carnegie's pioneering business philosophy of "countercyclical investing." Many business executives at the time invested their profits to upgrade facilities when business was booming; this was a costly endeavor. Carnegie, identifying the cyclical nature of the industry, undertook capital expenditures when the industry was in decline — this was less expensive. Investing when the industry was in a down cycle made his cost upgrades less expensive than investing during up cycles. This business practice greatly increased his company's profitability, and it's still used today.

Aluminum: Illuminating the Details

Aluminum is one of the most ubiquitous metals of modern society. Not just aluminum soda cans account for its widespread use — aluminum is also used in transportation (cars, trucks, trains, and airplanes), construction, and electrical power lines, to name just a few end uses. As a matter of fact, aluminum is the second most widely used metal in the world, right after steel. Because of its indispensability, you need to make room to include this metal in your portfolio. In this section, I show you how to do just that.

Aluminum is generally measured in *metric tons* (MT).

Just the aluminum facts

Aluminum is a lightweight metal that's resistant to corrosion. Because of these characteristics, it's widely used to create a number of products, from cars to jets. Consider a few items made out of aluminum:

- **Construction:** Aluminum has industrial uses as well, including a role in the construction of buildings, oil pipelines, and even bridges. Building constructors are attracted to it because it's lightweight, durable, and sturdy.

- **Packaging:** Almost a quarter of aluminum is used to create aluminum wrap and foil, along with beverage cans and rivets.

- **Transportation:** Aluminum is used to create the body, axles, and, in some cases, engines of cars. In addition, large commercial aircrafts are built using aluminum because of its light weight and sturdiness.

Table 16-3 breaks down total aluminum consumption by sector.

Table 16-3	Aluminum Consumption by Sector, 2009
Industry	*Aluminum Consumption (Percentage of Total)*
Transportation	26%
Packaging	22%
Construction	22%
Electrical	8%
Machinery	8%
Consumer goods	7%
Miscellaneous uses	7%

Source: London Metal Exchange (LME)

If you're interested in finding out more about the aluminum industry, I recommend checking out the following organizations:

- **The Aluminum Association:** www.aluminum.org
- **aluNET International:** www.alunet.net
- **International Aluminium Institute:** www.world-aluminium.org

Aluminum futures

You can invest in aluminum through the futures markets. Previously, two major contracts for aluminum were available. The first one is through the London Metal Exchange (LME); the second one used to trade in the COMEX division of the New York Mercantile Exchange (NYMEX). However, the COMEX contract was delisted in 2009, after the Chicago Mercantile Exchange (CME) acquired the exchange. As a result, the go-to contract is now the LME.

The London Metal Exchange (LME) aluminum contract is the most liquid in the world. It represents a size of 25,000 tons, and its price is quoted in U.S. dollars.

To give you an idea of the performance of aluminum in recent years, Figure 16-1 shows you the chart of LME aluminum. As you can see, the underlying demand from rapidly industrializing nations such as China and India has resulted in upward price pressures on the metal.

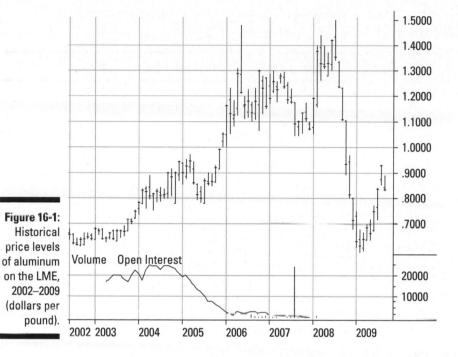

Figure 16-1:
Historical
price levels
of aluminum
on the LME,
2002–2009
(dollars per
pound).

Aluminum companies

Another way I recommend investing in aluminum is to invest in companies
that produce and manufacture aluminum products. A few companies make
the cut:

- ✔ **Alcoa (NYSE: AA):** Alcoa is the world leader in aluminum production.
  It's involved in all aspects of the aluminum industry and produces primary aluminum, fabricated aluminum, and alumina. The company has
  operations in more than 40 countries and services a large number of
  industries, from aerospace to construction. If you're looking to get the
  broadest exposure to the aluminum market, you can't go wrong with
  Alcoa.

- ✔ **Aluminum Corporation of China (NYSE: ACH):** As its name implies,
  ACH is primarily engaged in producing aluminum in the Chinese market.
  I recommend this company, which trades on the New York Stock
  Exchange (NYSE), because it gives you a foothold in the aluminum
  Chinese market, which may potentially be the biggest such market in the
  future. Besides this competitive advantage, ACH is a well-run company
  with profit margins that, during the writing of this book, were larger
  than 20 percent.

Paying a Visit to Dr. Copper

Copper, the third most widely used metal in the world, has applications in many sectors, including construction, electricity conduction, and large-scale industrial projects. Copper is sought after because of its high electrical conductivity, resistance to corrosion, and malleability. Copper played a huge role during the Industrial Revolution and in connecting and wiring the modern world. Because of the current trends of industrialization and urbanization across the globe (see Chapter 2), demand for copper has been — and will remain — very strong, making it a good investment.

Quick copper facts

Copper is used for a variety of purposes, from building and construction to electrical wiring and engineering. To get a better idea of its wide usage, check out the breakdown of copper use by sector in Table 16-4.

Table 16-4	Copper Consumption by Sector, 2009
Sector	*Copper Consumption (Percentage of Total)*
Building/construction	50%
Engineering	24%
Electrical	17%
Transportation	7%
Miscellaneous Uses	2%

Source: Copper Development Association (CDA)

You probably come across items made from copper on a daily basis but may have never thought much about its ubiquity. These everyday items, among others, are made from copper:

- Artistic items (bronze statues such as the Statue of Liberty)
- Coinage (U.S. coins such as the quarter and the dime, which are more than 90 percent copper)
- Construction tubes, pipes, and fittings
- Doorknobs

- Electrical wiring

- High-speed Internet cables

- Industrial sleeve bearings

- Musical instruments (brass instruments such as the trumpet and the tuba)

- Plumbing tubes

 Copper is often alloyed with other metals, usually with nickel and zinc (both covered in Chapter 17). When copper and nickel are alloyed, the resulting metal is *bronze;* when copper is alloyed with zinc, it results in *brass.* Ironically, the U.S. penny, the only U.S. coin that's a reddish/brown color (the color of copper), is the only coin that uses only 2.5 percent copper — 97.5 percent of the penny is made from zinc. The other coins in U.S. currency, which are all silvery/white, contain more than 90 percent copper.

If you're interested in finding out more about copper usage, I recommend that you consult the Copper Development Association, at www.copper.org.

Copper futures contracts

Like most of the other important industrial metals, there's a futures market available for copper trading. Large industrial producers and consumers of the metal account for most of this market, although you also can use it for investment purposes. You have two copper contracts to choose from:

- **CME/COMEX Copper (COMEX: HG):** This copper contract trades in the COMEX division of the Chicago Mercantile Exchange (CME). COMEX copper, which trades during the current month and subsequent 23 calendar months, is traded both electronically and through the open outcry system. It represents 25,000 pounds of copper and trades under the symbol HG.

- **LME Copper (LME: CAD):** The copper contract on the London Metal Exchange (LME) accounts for more than 90 percent of total copper futures activity. It represents a lot size of 25 tons. *Note:* Because the LME is located in the United Kingdom, the British Financial Services Authority (FSA) regulates it.

Demand for copper from China, India, and other advanced developing countries is increasing, and that has put upward pressure on the price of copper. In Figure 16-2, check out the price of copper futures on the CME/COMEX.

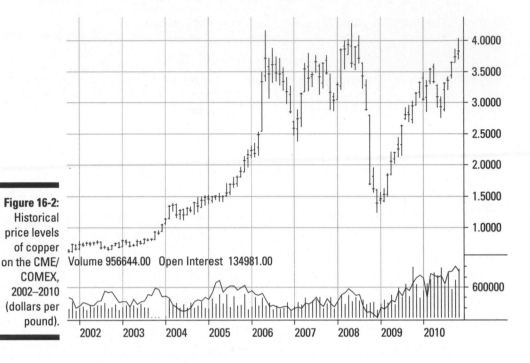

Figure 16-2:
Historical
price levels
of copper
on the CME/
COMEX,
2002–2010
(dollars per
pound).

Volume 956644.00   Open Interest 134981.00

Copper companies

Another investment vehicle I recommend is companies that specialize in
mining and processing copper ore. The companies I list here are leaders in
their industry and are involved in all aspects of the copper supply chain. The
only drawback of investing in companies is that you don't get direct exposure to the price fluctuations of the metals. Still, these companies are a good
option if you don't want to venture into the futures markets.

- **Freeport-McMoRan, Inc. (NYSE: FCX):** One of the reasons I like Freeport-
  McMoRan is that it's one of the lowest-cost producers of copper in the
  world. It has copper-mining and -smelting operations across the globe
  and has a significant presence in Indonesia and Papua New Guinea.
  The company specializes in producing highly concentrated copper ore,
  which it then sells on the open market. FCX also has some operations in
  gold and silver.

- **Phelps Dodge Corporation (NYSE: PD):** Founded in 1834, Phelps Dodge
  is one of the oldest mining companies in the United States. It's also one
  of the largest manufacturers and producers of copper and copper products in the world. The company has a global presence in copper mining,
  with operations in the United States, South Africa, the Philippines, and

Peru, among others. Because of its size and experience in the industry, Phelps Dodge is in a good position to capitalize on increased demand for copper.

I cover copper companies in depth in Chapter 18. I also examine integrated and diversified mining companies, to help you design an investment strategy that effectively allows you to "buy the market."

Chapter 17

Weighing Investments in Heavy and Not-So-Heavy Metals

*I*n this chapter, I go over a diverse group of metals: palladium, a precious metal, and two industrial metals, zinc and nickel. These metals are important components of the metals complex in their own right: palladium because of its precious metal status and as a part of the *platinum group of metals* (PGM), and nickel and zinc for their wide use in industry. These metals may not get much attention from the financial press, but you still need to consider including them in your portfolio: They're essential building blocks of the global economy. I outline the market characteristics of each of these metals so that you can determine whether they're right for you.

Palladium: Metal for the New Millennium

Palladium, which belongs to the platinum group of metals (PGM), is a popular alternative to platinum in the automotive industry and the jewelry industry. Its largest use comes into play in the creation of pollution-reducing catalytic converters. Palladium's malleability and resistance to corrosion make it the perfect metal for such use. In addition, because palladium is less expensive per troy ounce than platinum ($802 per ounce versus $1,793 per ounce, according to 2011 figures), it's increasingly becoming the metal of choice in manufacturing these devices.

Aside from its usage in catalytic converters and jewelry, palladium is used in dentistry and electronics. I list in Table 17-1 the main consumers of palladium.

Table 17-1   Palladium Consumption by Industry, 2009

Sector	Percentage of Total
Auto industry (catalytic converters)	58%
Jewelry	26%
Electronics	17%
Dentistry	15%
Other	4%

Source: U.S. Geological Survey

Palladium has benefited from more stringent fuel emission standards established by the *Environmental Protection Agency* (EPA) and other international environmental organizations. When pollution-reducing regulation was established in the 1970s, demand for palladium skyrocketed as a direct result. All things equal, if emissions standards are further improved and require a new generation of catalytic converters, demand for palladium will increase. Another reason to be bullish on palladium is that the number of automobiles, trucks, and other vehicles equipped with platinum- and palladium-made catalytic converters is increasing, particularly in China. If you invest in palladium, keep an eye on automobile-manufacturing patterns.

Two countries essentially dominate the palladium market: Russia and South Africa. These two countries account for more than 85 percent of total palladium production, as you can see in Table 17-2.

Table 17-2   Top Palladium-Producing Countries, 2009

Country	Production (Million Ounces)
Russia	3.7
South Africa	2.4
North America	0.8
Zimbabwe	0.2
Other	0.25

Source: U.S. Geological Survey

Because these two countries dominate palladium production, any supply disruption from either country has a significant impact on palladium prices. Such was the case in early 2000, when the Russian government announced it would halt shipments of palladium and other platinum group metals for the year. As you can see in Figure 17-1, the price of palladium in the year 2000 almost doubled, partly in response to Russian supply-side disruptions.

The Russian government eventually announced a resumption of palladium-mining activity, and prices dropped back to normal levels in 2001. As a result of this price shock, mining companies have tried to diversify their activities beyond Russia and South Africa. However, there's no way around the fact that most of the world's reserves of palladium ore are located in these two countries. As a matter of fact, perhaps no two countries dominate a commodity as much as Russia and South Africa dominate palladium.

Keep in mind the unique market structure as you consider investing in this precious metal.

Figure 17-1: Historical price levels of palladium on the CME/COMEX, 2002–2010 (dollars per 100 troy ounces).

One of the best — albeit indirect — methods of getting exposure to the palladium markets is investing in companies that mine the metal. A number of companies specialize in this activity, but I recommend taking a look at these two:

- **North American Palladium (AMEX: PAL):** North American Palladium, headquartered in Toronto, has a significant presence in the Canadian palladium ore–mining business. It's the largest producer of palladium in Canada, with production in 2005 totaling almost 200,000 ounces. North American palladium is your entry into the lucrative Canadian palladium-mining sector.

- **Stillwater Mining Company (NYSE: SWC):** Stillwater Mining, based in Montana, is the largest producer of palladium outside South Africa and Russia. Although it's involved in platinum and other PGM, its primary mining output is palladium. It produces approximately 500,000 ounces of palladium a year, primarily through North American mines.

Although these are the two largest companies that trade publicly on American exchanges, several international companies have significantly larger palladium-mining activities. Just make sure you're aware of the many regulatory differences between American and overseas markets before you invest in companies that trade in overseas stock markets.

You may also want to consider a couple international palladium companies:

- **Anglo Platinum Group (South Africa):** As its name suggests, Anglo Platinum Group invests in platinum group metals, but it's also one of the largest producers of palladium in the world. The company produced more than 2.5 million ounces of palladium in 2005 and is estimated to have reserves of more than 200 million ounces (this includes other PGM). With its operations located primarily in South Africa, Anglo Platinum Group is your gateway to South African palladium. Its shares are traded in the Johannesburg Stock Exchange (JSE) and the London Stock Exchange (LSE).

- **Norilsk Nickel (Russia):** Norilsk Nickel may not be a household name, but it's the largest producer of palladium in the world. It dominates the Russian palladium industry, which is the largest in the world (see Table 17-2). Beyond its large palladium-mining activities, the company is a major player in copper and nickel ore mining. The company's shares are available through the Moscow Inter-bank Currency Exchange (MICEX).

If you're comfortable in the futures markets (which I cover in Chapter 9), the Chicago Mercantile Exchange (CME) offers a futures contract that tracks palladium. This contract represents 100 troy ounces of palladium and trades both electronically and during the open outcry session. It trades under the symbol PA.

Zinc and Grow Rich

Zinc is the fourth most widely used metal, right behind iron/steel, aluminum, and copper (which I cover in Chapter 16). Zinc has unique abilities to resist corrosion and oxidation and is used for metal *galvanization,* the process of applying a metal coating to another metal to prevent rust and corrosion. As you can see from Table 17-3, galvanizing metals (particularly steel) is by far the largest application of zinc.

Table 17-3	Zinc Consumption by Sector
Sector	*Percentage of Market Consumption*
Galvanization	47%
Brass and bronze coatings	19%
Zinc alloying	15%
Other	14%

Source: London Metal Exchange

The best way to invest in zinc is to go through the futures markets. The London Metal Exchange (LME) offers a futures contract for zinc that has been trading since the early 1900s and is the industry benchmark for zinc pricing. The contract trades in lots of 25 tons and is available for trading during the current month and the subsequent 27 months. Figure 17-2 charts zinc's recent performance.

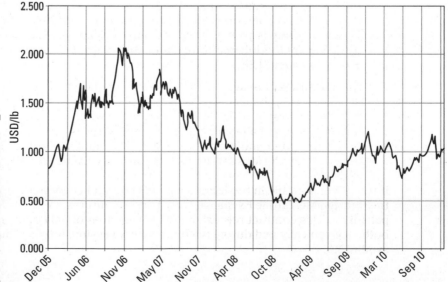

Figure 17-2: Historical price levels of zinc on the London Metal Exchange, 2005–2010 (dollars per 100 pounds).

You Won't Get Nickel and Dimed by Investing in Nickel

Nickel is a *ferrous metal,* which means it belongs to the iron group of metals. It's an important industrial metal that's used as an alloy with metals such as iron and copper, and it's sought after because of its ductility, malleability, and resistance to corrosion.

One of nickel's primary applications is in creating stainless steel. When steel is alloyed with nickel, its resistance to corrosion increases dramatically. Because stainless steel is a necessity of modern life, and a large portion of nickel goes toward creating this important metal alloy, you can rest assured that demand for nickel will remain strong. As you can see from Table 17-4, although nickel has many important uses, the creation of stainless steel remains its primary application.

Table 17-4	Nickel Consumption by Sector
Sector	*Percentage of Market Consumption*
Stainless steel	65%
Nonferrous alloys	12%
Ferrous alloys	10%
Electroplating	8%
Other	5%

Source: London Metal Exchange

Australia has the largest reserves of nickel, and its proximity to the rapidly industrializing Asian center — China and India — is a strategic advantage. Another major player in the nickel markets is Russia; the Russian company Norilsk Nickel (covered in the section on palladium earlier in this chapter) is the largest producer of nickel in the world. Nickel mining is a labor-intensive industry, but countries that have large reserves of this special metal are poised to do very well. Check out the countries with the largest reserves of nickel in Table 17-5.

Table 17-5	Largest Nickel Reserves, 2010
Country	*Percentage of Total*
Australia	37%
Russia	14%
Indonesia	12%
New Caledonia	8%
Canada	5%
Cuba	3%
Philippines	2.5%
Papua New Guinea	2%
Brazil	2%
China	1.5%

Source: U.S. Geological Survey

The LME offers a futures contract for nickel. The nickel futures contract on the LME gives you the most direct access to the nickel market. It trades in lots of 6 tons, and its tick size is $5 per ton. As with zinc, it trades during the first month, as well as 27 subsequent months.

Check out the historical performance of nickel on the LME in Figure 17-3.

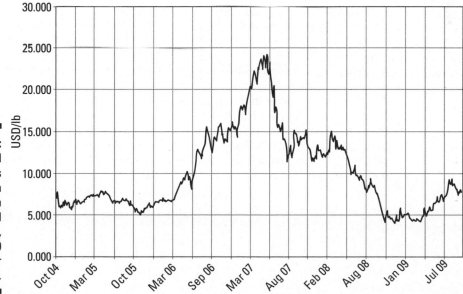

Figure 17-3: Historical price levels of nickel on the London Metal Exchange, 2004–2009 (dollars per pound).

The London Metal Exchange

The *London Metal Exchange* (LME), where the nickel and zinc contracts are traded, is one of the oldest futures exchanges in the world. It traces its origins back to Britain's Industrial Revolution in the late 19th century. The Industrial Revolution was partly fueled by large consumption of metals, and metals producers and consumers needed a place to establish benchmark prices and transact with each other. That's where the LME came to play an important role. Today the LME is one of the only exchanges dedicated to trading nonferrous metals. Besides nickel and zinc, the exchange offers futures contracts for aluminum, copper, lead, and tin. The LME still has open outcry trading sessions, although it has introduced electronic trading as well.

The term *nickel,* used to denote the 5-cent coin, is misleading because the coin actually consists primarily of copper (75 percent). Nickel, the metal, makes up only 25 percent of nickel, the coin.

Chapter 18

Mine Your Own Business: Unearthing the Top Mining Companies

*T*rading metals outright — through the futures markets — can be tricky for the uninitiated trader. You have to keep track of a number of moving pieces, such as contract expiration dates, margin calls, trading months, and other variables. In addition, metals on the futures markets can be subject to extreme price volatility, and you can set yourself up for disastrous losses. So it's understandable if you don't want to trade metals futures contracts, which I cover in Chapter 9. But this doesn't mean that you should ignore the whole metals subasset class altogether, because you may miss out on some substantial returns.

One possible avenue for opening up your portfolio to metals is to invest in companies that specialize in mining metals and minerals. A number of such companies exist, and their performance has been stellar in recent years. For example, Rio Tinto (NYSE: RTP), a mining conglomerate that I discuss in this chapter, saw its stock price surge from $60 in 2002 to more than $200 in 2006. Although not all mining companies have had similar performances, ignoring such a large group of the market is not advisable.

In this chapter, I look at the top mining companies — both the conglomerates and the specialized ones — to help you identify the best ones to include in your portfolio.

I provide you only a snapshot of recent financial performance here. Before you invest in any company, you want to look at a number of metrics to determine its financial health. Go through the balance sheet, income statement, and statement of cash flows — among other key financial statements — with a fine-toothed comb. Only if you determine that the company has a clean financial bill of health and is poised for growth should you proceed with your investment. Turn to Chapter 7 for more on the due diligence process.

Considering Diversified Mining Companies

Like the large integrated energy companies — ExxonMobil and BP, covered in Chapter 10 — diversified mining companies are involved in *all* aspects of the metals production process. These companies, which often employ tens of thousands of people, have operations in all four corners of the globe. They're involved in excavating metals — both *precious* and *base* metals, *ferrous* and *nonferrous* — as well as transforming these metals into finished products and subsequently distributing the end products to consumers.

Investing in one of these companies gives you exposure not only to a wide variety of metals, but also to the whole mining supply chain. I've selected the "best of breeds," and I evaluate their investment suitability in the following sections.

BHP Billiton

BHP Billiton is one of the largest mining companies in the world. It formed as a result of the 2001 merger between Broken Hill Proprietary, an Australian company, and Billiton, an Anglo-Dutch company. BHP Billiton, headquartered in Melbourne, Australia, has mining operations in more than 25 countries, including Australia, Canada, the United States, South Africa, and Papua New Guinea. The company processes a large number of metals, including aluminum, copper, silver, and iron; it also has small oil and natural gas operations in Algeria and Pakistan. The company is listed on the New York Stock Exchange (NYSE) under the symbol BHP.

One of the reasons I like BHP Billiton is that it offers economies of scale, meaning large-scale exposure to various sectors of the supply chain, which enhances its pricing capabilities. This is a large company, by any standard. Here's a snapshot of the company's financial performance. (All figures are for 2010.)

- **Revenues:** $53.3 billion
- **Net income:** $12.7 billion

✔ **Free cash flow:** $16.5 billion

✔ **Profit margins:** 21.4 percent

The company has benefited handsomely from the increasing prices of commodities such as copper and aluminum. As a result, BHP Billiton's profit increased by a staggering 90 percent between 2004 and 2005. The company has been operating on a historical profit margin in the neighborhood of 20 percent. This solid financial profile is reflected in its stock price, illustrated in Figure 18-1.

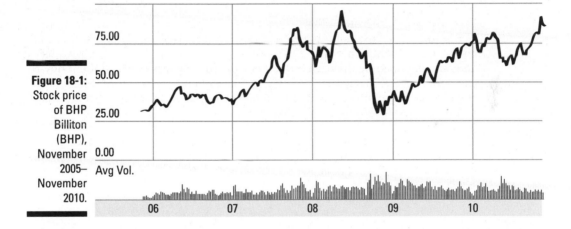

Figure 18-1: Stock price of BHP Billiton (BHP), November 2005– November 2010.

Remember that past results don't guarantee future performance. Commodity prices are cyclical in nature, and prices for metals such as copper, silver, and aluminum can't go up in a straight line forever. Make sure that you take into account the cyclicality factor as you move forward with your commodity investments. As evidence, consider the Global Financial Crisis of 2008 and the subsequent effect it had on global equities, including BHP.

Rio Tinto

Rio Tinto is a mining company rich in both minerals and history. The Rothschild banking family founded the company in 1873 to mine ore deposits in Spain. Today Rio Tinto boasts operations in Africa, Australia, Europe, the Pacific Rim, North America, Australia, and South America. It is a true mining conglomerate that's involved in all facets of the mining supply chain, from extraction to transformation and distribution.

The company is involved in the production of a number of commodities, including iron ore, copper, aluminum, and titanium. In addition, Rio Tinto has interests in diamonds, manufacturing almost 30 percent of global natural diamonds, processed primarily through its mining activities in Australia.

By investing in Rio Tinto, you get not only a company that has extensive operations across the mining complex, but also one that's in a solid financial position. Check out some numbers the company posted in 2009:

- ✔ **Revenues:** $41.8 billion
- ✔ **Net income:** $4.8 billion
- ✔ **Free cash flow:** $3.80 billion
- ✔ **Profit margins:** 10 percent

These strong numbers, which reflect increased demand for the commodities the company is involved in, have had a positive mid- to long-term impact on the company's stock, as you can see in Figure 18-2. Rio Tinto trades on the NYSE under the ticker symbol RTP.

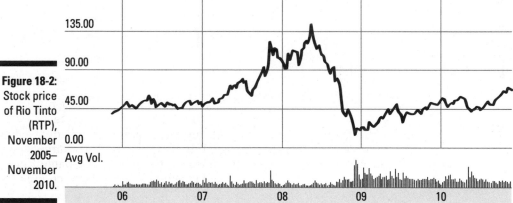

Figure 18-2: Stock price of Rio Tinto (RTP), November 2005– November 2010.

Anglo-American

Anglo-American PLC began mining gold in South Africa in 1917. It was a venture by British and American entrepreneurs (hence the name) who saw an opportunity in developing South African mines. Ever since, it has played an important role in the development of South Africa's gold-mining industry. Today Anglo-American has operations in all four corners of the globe and operates in more than 20 countries. It's involved in producing and distributing a wide array of metals, minerals, and natural resources, including gold, silver, and platinum, but also diamonds and paper packaging (it owns 45 percent of DeBeers, the diamond company).

I recommend Anglo-American as a long-term investment because it has been in the business for almost a century, it's involved in almost all aspects of the mining industry, and the scale of its operations is global.

The company is listed in the London Stock Exchange under the ticker symbol AAL. In addition, it has American Depository Receipts listed in the NASDAQ National Market that trade under the symbol AAUK.

When a foreign company wants to access the American capital markets, it has the option of issuing its shares as *American Depository Receipts* (ADRs). A domestic bank (such as the Bank of New York, which is the largest issuer of ADRs) issues ADRs to the American investing public, while the bank holds shares of the foreign company overseas. The advantage of the ADR is that it allows American investors to invest in foreign companies without going through foreign exchanges. The ADRs trade in such a way that they reflect the daily price movements of the underlying stock as it is traded in a stock exchange overseas. For more information, you can check out the Bank of New York's Web site on ADRs, at www.adrbny.com.

Checking Out Specialized Mining Companies

The benefit of investing in diversified mining companies, like those profiled in the previous section, is that you get to "buy the market" in one fell swoop. However, what if you spot a rally in gold, copper, or another individual metal and want to profit from this specific trend? In this case, the most direct exposure through the equity markets comes by investing in companies that specialize in specific metals. I identify and evaluate some of these companies in this section.

Newmont Mining: Gold

Newmont is headquartered in Colorado but operates gold mines all over the world. It's the largest producer of gold in South America, one of the most important gold regions, and has wholly owned subsidiaries or joint ventures in Australia, Canada, and Uzbekistan.

I recommend Newmont because it's a premier player in the competitive gold-mining industry. It has some competitive advantages, including its control of

50,000 square miles of land containing more than 90 million equity ounces of gold. (*Equity ounces* is the amount of gold measured in troy ounces multiplied by the current market price of gold as measured in U.S. dollars.) In addition, it has a strong balance sheet and is in solid financial condition. Check out some of Newmont's numbers (2009 figures):

- ✔ **Revenues:** $7.7 billion
- ✔ **Net income:** $1.3 million
- ✔ **Free cash flow:** $1.1 million
- ✔ **Profit margins:** 16.8 percent

If you're looking for a well-managed company with extensive experience and operations in the gold-mining industry, you can't go wrong with Newmont. (Be sure to read Chapter 15 for in-depth coverage of the gold industry.)

Silver Wheaton: Silver

Silver Wheaton focuses on one thing only: silver. Some mining companies have small operations in secondary metals, but Silver Wheaton generates 100 percent of its revenues from silver mining. The company operates mines primarily in Mexico and Sweden. Its modus operandi is to purchase silver directly from the mines and sell it on the open market for a profit. As a result, the company has very little, if any, operating overhead. This results in strong revenues and cash flows, as you can see from 2009 operations:

- ✔ **Revenues:** $239 million
- ✔ **Net income:** $118 million
- ✔ **Operating cash flow:** $166 million
- ✔ **Profit margins:** 49 percent

Silver Wheaton may not generate the same kinds of revenues as Anglo-American or other large mining conglomerates, but it's a well-run company with high profit margins and stable revenues.

Silver Wheaton's numbers reflect a strong operating background. It's actually the second-largest producer of silver, in terms of annual output measured in troy ounces. It produced more than 15 million troy ounces in 2005.

For more information on the silver industry, including the top producers, the largest-consuming segments, and an analysis of additional investment methodologies, turn to Chapter 15.

Freeport McMoRan: Copper

Freeport McMoRan (NYSE: FCX) is the largest independent copper producer in the world and also has significant operations in gold mining. Freeport started operations in Texas and rapidly expanded to include other locations in the continental United States and, later, internationally; the company has a strong footprint in Asia. In 2007, Freeport acquired its main rival, Phelps Dodge.

Phelps Dodge had quite a history in the mining industry, having been in the copper business for more than 150 years. It started as a mining concern and played a key role in the industrialization of the United States. Copper was in high demand by the growing nation, and Phelps Dodge was there to supply it. The Phelps Dodge acquisition was a huge coup for Freeport, and today the combined company is the market leader in copper production, with significant operations in the production of molybdenum and molybdenum-based chemicals.

Molybdenum (pronounced mah-*lib*-den-um) is known as a transition metal because it's principally used as an alloy with a number of metals. It has wide applications in industry — for instance, it's used in the construction of oil pipelines, aircraft engines, and missiles.

Freeport is also known for operating the largest copper mine ever discovered, the Grasberg mine in Indonesia; the proceeds from Grasberg are so prolific that Freeport is the largest individual taxpayer to the Indonesian government. Freeport is large by any standards, as evidenced by its 2010 financial performance:

- ✔ **Revenues:** $15 billion
- ✔ **Net income:** $2.7 billion
- ✔ **Operating cash flow:** $2.8 billion
- ✔ **Profit margins:** 18 percent

Overall, Freeport's performance has been positive over the last five years, although not without turbulence, due to the global financial downturn that has directly impacted its bottom line (see Figure 18-3).

Phelps Dodge has an active hedging program, in which it enters into agreements with other market participants through the futures markets, to hedge against price risk. However, not all hedgers are created equal, and Phelps Dodge has taken some hits in the past as a result of its hedging activities. During the second quarter of 2006, for instance, the company's net income fell to $471.1 million from $682.3 million the previous year-over-year quarter. This was a direct result of losses it incurred in hedging-related activity. So even though the price of copper was robust during this period, and the company would have benefited from these strong prices, its external activities were negatively affected. Always make sure that you know what's going on with a company before you invest in it.

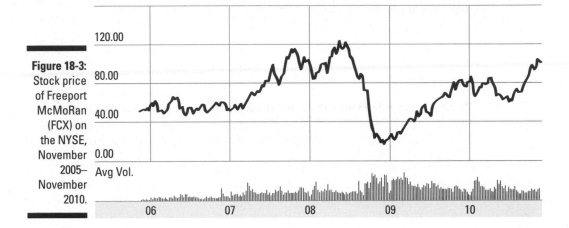

Figure 18-3: Stock price of Freeport McMoRan (FCX) on the NYSE, November 2005– November 2010.

You can find more information about the copper market and industry in Chapter 16.

Alcoa: Aluminum

Alcoa is a household name, and for good reason: It's the largest producer of aluminum, which is the most ubiquitous metal in the modern world. Cars, soda cans, and fighter jets are all partly made from aluminum, and Alcoa is the primary supplier of this metal in the market today. Alcoa (an acronym that stands for Aluminum Company of America) is involved in all phases of the aluminum supply chain. It provides aluminum-based products to a wide range of customers, including the aerospace and automotive industries, individual and commercial enterprises, the manufacturing sector, and the military.

Another reason I like Alcoa is that it's making some aggressive moves overseas and signing strategic, long-term pacts with some of the top aluminum producers. It recently entered into a partnership with the Aluminum Corporation of China (NYSE: ACH), China's largest aluminum producer, and is positioning itself to capitalize on the Chinese market, possibly the largest aluminum market in the future. Alcoa has undergone some strategic changes and made some strategic acquisitions — such as purchasing its main competitor, Alcan — that have acted as a drag on its financial perfor-mance in the short term. Capturing these market synergies and experienc-ing some weakness in the aluminum market short term have pressured its profitability. That said, I believe these circumstances present a good oppor-tunity to buy a solid company at a discount:

- ✔ **Revenues:** $18.4 billion
- ✔ **Net income:** –$1.1 billion
- ✔ **Free cash flow:** $257 million
- ✔ **Profit margins:** –1.4 percent

As you can see in Figure 18-4, the stock's performance has been choppy in recent years, so make sure that you research the company as much as pos-sible before you take the plunge.

Be sure to read Chapter 16 for a close examination of the aluminum market.

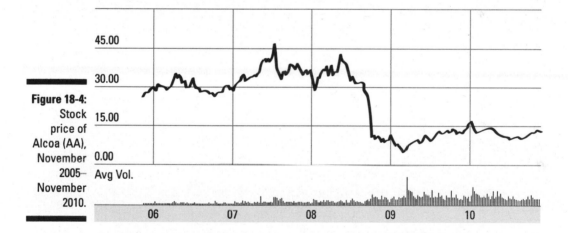

Figure 18-4: Stock price of Alcoa (AA), November 2005– November 2010.

Arcelor-Mittal: Steel

Mittal Steel, under the management of Indian-born steel magnate Lakshmi Mittal, launched an unsolicited bid to acquire Arcelor, the Luxembourg-based high-end steel manufacturer, in January 2006. After a five-month takeover battle, which involved *poison pill* and *white knight* takeover defense strategies, the boards of both companies agreed to a merger of equals. The combined entity created one of the largest independent steel companies in the world.

In mergers and acquisitions (M&A), companies use a number of strategies to fend off hostile takeovers. One of the most popular defense strategies includes pursuing a merger or acquisition with a "friendly" company, known as a white knight. Another strategy, the poison pill strategy, takes a different approach. This option involves making the company unattractive to an acquirer, such as by increasing levels of debt or increasing the number of shares outstanding to dilute their value.

The new company combines the number one and number two steel producers in the world and will control more than 10 percent of global steel output. Arcelor-Mittal will be a truly global steel manufacturer, with operations in all four corners of the globe and across all stages of the steel-making process. If the performance of the new company is anything like the recent performance of Mittal stock, shown in Figure 18-5, you don't want to miss out on healthy returns to come.

Turn to Chapter 16 for an in-depth examination of the global steel industry.

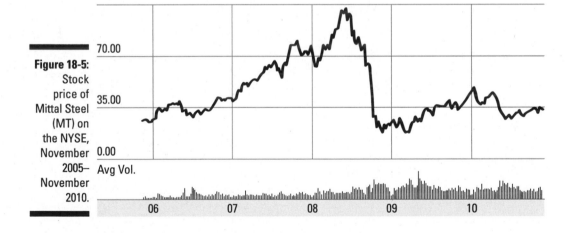

Figure 18-5: Stock price of Mittal Steel (MT) on the NYSE, November 2005– November 2010.

Making Money during the Mining Merger Mania

Profiting from the merger activity in the mining industry can be a good investment strategy. Since the year 2000, a number of large companies have entered into merger agreements (the marriage of the Australian BHP and the British Billiton, which resulted in BHP Billiton, is a good example), and this trend is likely to continue as mining companies seek to add new capacity by merging their activities or acquiring smaller rivals. In 2004, for instance, a total of 49 deals were made in the mining industry, valued at $5.6 billion; in 2005, the number of deals increased to 85, with a total value of $7.4 billion.

Due to the sustained levels of high commodity prices, mining companies have large cash reserves and are looking to spend them to beef up their operations by acquiring other companies. Mergers and acquisitions present long-term value opportunities to these companies and their shareholders, and are likely to continue in the years to come. During the writing of this book, for example, Phelps Dodge (one of the largest copper-mining companies) launched a simultaneous double bid to acquire Inco and Falconbridge, both independent Canadian mining companies, in a synchronized transaction valued at more than $40 billion.

The caveat of profiting from merger announcements, of course, is identifying the "hunter" and the "hunted," the acquirer and the target. Doing so isn't easy; theoretically, any given sector has an infinite number of merger and acquisition combinations. The best plan is to regularly monitor the industry for news, special announcements, or unusual trading activity. Specifically, keep your eye out for any announcements by companies in Forms 8K (filings with the SEC that announce special situations); read news stories about the companies in the industry (I recommend reading *The Wall Street Journal's* "Heard on the Street" column); and remain alert to any sudden and unusual movements in the companies' stock activity, such as an unusual spike in volume. (Check out Chapter 10 for more on volume and other technical metrics.)

Identifying possible merger announcements isn't an exact science, but it can yield some phenomenal returns. A lot of folks try to profit from insider information regarding merger deals, which is illegal and has led to some huge financial scandals. If you trade on information that's not public, you could end up going to jail — don't do it! Also remember that, as a general rule, you want to buy the "hunted" before any merger announcements because the stock price of a target company tends to increase with any merger announcement, while that of the acquiring company decreases. The logic here is that the acquiring company is paying a premium for its acquisition and will have to bear the costs of incorporating this new entity within its corporate and operational structure.

Part V
Going Down to the Farm: Trading Agricultural Products

The 5th Wave   By Rich Tennant

"Eat your cereal. Your father's heavily invested in grain."

In this part . . .

Food is the most essential resource in human life. Investing in this sector can also help improve your bottom line. In this part, I introduce the major sectors in this subasset class and show you how to profit from grains such as corn and wheat; tropical commodities like coffee and orange juice; and livestock such as live cattle, feeder cattle, and frozen pork bellies.

Chapter 19

Breakfast of Champions: Profiting from Coffee, Cocoa, Sugar, and Orange Juice

The commodities I cover in this chapter — coffee, cocoa, sugar, and frozen concentrated orange juice — are known as *soft commodities*. Soft commodities are commodities that are usually grown, as opposed to those that are mined (such as metals) or those that are raised (such as livestock). The *softs,* as they're sometimes known, represent a significant portion of the commodities markets. They're indispensable and cyclical, just like energy and metals, but they're also unique because they're edible and seasonal. *Seasonality* is a major distinguishing characteristic of soft commodities because they can be grown only during specific times of the year and in specific geographical locations — usually in tropical areas. (This is why these commodities are also known as *tropical commodities*.) In this chapter, I show you that there's nothing soft about these soft commodities.

Giving Your Portfolio a Buzz by Investing in Coffee

Coffee, which originated in Arabia sometime in the 15th century, is today the second most widely traded commodity in terms of physical volume — behind only crude oil. Coffee is an important global commodity because folks just love a good cup of coffee. In this section, I show you how to stay grounded while investing in this market.

Coffee: It's time for your big break

As with a number of other commodities, coffee production is dominated by a handful of countries. Brazil has historically been the top producer of coffee in the world and has held this position for several decades. Traditionally, Colombia has held the number two spot, but it's lost that position to up-and-comers such as Vietnam and Indonesia. Table 19-1 lists the largest coffee-producing countries.

Table 19-1	Top Coffee Producers, 2009
Country	*Production (Thousands of Bags)*
Brazil	39,470
Vietnam	18,000
Indonesia	11,380
Colombia	8,500
India	4,827
Ethiopia	4,500
Mexico	4,200
Honduras	3,527
Guatemala	3,500
Uganda	3,000

Source: International Coffee Organization

Large-scale coffee production is measured in *bags*. One bag of coffee weighs 60 kilograms, or approximately 132 pounds.

If you want to further investigate the ins and outs of the coffee markets, I recommend Mark Pendergrast's excellent book *Uncommon Grounds: The History of Coffee and How It Transformed Our World* (Basic Books), to help you understand the mechanics of the global coffee trade. You may also want to visit these websites for more information:

✔ **International Coffee Organization:** www.ico.org

✔ **National Coffee Association of the USA:** www.ncausa.org

Just as choosing the right flavor is important when buying your cup of coffee, knowing the different types of coffees available for investment is crucial. The world's coffee production is pretty much made up of two types of beans:

- **Arabica:** Arabica coffee is the most widely grown coffee plant in the world, accounting for more than 60 percent of global coffee production. Arabica is grown in countries as diverse as Brazil and Indonesia. It's the premium coffee bean, adding a richer taste to any brew, and, as a result, is the most expensive coffee bean in the world. Because of its high quality, it serves as the benchmark for coffee prices all over the world.

- **Robusta:** Robusta accounts for about 40 percent of total coffee production. Because it's easier to grow than Arabica coffee, it's also less expensive.

You have several ways to invest in coffee production. One way is to buy coffee in the futures markets; the other is to invest in companies that specialize in running gourmet coffee shops.

The coffee futures contract: It may be your cup of tea

The coffee futures markets determine the future price of coffee and, more important, protect producers and purchasers of coffee from wild price swings (see Chapter 9 for more on futures contracts). In addition to hedging opportunities, the coffee futures markets allow individual investors to profit from coffee price variations. The most liquid coffee futures contract is available on the Intercontinental Exchange (ICE), which assumed tradability of the coffee contract when it acquired the New York Board of Trade (NYBOT).

Take a look at its contract specs:

- **Contract ticker symbol:** KC
- **Contract size:** 37,500 pounds
- **Underlying commodity:** Pure Arabica coffee
- **Price fluctuation:** $0.0005 per pound ($18.75 per contract)
- **Trading months:** March, May, July, September, and December

The price chart in Figure 19-1 gives you an idea of the performance of the coffee futures contract in recent years.

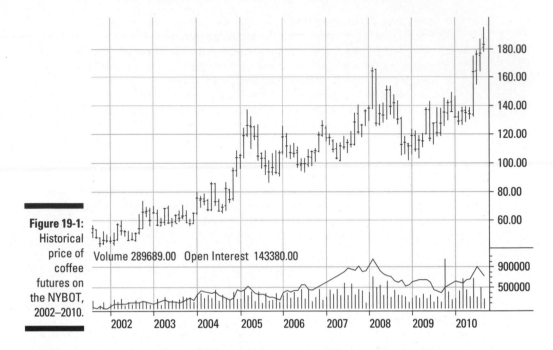

Figure 19-1:
Historical price of coffee futures on the NYBOT, 2002–2010.

Volume 289689.00   Open Interest 143380.00

Because of seasonality, cyclicality, and geopolitical factors, coffee can be a volatile commodity subject to extreme price swings. Be sure to research the coffee markets inside and out before investing.

Ordering up investments in gourmet coffee shops

In New York City, where I live, as in most other metropolitan areas, you can't walk a block without spotting two or three gourmet coffee shops, especially Starbucks. Coffee shops are nothing new — Arabian coffee shops sprang up in the Middle East as early as the 15th century. Today coffee shops are still a place where you can enjoy a nice (and big) cup of joe while socializing with friends.

But behind the relaxed, laid-back atmosphere is a complex moneymaking operation. Coffee is serious business, and you can profit from the coffee craze that has gripped the United States (the largest consumer of coffee in the world) and is spreading throughout Europe and newly developing countries such as India and China: Simply invest in the companies that are capitalizing on this trend. Find out where your $4.50 for a cup of coffee is going, and profit from it.

You're probably familiar with Starbucks; a number of other gourmet coffee shops and distributors provide you with good investment opportunity as well. These purveyors of coffee include the following:

✓ **Starbucks Corp. (NASDAQ: SBUX):** Perhaps no other brand has come to represent an entire industry as Starbucks has coffee. (The only other brands that come to mind are Kleenex with tissues and Xerox with photocopiers.) Starbucks is a cultural phenomenon, but, more important, it's also a financial juggernaut. This is a $20-billion company with about $10 billion in revenue (according to 2009 figures). Starbucks dominates the entire coffee supply chain, from purchasing and roasting to selling and marketing. It has more than 10,000 stores worldwide, primarily in the United States and Europe, but also in China, Singapore, and even Saudi Arabia.

✓ **Peet's Coffee and Tea, Inc. (NASDAQ: PEET):** Peet's Coffee operates only about 100 coffee shops, but its strength lies in distribution. The company sells a large selection of coffees, produced in countries as diverse as Guatemala and Kenya, to customers across the United States, including restaurants and grocery stores.

✓ **Green Mountain Coffee Roaster, Inc. (NASDAQ: GMCR):** Green Mountain Coffee, with headquarters in Vermont, distributes specialized coffee products. It sells premium Arabica coffee to a number of entities, such as convenience stores, specialty retailers, and restaurants. It has a large presence on the East Coast and has a partnership with Paul Newman's company, Newman's Own, to provide organic coffee to customers. This company is a good one if you want exposure to the high-end coffee distribution market in the Northeast.

The New York Board of Trade: The place for trading places and soft commodities

Besides being tropical commodities, the commodities I analyze in this chapter have another common characteristic: They all trade on the *New York Board of Trade* (NYBOT). The NYBOT is one of the oldest exchanges in the United States and is the premier location for the trade of agricultural commodities. The NYBOT also offers futures contracts that track cotton, ethanol, and wood pulp (*pulp* is used to make paper), as well as products that track several financial futures, such as the euro (the currency), the New York Stock Exchange Composite Index, and the Reuters/Jefferies CRB Index. (The NYBOT is also where the movie *Trading Places,* with Eddie Murphy and Dan Aykroyd, was shot. In the final scene of the movie, Murphy and Aykroyd corner the orange juice market and, in the process, wipe out Randolph and Mortimer Duke.)

As a sign of the times and the advent of electronic trading, in 2007, the ICE, an all-electronic trading platform, acquired the NYBOT. Although the ICE has integrated many of the commodities offered on the NYBOT with its electronic platform, many traders still refer to the original NYBOT commodities as ICE/NYBOT.

Warming Up to Cocoa

Cocoa is a fermented seed from the cacao tree, which is usually grown in hot and rainy regions around the equator. The first cacao tree is said to have originated in South America, where cocoa beans were used for both consumption and monetary purposes. European traders came across the cacao tree and were so impressed with the tasty beverages made from cocoa beans that they brought some back to Europe, where cocoa beans were then turned into chocolate. From Europe, the cacao tree was introduced to Africa. Today African countries dominate the cocoa trade, as you can see in Table 19-2.

Table 19-2	Top Cocoa Producers, 2009
Country	*Production (Thousands of Tons)*
Ivory Coast	1,190
Ghana	650
Indonesia	535
Nigeria	260
Cameroon	200
Brazil	155
Ecuador	150
Colombia	50
Mexico	45
Papua New Guinea	40

Source: International Cocoa Organization

Cocoa production for import and export purposes is measured in metric tons. To put things in perspective, 3.6 million tons of cocoa were produced worldwide in 2009.

For a more nuanced understanding of the cocoa market and the companies that control it, check out these resources:

- **Cocoa Producer's Alliance:** www.copal-cpa.org
- **International Cocoa Organization:** www.icco.org
- **World Cocoa Foundation:** www.worldcocoafoundation.org

The ICE offers a futures contract for cocoa. Consider some useful information regarding this cocoa futures contract, which is the most liquid in the market:

- ✓ **Contract ticker symbol:** CC
- ✓ **Contract size:** 10 metric tons
- ✓ **Underlying commodity:** Generic cocoa beans
- ✓ **Price fluctuation:** $1 per ton ($10 per contract)
- ✓ **Trading months:** March, May, July, September, and December

As with coffee, the cocoa market is subject to seasonal and cyclical factors that have a large impact on price movements. Check out the price of the ICE cocoa futures contract in recent years in Figure 19-2. As you can see, it can be pretty volatile.

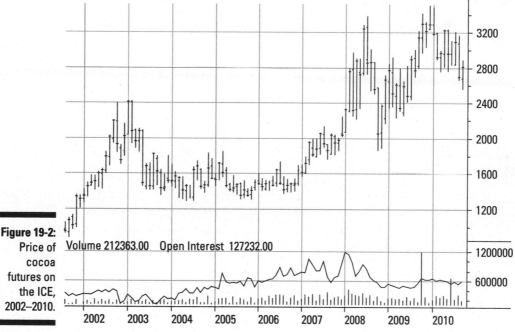

Figure 19-2: Price of cocoa futures on the ICE, 2002–2010.

Volume 212363.00   Open Interest 127232.00

Investing in Sugar: Such a Sweet Move!

Sugar production reportedly started more than 9,000 years ago in southeastern Asia, where it was used in India and China for medicinal purposes. It then spread to southern Europe through Persia and Arabia around 400 B.C. In Europe and the Middle East, sugar became a popular food sweetener. From Europe, sugar spread to the New World in the 15th century and was particularly suitable for growing in Latin America. Today Latin American countries dominate the sugar trade; Brazil is the largest sugar producer in the world, as you can see in Table 19-3. In 2009, the top ten sugar producers accounted for 74 percent of global production.

Table 19-3	Top Sugar Producers, 2009
Country	Production (Millions of Tons)
Brazil	36
E.U.	18
India	17
China	13
Thailand	8
United States	7
South Africa	6
Mexico	5
Australia	4.5
Russia	4

Source: United States Department of Agriculture

If you're interested in investing in sugar, the ICE offers two futures contracts that track the price of sugar: Sugar #11 (world production) and sugar #14 (U.S. production). Consider the contract specs for these two sugar contracts:

✔ **Sugar #11 (World)**

- **Contract ticker symbol:** SB
- **Contract size:** 112,000 pounds

- **Underlying commodity:** Global sugar
- **Price fluctuation:** $0.01 per pound ($11.20 per contract)
- **Trading months:** March, May, July, and October

✔ **Sugar #14 (USA)**

- **Contract ticker symbol:** SE
- **Contract size:** 112,000 pounds
- **Underlying commodity:** Domestic (U.S.) sugar
- **Price fluctuation:** $0.01 per pound ($11.20 per contract)
- **Trading months:** January, March, May, July, September, and November

On a historical basis, sugar #14 produced in the United States tends to be more expensive than sugar #11. However, sugar #11 accounts for most of the volume in the ICE sugar market. Check out the historical price of sugar #11 on the ICE in Figure 19-3.

Figure 19-3: Price of sugar futures on the NYBOT, 2002–2010.

Volume 2869454.00   Open Interest 651985.00

Orange Juice: Refreshingly Good for Your Bottom Line

Orange juice is one of the only actively traded contracts in the futures markets that's based on a tropical fruit: oranges. Oranges are widely grown in the Western Hemisphere, particularly in Florida and Brazil. As you can see in Table 19-4, Brazil is by far the largest producer of oranges, although the United States — primarily Florida — is also a major player.

Table 19-4	Top Orange Producers, 2009
Country	*Production (Tons)*
Brazil	18,389,000
United States	9,120,000
India	4,396,700
Mexico	4,306,600
China	3,450,120

Source: United Nations Statistical Database

Because oranges are perishable, the futures contract tracks *frozen concentrated orange juice* (FCOJ). This particular form is suitable for storage and fits one of the criteria for inclusion in the futures arena: that the underlying commodity be deliverable. This contract is available for trade on the ICE. The ICE includes two versions of the FCOJ contract: one that tracks the Florida/Brazil oranges and another one based on global production.

Consider the contract specs of FCOJ on the ICE:

✔ **FCOJ-A (Florida/Brazil)**

- **Contract ticker symbol:** OJ

- **Contract size:** 15,000 pounds

- **Underlying commodity:** FCOJ from Brazil and/or Florida only

- **Price fluctuation:** $0.0005 per pound ($7.50 per contract)

- **Trading months:** January, March, May, July, September, and November

↙ **FCOJ-B (World)**

- **Contract ticker symbol:** OB
- **Contract size:** 15,000 pounds
- **Underlying commodity:** FCOJ from any producing country
- **Price fluctuation:** $0.0005 per pound ($7.50 per contract)
- **Trading months:** January, March, May, July, September, and November

The production of oranges is very sensitive to weather. For instance, the hurricane season common in the Florida region can have a significant impact on the prices of oranges both on the spot market and in the futures market. In Figure 19-4, you can clearly see a spike in the price of the FCOJ contract during the 2004–2005 period, which saw heavy hurricane activity. Be sure to consider weather and seasonality when investing in FCOJ futures.

Figure 19-4: Price of orange juice futures on the NYBOT, 2002–2010.

Chapter 20

How to Gain from Grains: Trading Corn, Wheat, and Soybeans

*I*n this chapter, I look at some of the major agricultural commodities that trade in the futures markets. These commodities, sometimes simply known as *ags,* are a unique component of the broader commodities markets. They're labor intensive and subject to volatility because of underlying market fundamentals, which I explore in the following sections. However, they also present solid investment opportunities. Corn, for example, is a major food staple; wheat is an absolutely necessary commodity and, according to archaeologists, may be the first commodity grown and traded; and soybeans have a growing number of applications, ranging from fuel additives, to feedstock, to trendy food products. I examine all three of these commodities and their investment opportunities in depth.

For additional information on agricultural commodities in general, I recommend checking out the following resources:

▶ **National Grain and Feed Association:** www.ngfa.org

▶ **U.S. Department of Agriculture (USDA):** www.usda.gov

▶ **USDA National Agriculture Library:** www.nal.usda.gov

▶ **USDA National Agricultural Statistics Service:** www.nass.usda.gov

Field of Dreams: Investing in Corn

In 2009, world corn production stood at about 790 million metric tons. Approximately 35 million hectares of land are used exclusively for the production of corn worldwide, a business that the U.S. Department of Agriculture values at more than $20 billion a year. Corn is an important food source for both humans and animals and, unlike other grains, can be grown in a wide variety of climates and conditions, making it an important cash crop for many countries. Corn isn't used just as a feedstock; it has other important applications and is processed into starches, corn oil, and even fuel ethanol. Corn is definitely big business. In this section, I give you all the information you need to invest in this major crop.

Corn, like other commodities, such as crude oil (see Chapter 10) and coffee (see Chapter 19), comes in different qualities. The most important types of corn to be familiar with are *high-grade number 2* and *number 3 yellow corn,* which are both traded in the futures markets.

The most direct way of investing in corn is to go through the futures markets. A corn contract, courtesy of the Chicago Mercantile Exchange (CME), helps farmers, consumers, and investors manage and profit from the underlying market opportunities. Take a look at the contract specs:

- ✔ **Contract ticker symbol (open outcry):** C
- ✔ **Electronic ticker (CME Globex):** ZC
- ✔ **Contract size:** 5,000 bushels
- ✔ **Underlying commodity:** High-grade no. 2 or no. 3 yellow corn
- ✔ **Price fluctuation:** $0.0025 per bushel ($12.50 per contract)
- ✔ **Trading hours:** 9:05 a.m. to 1:00 p.m. open outcry; 6:30 p.m. to 6:00 a.m. electronic (CST)

   It's important to know the trading hours for corn and other commodities that trade both on the open outcry and through electronic trading. Open outcry hours are a legacy from the pre-Internet age, when people traded all contracts on the trading floor; you can still participate in this trading method during the hours noted in this chapter. The electronic trading system is the latest addition and is much quicker, so you can be sure to get your orders placed quickly and efficiently. As of the writing of this book, the open outcry system is slowly being phased out; eventually, electronic trading will permanently replace it.

- ✔ **Trading months:** March, May, July, September, and December

Corn futures contracts are usually measured in bushels (as with the corn contract the CME offers). Large-scale corn production and consumption is generally measured in metric tons.

Historically, the United States has dominated the corn markets — and still does, thanks to abundant land and helpful governmental subsidies. China is also a major player and exhibits potential for becoming a market leader in the future. Other notable producers include Brazil, Mexico, Argentina, and France. Table 20-1 lists the top producers in 2009.

Table 20-1	Top Corn Producers, 2009
Country	*Production (Millions of Tons)*
United States	307
China	165
Brazil	51
Mexico	25
India	18.5
South Africa	12.7
Argentina	12.6
Ukraine	11 4
Canada	10.5

Source: U.S. Department of Agriculture

Similar to other agricultural commodities, corn is subject to seasonal and cyclical factors that have a direct, and often powerful, effect on prices. Prices for corn can go through roller-coaster rides, with wild swings in short periods of time, as you can see in Figure 20-1.

The Chicago Board of Trade

Established in 1848, the *Chicago Board of Trade* (CBOT) used to be the oldest commodity exchange in the world. All the commodities covered in this chapter used the CBOT as the go-to exchange for grains and other agricultural products, such as oats, ethanol, and rice. The exchange also offered several metals contracts targeted at individual investors, including the mini gold and mini silver contracts.

In 2007, the Chicago Mercantile Exchange (CME) acquired the CBOT as part of a great consolidation wave (the CME also acquired NYMEX/COMEX). CME rolled up the CBOT's popular grain contracts and now offers them on its electronic platform. Many traders still refer to some of these contracts as CBOT grains.

For more information on the corn markets, check out the following sources:

- **Corn Refiners Association:** www.corn.org
- **National Corn Growers Association:** www.ncga.com
- **USDA Corn Research Service:** www.ers.usda.gov/briefing/corn

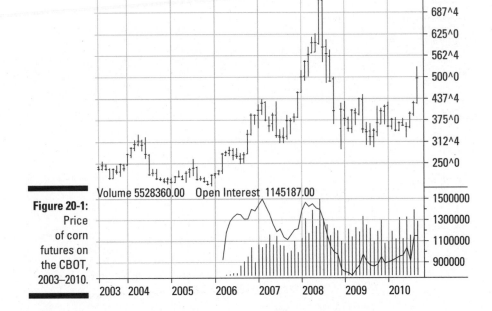

Figure 20-1: Price of corn futures on the CBOT, 2003–2010.

Welcome to the Bread Basket: Investing in Wheat

According to archaeologists, wheat is one of the first agricultural products grown by man. Evidence suggests that wheat production developed in the Fertile Crescent region, an area that encompasses modern-day Turkey and Syria. Today wheat is the second most widely produced agricultural commodity in the world (on a per-volume basis), right behind corn and ahead of rice. World wheat production came in at 682 million metric tons in 2009, according to the U.S. Department of Agriculture (USDA).

Unlike other commodities that are dominated by single producers — Saudi Arabia and oil, the Ivory Coast and cocoa, Russia and palladium, for example — no single country dominates wheat production. As you can see from Table 20-2, the major wheat producers are a surprisingly eclectic group. The advanced developing countries of China and India are the two largest producers, and industrial countries like Canada and Germany also boast significant wheat-production capabilities.

Table 20-2	Top Wheat Producers, 2009
Country	**Production (Millions of Tons)**
China	115
India	81
Russia	61
United States	60
France	38
Canada	26.5
Germany	25.2
Pakistan	24
Australia	21
Ukraine	21

Source: U.S. Department of Agriculture

Wheat is measured in bushels, for investment and accounting purposes. Each bushel contains approximately 60 pounds of wheat. As for most other agricultural commodities, metric tons are used to quantify total production and consumption figures on a national and international basis.

The most direct way of accessing the wheat markets, short of owning a wheat farm, is to trade the wheat futures contract. As with the other agricultural commodities discussed in this chapter, the CME offers a futures contract for those interested in capturing profits from wheat price movements — whether for hedging or speculative purposes. Here are the specs for the CME futures contract:

- **Contract ticker symbol (open outcry):** W
- **Electronic ticker (CME Globex):** ZW
- **Contract size:** 5,000 bushels

- **Underlying commodity:** Premium wheat
- **Price fluctuation:** $0.0025 per bushel ($12.50 per contract)
- **Trading hours:** 9:30 a.m. to 1:15 p.m. open outcry; 6:32 p.m. to 6:00 a.m. electronic (CST)
- **Trading months:** March, May, July, September, and December

Wheat production, like that of corn and soybeans, is a seasonal enterprise that's subject to various output disruptions. For instance, Kazakhstan, an important producer, has faced issues with wheat production in the past related to underinvestment in machinery and the misuse of fertilizers. This mismanagement of resources has an impact on the acreage yield, which then impacts prices. Such disruptions on the supply side can have a magnified effect on futures prices, as evidenced by the numbers in Figure 20-2.

Interested in finding out more about the wheat market? I recommend the following sources:

- **National Association of Wheat Growers:** www.wheatworld.org
- **U.S. Wheat Associates:** www.uswheat.org
- **Wheat Foods Council:** www.wheatfoods.org

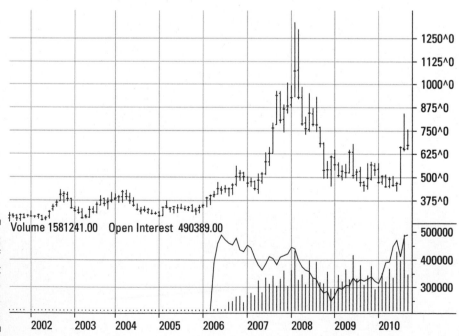

Figure 20-2:
Price of
wheat
futures on
the CBOT,
2001–2010.

Many organizations that offer information on specific commodities, such as corn and wheat, are specialized lobby groups whose agenda — alongside providing information to the public — includes promoting the consumption of the products they represent. Keep this in mind as you consult any outside resource for research purposes, and consider the source before you act on any information.

It's Not Just Peanuts: Trading Soybeans

Soybeans have been cultivated for centuries, starting in Asia. Soybeans are a vital crop for the world economy, used in everything from producing poultry feedstock to creating vegetable oil. In this section, I introduce you to the different soybean extracts you can trade: soybeans, soybean oil, and soybean meal.

If you're interested in getting more background information on the soybean industry, check out the following reputable resources:

- ✔ **American Soybean Association:** www.soygrowers.org
- ✔ **Iowa Soybean Association:** www.iasoybeans.com
- ✔ **Soy Protein Council:** www.spcouncil.org
- ✔ **Soy Stat Reference Guide:** www.soystats.com

Soybeans

Although most soybeans are used to extract soybean oil (used as vegetable oil for culinary purposes) and soybean meal (used primarily as an agricultural feedstock), whole soybeans are also a tradable commodity. Soybeans are edible: If you've ever gone to a sushi restaurant, you may have been offered soybeans as appetizers, under the Japanese name *edamame*.

The United States dominates the soybean market, accounting for more than 50 percent of total global production. Brazil is a distant second, with about 20 percent of the market. The crop in the United States begins in September, and soybean production is cyclical, as you can see from the price patterns in Figure 20-3.

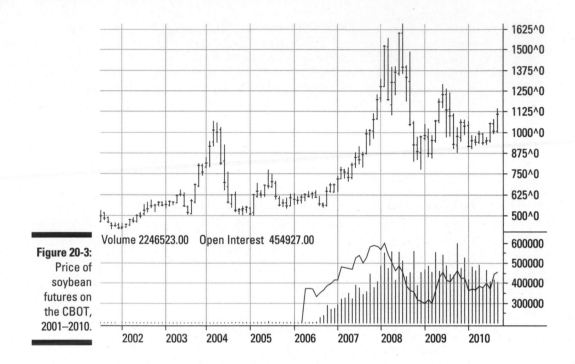

Figure 20-3:
Price of
soybean
futures on
the CBOT,
2001–2010.

The most direct way to trade soybeans is through the CME soybean futures contract. Here's the contract information:

- ✔ **Contract ticker symbol (open outcry):** S
- ✔ **Electronic ticker (CME Globex):** ZS
- ✔ **Contract size:** 5,000 bushels
- ✔ **Underlying commodity:** Premium no. 1, no. 2, and no. 3 yellow soybean bushels
- ✔ **Price fluctuation:** $0.0025 per bushel ($12.50 per contract)
- ✔ **Trading hours:** 9:30 a.m. to 1:15 p.m. open outcry; 6:31 p.m. to 6:00 a.m. electronic (CST)
- ✔ **Trading months:** January, March, May, July, August, September, and November

Soybean oil

Soybean oil is an extract of soybeans that you and I know as vegetable oil. Soybean oil is the most widely used culinary oil in the United States and around the world, partly because of its healthy, nutritional characteristics. It contains about 85 percent unsaturated fat and very little saturated fat, which makes it appealing to health-conscious consumers.

In addition to its gastronomic uses, soybean oil is becoming an increasingly popular additive in alternative energy sources technology, such as biodiesel. For example, an increasing number of cars in the United States and abroad are being outfitted with engines that allow them to convert from regular diesel to soybean oil during operation. Because of their economic fuel mileage and low environmental impact, these soybean oil–enabled cars, known as *frybrids,* are becoming more popular.

Demand for soybean oil has increased in recent years as demand for these cleaner-burning fuels increases and as the automotive technology becomes better able to accommodate the usage of such biodiesels. According to the Commodity Research Bureau (CRB), production of soybean oil increased from an average of 15 billion pounds in the mid-1990s to more than 35 billion pounds in 2009.

If you want to trade soybean oil, you need to go through the CME, which offers the standard soybean oil contract. Here's the contract information:

- **Contract ticker symbol (open outcry):** BO
- **Electronic ticker (CME Globex):** ZL
- **Contract size:** 60,000 pounds
- **Underlying commodity:** Premium crude soybean oil
- **Price fluctuation:** $0.0001 per pound ($6 per contract)
- **Trading hours:** 9:30 a.m. to 1:15 p.m. open outcry; 6:31 p.m. to 6:00 a.m. electronic (CST)
- **Trading months:** January, March, May, July, August, September, October, and December

For more information on investing in soybean oil, turn to the National Oilseed Processors Association, an industry group, at www.nopa.org.

Soybean meal

Soybean meal, like soybean oil, is an extract of soybeans. Basically, whatever is left after soybean oil is extracted from soybeans can be converted to soybean meal. Soybean meal is a high-protein, high-energy-content food used primarily as a feedstock for cattle, hogs, and poultry. (I cover trading such livestock in Chapter 21.)

To invest in soybean meal, you can trade the soybean meal futures contract on the CME. Here's the information to help you get started trading this contract:

- ✔ **Contract ticker symbol (open outcry):** SM
- ✔ **Electronic ticker (CME Globex):** ZM
- ✔ **Contract size:** 100 tons
- ✔ **Underlying commodity:** 48% protein soybean meal
- ✔ **Price fluctuation:** $0.10 per ton ($10 per contract)
- ✔ **Trading hours:** 9:30 a.m. to 1:15 p.m. open outcry; 6:31 p.m. to 6:00 a.m. electronic (CST)
- ✔ **Trading months:** January, March, May, July, August, September, October, and December

You can get more information regarding soybean meal from the Soybean Meal Information Center, at www.soymeal.org.

Chapter 21

Alive and Kicking! Making Money Trading Livestock

● ●

In This Chapter

▶ Identifying opportunities in the cattle markets

▶ Deciding whether trading lean hogs is right for you

▶ Examining the frozen pork bellies market

● ●

According to the U.S. Department of Agriculture (USDA), consumers spend roughly 20 percent of their total food and beverage allowance on meat products, such as cattle and pork. Think of all those hamburgers and BLTs you've had over the years. Livestock, like the tropical and grain commodities, is a unique category in the agricultural commodities subasset class. It's not a widely followed area of the commodities markets — unlike crude oil, for example, you're not likely to see feeder cattle prices quoted on the nightly news — but this doesn't mean that you can ignore this area of the markets.

That said, raising livestock is a time-consuming and labor-intensive undertaking, and the markets are susceptible and sensitive to minor disruption. These contracts are volatile (see the performance of frozen pork bellies in Figure 21-4), so venture into this area of the market only if you have an ironclad grasp on the concepts behind futures trading — along with a high tolerance for risk. In this chapter, I analyze the markets for cattle (both live cattle and feeder cattle), lean hogs, and frozen pork bellies.

Even by agricultural futures standards, livestock futures are notoriously volatile; only traders with a high level of risk tolerance will want to trade in this area. Keep in mind that trading agricultural futures requires understanding the cyclicality and seasonality of the underlying commodity, as well as large capital reserves to help offset any margin calls that may arise from a trade gone bad. If you don't have an elevated risk tolerance or you aren't comfortable in the futures arena, I recommend skipping these contracts; otherwise, you may be setting yourself up for disastrous losses.

The Chicago Mercantile Exchange

The *Chicago Mercantile Exchange* (CME), where all the commodities discussed in this chapter are traded, is the largest and most liquid futures exchange in the world. The CME has the heaviest trading activity — and open interest — of any exchange, partly because of the depth of its products offerings. Besides agricultural commodities, it trades *economic derivatives* (contracts that track economic data such as U.S. quarterly GDP and nonfarm payrolls), foreign currencies (it offers a broad currency selection, ranging from the Hungarian forint to the South Korean won), interest rates (including the London Inter Bank Offered Rate, the LIBOR), and even *weather derivatives* (contracts that track weather patterns in various regions of the world).

Because of its broad products listing, the CME is perhaps the most versatile of the commodity exchanges. In addition, the CME was one of the first exchanges to launch an electronic trading platform, the CME Globex, which became an instant hit with traders. It now accounts for more than 60 percent of the exchange's total volume. In 2006, the New York Mercantile Exchange (NYMEX) entered into an agreement with the CME to trade its marquee energy and metals contracts on the CME electronic platform (see www.nymexoncmeglobex.com). In 2008, the CME went on a series of acquisitions and purchased the NYMEX, COMEX, and Chicago Board of Trade (CBOT). The CME is also the first exchange to go public. Investors greeted the initial public offering with enthusiasm, raising the stock from $40 in 2003 to more than $500 in 2006. (See Chapter 8 for more on the exchanges.) For more on the CME, check out its Web site at www.cme.com, which also includes helpful tutorials on all its products.

One recommended resource that provides fundamental data relating to the consumption and production patterns of pork bellies, livestock, and other commodities is the *Commodity Research Bureau Yearbook*. This book, compiled by the Commodity Research Bureau (CRB), includes much data on some of the most important commodities, including how to identify seasonal and cyclical patterns affecting the markets. For more information on this publication, visit www.crbtrader.com.

Holy Cow! Investing in Cattle

Some historians claim that cattle were the first animals domesticated by humans. One thing is certain: Cattle have played a unique role in history. Throughout the ages, cows have been valued not only for their dietary value, but also for their monetary worth. Cows are a special breed because they're low-maintenance animals with high-product output: They eat almost nothing but grass, yet they produce milk, provide meat, and, in some cases, create leather goods. This input-to-output ratio means that cows occupy a special place in the agricultural complex.

Two futures contracts exist for the cattle trader and investor: the live cattle and the feeder cattle contracts. Both trade on the Chicago Mercantile Exchange (CME).

Live cattle

The live cattle futures contract, traded on the CME, is unique because it was the first contract the CME launched to track a commodity that's actually alive. Before the live cattle futures, all futures contracts were for storable commodities, such as crude oil, copper, and sugar. The CME live cattle futures contract, launched in 1964, heralded a new era for the exchanges. Various market players, including cattle producers, packers, consumers, and independent traders, now widely trade this futures contract.

Consider the specs of this futures contract:

- **Contract ticker symbol (open outcry):** LC
- **Electronic ticker (CME Globex):** LE
- **Contract size:** 40,000 pounds
- **Underlying commodity:** Live cattle (55% choice, 45% select, Yield Grade 3 live steers)
- **Price fluctuation:** $0.00025 per pound ($10 per contract)
- **Trading hours:** 9:05 a.m. to 1:00 p.m. (CST), electronic and open outcry
- **Trading months:** February, April, June, August, October, and December

The live cattle contract is popular partly because it allows all interested parties to hedge their market positions, to reduce the volatility and uncertainty associated with livestock production in general and live cattle growing in particular.

If you decide to trade this contract, keep the following market risks in mind: seasonality, fluctuating prices of feedstock, transportation costs, changing consumer demand, and threat of diseases (such as mad cow disease). The market for the live cattle contract can be fairly volatile.

Check out the performance of the live cattle futures contract on the CME in Figure 21-1.

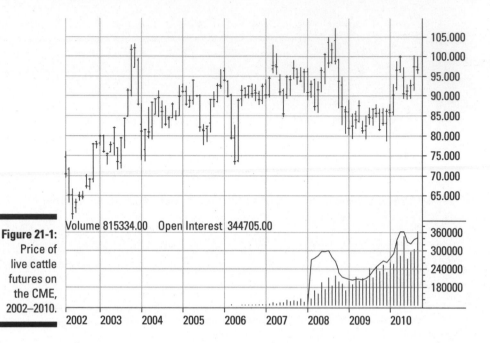

Figure 21-1:
Price of
live cattle
futures on
the CME,
2002–2010.

Feeder cattle

The CME launched a feeder cattle futures contract in 1971, only a few years after the launch of the groundbreaking live cattle contract. The feeder cattle contract is for calves that weigh in at 650–849 pounds, which are sent to the feedlots to get fed, fattened, and then slaughtered.

Because the CME feeder cattle futures contract is settled on a cash basis, the CME calculates an index for feeder cattle cash prices based on a seven-day average. This index, known in the industry as the *CME Feeder Cattle Index,* is an average of feeder cattle prices from the largest feeder cattle–producing states in the United States, as compiled by the U.S. Department of Agriculture (USDA). These producing states are (in alphabetical order) Colorado, Iowa, Kansas, Missouri, Montana, Nebraska, New Mexico, North Dakota, Oklahoma, South Dakota, Texas, and Wyoming. You can get information on the CME Feeder Cattle Index through the CME Web site, at www.cme.com.

To get livestock statistical information, check out the U.S. Department of Agriculture's statistical division, at www.marketnews.usda.gov/portal/lg.

Look over the specs of this futures contract:

- **Contract ticker symbol (open outcry):** FC
- **Electronic ticker (CME Globex):** GF
- **Contract size:** 50,000 pounds
- **Underlying commodity:** Feeder cattle (650–849 pound steers, medium-large #1 and medium-large #1–2)
- **Price fluctuation:** $0.00025 per pound ($12.50 per contract)
- **Trading hours:** 9:05 a.m. to 1:00 p.m. (CST), electronic and open outcry
- **Trading months:** January, March, April, May, August, September, October, and November

Two important traits characterize the feeder cattle contract:

- Like many meat commodities, it's fairly volatile.
- It's a thinly traded contract — in other words, it doesn't have as much liquidity as some of the other CME products. I illustrate this point in Figure 21-2.

Figure 21-2: Price of feeder cattle futures on the CME, 2006–2010.

Don't get mad: Considering the effect of mad cow disease on the livestock market

The live cattle and feeder cattle futures contracts are sensitive to any supply-side disruptions or demand variations. News of a mad cow disease outbreak in the United Kingdom in 2004 had a major impact on U.S. live cattle futures prices. This event brought much uncertainty to the markets and generated volatility. News of this sort is like a one-two punch to the markets because demand and supply are affected simultaneously: Demand drops dramatically because folks no longer want to buy the products, and supply decreases as measures are taken to eliminate affected cattle.

For U.S. beef producers, the threat of mad cow disease also affects their bottom line because their exports decrease dramatically. For instance, when word came out of potential mad cow disease in U.S. herds, Japan — which buys more than $1 billion of U.S. beef a year — placed restrictions on the imports of U.S. beef. This pained U.S. beef producers as they confronted declining demand both at home and abroad.

Lean and Mean: Checking Out Lean Hogs

The lean hog futures contract (which is a contract for the hog's carcass) trades on the CME and is used primarily by producers of lean hogs — both domestic and international — and pork importers/exporters. Launched in 1997, the lean hog contract is a fairly new addition to the CME, intended to replace the live hog futures contract that was retired. The lean hog contract replaced the live hog contract because producers and consumers of these products don't transact the live animal (live hog); it made more sense for the futures contract to track the product traded in the marketplace.

Here are the contract specs for lean hogs:

- **Contract ticker symbol (open outcry):** LH
- **Electronic ticker (CME Globex):** HE
- **Contract size:** 40,000 pounds
- **Underlying commodity:** Lean hogs (hog barrow and gilt carcasses)
- **Price fluctuation:** $0.00025 per pound ($10 per contract)
- **Trading hours:** 9:10 a.m. to 1:00 p.m. (CST), electronic and open outcry
- **Trading months:** February, April, May, June, July, August, October, and December

WARNING!

Perhaps no other commodity, agricultural or otherwise, exhibits the same level of volatility as the lean hogs futures contract (see Figure 21-3). One of the reasons is that, compared to other products, this contract isn't very liquid: It's primarily used by commercial entities seeking to hedge against price risk. Other commodities that are actively traded by individual speculators as well as the commercial entities (such as crude oil) are far more liquid and, therefore, less volatile. If you're intent on trading this contract, keep in mind that you're up against some large and very experienced players in this market.

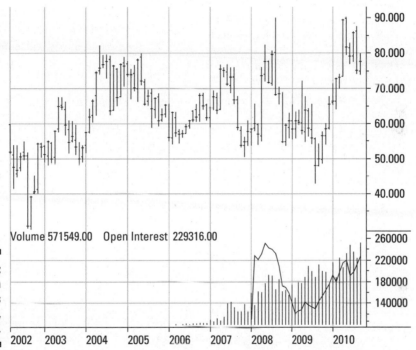

Figure 21-3:
Price of lean
hogs futures
on the CME,
2002–2010.

You Want Bacon with That?
Trading Frozen Pork Bellies

Essentially, the term *pork bellies* is the traders' way of referring to bacon. Physically, pork bellies come from the underside of a hog and weigh approximately 12 pounds. These pork bellies are generally stored frozen for extended periods of time, pending delivery to consumers.

As with most other livestock products, the CME offers a futures contract for frozen pork bellies. This contract, launched by the CME in 1961, is the first-ever contract on a commodity exchange for which the underlying deliverable commodity is a meat — albeit, dead meat. (The CME live cattle contract was the first contract based on a live animal; refer to that section earlier in this chapter for more information.)

Here are the specs for the CME frozen pork bellies futures contract:

- ✔ **Contract ticker symbol (open outcry):** PB
- ✔ **Electronic ticker (CME Globex):** GPB
- ✔ **Contract size:** 40,000 pounds
- ✔ **Underlying commodity:** Pork bellies, cut and trimmed (12- to 18-pound frozen pork bellies)
- ✔ **Price fluctuation:** $0.00025 per pound ($10 per contract)
- ✔ **Trading hours:** 9:10 a.m. to 1:00 p.m. (CST), electronic and open outcry
- ✔ **Trading months:** February, March, May, July, and August

The pork bellies market is a seasonal market subject to wild price fluctuations. Although production of pork bellies is a major determining factor of market prices, other variables have a significant impact on prices. A buildup in pork belly inventories usually takes place at the beginning of the calendar year, resulting in lower prices. But as inventories are depleted, the market moves to a supply-side bias, placing upward pressure on market prices. On the other side of the equation, consumer demand for bacon and other meats isn't easily predictable and fluctuates with the seasons.

Because of the cyclicality of the supply-side model, coupled with the seasonality of the demand model, pork belly prices are subject to extreme volatility. As a matter of fact, the pork bellies futures contract is one of the most volatile contracts trading in the market today. Check out the price of frozen pork bellies per pound in Figure 21-4.

Demand for bacon and other high-fat, high-cholesterol foods appears to be waning as a result of the health-conscious eating trends sweeping the nation. These dietary changes could have an impact on the prices of frozen pork bellies and other meats. Be aware of the impact of these dietary trends on the prices of pork bellies and other meats before you invest.

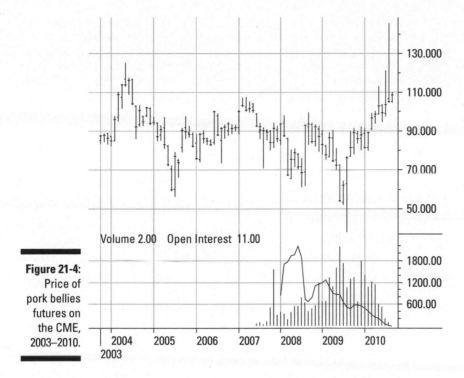

Figure 21-4:
Price of
pork bellies
futures on
the CME,
2003–2010.

Man against machine: The battle over the future of trading

All the contracts I discuss in this chapter are available for trading on the Chicago Mercantile Exchange's electronic trading platform, the CME Globex. Until a few years ago, humans buying and selling contracts during the open outcry sessions did most of the trading in the futures markets. Recently, electronic trading — which matches buyers and sellers electronically — has overtaken the open outcry sessions as the main venue for trading. In the CME, for example, more than 60 percent of trading is now conducted electronically. The advantages of electronic trading are that it's more efficient and it can be performed from remote locations.

The New York Mercantile Exchange (NYMEX) and the New York Board of Trade (NYBOT) are the only exchanges that still rely heavily on the open outcry sessions. However, that's on the decline. The NYMEX recently signed an agreement to have its contracts offered on the CME Globex. Some exchanges, such as the Intercontinental Exchange, don't even own physical trading facilities — all the trading occurs electronically through computer terminals. The age in which humans interact with each other to establish prices for the world's most important commodities will soon be part of a bygone era.

Part VI
The Part of Tens

The 5th Wave   By Rich Tennant

"I agree with you on pork bellies and tin futures, but I think you're overestimating corn."

In this part . . .

1 include here the legendary *For Dummies* Part of Tens. In these chapters, I uncover the major market indicators you need to monitor to get a sense of where the markets are heading; identify the top resources to use when you invest in the markets; and share the top exchange-traded funds (ETFs), to give you the easiest and most direct market access. This part also includes invaluable advice on top investment vehicles that will help make you a better investor.

Chapter 22

Ten or So Investing Resources You Can't Do Without

In This Chapter

▶ Using trade journals effectively

▶ Reading the financial press

▶ Getting help from the government

*L*iving in the Information Age can be both a blessing and a curse. The advantage of the information revolution is that you have so many sources of information to choose from; the drawback is knowing which ones to use. It's easy to get overwhelmed by the amount of information out there.

In this chapter, I list the top ten or so resources to turn to when investing in commodities. Although not all these resources deal specifically with commodities, they're indispensable sources of information because they help you get a sense of where the financial markets are heading. Information and its application ultimately separate successful investors from the rest.

Using these resources helps you stay up-to-date on the major events that move markets and gives you an edge over the competition.

The Wall Street Journal

For daily intakes of financial news, nothing beats *The Wall Street Journal*. If you want to be a successful trader, you need to keep abreast of all the information that's worth knowing. *The Journal* does a good job of presenting solid analysis and in-depth coverage of the day's main events. Its coverage of the commodities markets in its online edition at www.wsj.com is fairly extensive (a subscription is required), with interactive charts and graphs for both cash prices and futures markets. Also keep an eye out for the section "Heard on the Street," which includes a wealth of information to help you develop winning strategies that take advantage of the market fundamentals. I read *The Journal* every single day and can't imagine my day without it.

Bloomberg

The Bloomberg Web site, at www.bloomberg.com, is one of the best sources of raw information and data available to investors. Visiting this site once a day keeps you up on important developments in the markets. The Web site's commodity section, at www.bloomberg.com/markets/commodities/ cfutures.html, contains comprehensive information on all the major commodities, from crude oil and cocoa to natural gas and aluminum, including regular price updates on the futures markets. If you trade futures, this is an indispensable resource.

Commodities-Investors.com

I set up this Web site, located at www.commodities-investors.com, to serve as an online companion to *Commodities For Dummies*. The book gives you a broad-based fundamental and technical approach to commodities; the Web site offers you up-to-date information on the markets. The world of commodities is fast paced, and staying on top of all the developments helps you improve your bottom line. Make sure you check out the Web site for regular updates, unique investment strategies, and tips on trading techniques.

Nightly Business Report

I try to tune in every weeknight to my local PBS network to watch NBR's Paul Kangas, Susie Gharib, and the gang analyze the day's events. Their special features and market analysts are insightful. Plus, it's commercial free! Check your PBS station for local listings.

Morningstar

Morningstar is a heavyweight in the mutual funds analysis industry. Its Web site, at www.morningstar.com, includes a plethora of information on the latest mutual funds, exchange-traded funds, and other investment vehicles popular with investors. If you want to invest in commodities through a managed fund, consult the Morningstar Web site before you do so.

Yahoo! Finance

Yahoo! Finance, at `finance.yahoo.com`, is my browser's default home page, and I don't plan on changing it anytime soon. I love this Web site because it includes so many different sources of information, all conveniently located in one site. You get market analysis updated hourly, regular news alerts (you can sign up to receive these in your inbox), and one of the best chart services on the Web. If you're considering investing in companies that produce commodities, Yahoo! Finance is your one-stop shop for information on the stock's technical performance and its fundamental outlook.

Commodity Futures Trading Commission

The Commodity Futures Trading Commission (CFTC) is the federal regulatory body responsible for monitoring activities in the commodities markets. Before you do anything related to commodities, take a look at the Web site, at `www.cftc.gov`. Before you invest, you need to know your rights as an investor, and the CFTC does a magnificent job of informing you of them. Also check out the comprehensive glossary.

The Energy Information Administration

The Energy Information Administration (EIA) is part of the U.S. Department of Energy and is the official source of energy statistics for the U.S. government. The Web site, located at `www.eia.doe.gov`, is your number one source for information on energy markets. It covers everything from crude oil production and consumption to gasoline inventories and natural gas transportation activity. If you want to invest in energy, check out the EIA's Country Analysis Briefs, which give an overview of the global energy supply chain country by country. That section of the site is located at `www.eia.doe.gov/emeu/cabs/contents.html`.

Stocks and Commodities Magazine

If you want to become a serious commodity futures trader, you can't go without reading *Stocks and Commodities* magazine. Its articles include market-tested trading strategies to help you place and execute trades. The Web site is at `www.traders.com`.

Oil & Gas Journal

Oil & Gas Journal is a subscription-based magazine that features in-depth articles about the energy industry. If you want to trade the energy markets, read O&G, at `ogj.pennnet.com`.

National Futures Association

The National Futures Association (NFA) is the industry's self-regulatory organization. If you're interested in investing in the futures markets, I highly recommend that you check out the Web site at `www.nfa.futures.org` before you start trading. Specifically, check out the database of registered investment advisors if you're planning to go through a manager. NFA has comprehensive information on all managers (who are required to register with the NFA before handling client accounts) through its Background Affiliation Status Information Center (BASIC) service. BASIC is located at `www.nfa.futures.org/basicnet`.

Chapter 23

Top Ten Market Indicators You Should Monitor

*T*he commodity waters can be perilous at times, and knowing how to navigate them is crucial. Keeping your eye on where the markets are heading — and where they've been — will help you develop a winning investment strategy. One way to identify where the markets are heading is to watch certain market indicators. The ten key metrics highlighted in this chapter provide insight into what the markets are doing and help you design and calibrate an investment strategy based on the market fundamentals.

Consumer Price Index

The *Consumer Price Index* (CPI), compiled by the Bureau of Labor Statistics (BLS), is a statistically weighted average of a basket of goods and services purchased by consumers around the country. The CPI is the closest thing to a cost-of-living index and is sometimes used to gauge inflationary trends. If the CPI is rising, economists — especially the ones at the Federal Reserve — start worrying that inflation is creeping up. A rising CPI may then result in an increase in the *Federal Funds Rate* (see the relevant section later in the chapter). The CPI is sometimes broken down further into the *Core CPI,* which excludes items like food and energy. Comparing the CPI with the Core CPI can give you a good idea of how much consumers, who account for two-thirds of economic activity, are spending on commodities such as energy and agricultural products. Visit www.bls.gov/cpi for the latest data on the CPI.

EIA Inventory Reports

Energy traders are glued to their Bloomberg terminals every Wednesday morning (at 10:30 a.m. EST, to be precise), waiting for the latest inventory reports. Those inventory reports come from the Energy Information Administration (EIA), which is the statistical branch of the Department of Energy (DOE), and they detail activity in the country's energy sector. They include a summary of weekly supply estimates, crude oil supply, and disposition rates (consumer consumption), as well as production, refinery utilization, and any movement in stock changes. The EIA petroleum inventory reports may not get wide coverage in the press, but they have a direct impact on the price of crude oil and other energy products. Naturally, you'll want to monitor them regularly. You can find all the information about these reports by going to the EIA Web site at www.eia.doe.gov.

Federal Funds Rate

Perhaps no other market indicator is as closely watched by investors as the *Federal Funds Rate*. When the financial press talks about interest rates going up or down, they're almost always referring to the Federal Funds Rate, which is established by the Federal Open Market Committee (FOMC). This is the short-term interest rate banks charge each other overnight for Federal Reserve balances. When the Fed wants to stimulate a sluggish economy, it tends to decrease this short-term rate. On the other hand, if the Fed believes that the economy is overheating — and, therefore, subject to inflation — it increases this rate, which makes borrowing money more expensive.

Gross Domestic Product

Gross domestic product (GDP) is one of the most closely watched economic indicators. GDP is essentially a measure of all the goods and services produced in a country by private consumers, the government, the business sector, and trade (exports/imports). GDP, especially *per-capita GDP* (which essentially measures purchasing power on an individual level), is a good indication of the likely demand for and activity in commodities. The higher the GDP growth, the more likely a country is to spend more money on purchasing crude oil, natural gas, and other natural resources. Of course, GDP gives you a big picture of the economic landscape and may not necessarily identify specific trends. That said, solid and growing GDP is a good measure of economic health and is a bullish indicator for commodities. Theoretically, you can analyze the GDP of all countries, but I recommend looking closely at U.S. GDP, the largest economy on the planet, and the Chinese GDP, the fastest-growing economy in the world. These two countries are also the biggest purchasers of commodities such as crude oil and steel.

London Gold Fix

Gold is a special commodity because it's one of the only commodities that has a monetary role. For decades, many currencies — including the U.S. dollar and the British pound — were fixed to gold. Even though President Richard Nixon took the United States off the gold standard in 1971, thereby heralding a floating exchange rate regime, gold is still used as a global monetary benchmark. The Federal Reserve and other central banks hold gold bullion in vaults for monetary purposes, and economists sometimes use gold as a measure of inflation. Monitoring gold, both as a possible measure of inflation and for its monetary stability, is a good idea. Spot gold prices are fixed in London daily — in what is known as *London gold fixing* — by five leading members of the financial community. Precious metals dealers closely monitor the London gold fix and use it as a global benchmark for gold spot prices. You can also get an idea of where gold prices are heading by consulting the futures markets, specifically the COMEX gold futures prices provided by the Chicago Mercantile Exchange (CME/COMEX). Visit www.nymex.com for more on gold futures and www.goldfixing.com for the London gold fix.

Nonfarm Payrolls

As with the Consumer Price Index, nonfarm payrolls are compiled by the Bureau of Labor Statistics. Statistically, *nonfarm payrolls* include the number of individuals with paid salaries employed by businesses around the country. It does not include government employees, household employees (homemakers), individuals who work in the nonprofit sector, and workers involved in agriculture. Nonfarm payrolls include information on about 80 percent of the nation's total workforce, and this number is often used to determine unemployment levels. The nonfarm payroll report is released monthly, on the first Friday of the month, and does not include total employment; instead, it shows a change between the current employment levels and previous employment levels, as measured by the *new* number of jobs added. The higher the number, the stronger the economy and the more people hired by businesses — which all means that consumers have more money to spend. Although the link is indirect, higher nonfarm payroll numbers can be interpreted as a bullish sign for the commodities markets. Visit www.bls.gov/ces for more information on nonfarm payrolls.

Purchasing Managers Index

The *Purchasing Managers Index* (PMI), released by the Institute of Supply Management (ISM), is a composite index and a good indicator of total manufacturing activity, which, in turn, is an important barometer of overall economic activity. The manufacturing sector is a large consumer of commodities, such as crude oil and natural gas, and a strong PMI signals that manufacturers are doing well and are likely to spend additional dollars on commodities. The PMI is released at 10 a.m. EST on the first business day of every month. You can view the reports at `www.ism.ws/ISMReport`.

Reuters/Jefferies CRB Index

The *Reuters/Jefferies CRB Index* is the oldest commodity index and is one of the most widely followed commodity benchmarks in the market. Although commodity indexes have their shortcomings — for example, they track only commodities on futures contracts, thereby ignoring important commodities such as steel — they're the best measure of where the commodities markets as a whole are heading. The Reuters/Jefferies CRB Index tracks 19 commodities, everything from crude oil and silver to corn and nickel. Read Chapter 6 for more on commodity indexes.

U.S. Dollar

Keeping your eye on what the U.S. dollar is doing is critical for a variety of reasons. U.S. dollars are the world's de facto currency, so most of the world's crucial commodities, from crude oil and gold to copper and coffee, are priced in them. Any shift in the dollar has an indirect impact on these important markets. For example, the integrated energy companies (the majors) have operations around the globe and often deal with the local currency in the area they're operating. Any shift in the local currency/U.S. dollar exchange rate has a direct impact on how the companies account for profits and expenses, as well as other metrics.

WTI Crude Oil

West Texas Intermediate (WTI) crude oil is one of the most widely followed benchmarks in the energy complex. WTI is a high-grade, low-sulfur, premium crude produced in West Texas. This light, sweet crude is traded on the NYMEX section of the Chicago Mercantile Exchange (CME/NYMEX) through a futures contract, which is widely quoted in the financial press and in analyst reports as a benchmark for global oil prices. More important, industry players use it as a benchmark for global oil prices. Of course, because the price of the CME/NYMEX WTI refers only to light, sweet crudes, the price of heavy, sour crudes is going to be different. Currently, most heavy, sour crudes are priced relative to their lighter and sweeter counterparts. (Turn to Chapter 10 for more on the different grades of crude oil.)

An alternative global crude benchmark is the North Sea Brent, which is also a high-quality crude that's produced in the Norwegian/British North Sea. This contract trades on the Intercontinental Exchange (ICE). For more on the WTI contract, visit www.cme.com. See www.theice.com for additional information on the North Sea Brent contract.

Chapter 24

Top Ten Commodity ETFs

*E*xchange-traded funds (ETFs) are a relative newcomer in the asset-management product space. ETFs have become extremely popular with investors, especially individual investors, because of their relative ease-of-use and the type of exposure they can offer. With ETFs, you can now access investment products that were once the purview of expert industry insiders.

Because ETFs are now in a position to offer easy access to commodities, and because the number and type of commodities they cover has expanded, you can benefit from seeing which ETFs are out there to help with your investment needs. In this chapter, I cover a broad range of top ETFs and the type of exposure they can give you.

PowerShares DB Commodity Index

The DB Commodity Index (NYSE: DBC) was the first ETF of its kind to track a commodity index. Launched in 2006, it tracks the performance of the index with the same name, a product courtesy of Deutsche Bank. This ETF gives you broad exposure to this index, which holds several of the most liquid commodities traded in the market, including crude oil, gasoline and heating oil, gold, copper, zinc, and sugar. If you're looking for broad-based commodity exposure via an ETF, I recommend considering the DBC for your portfolio.

iPath DJ-UBS Commodity Index

The DJ-UBS Commodity Index ETF (NYSE: DJP) tracks the index of the same name, which is jointly managed by news service Dow Jones and investment bank UBS. Like the DBC (see the preceding section), the DJP gives you broad exposure to the commodity markets. However, unlike the DBC, this index ETF gives you a different mix of exposure, which is generally more overweight industrial commodities such as energy and base metals. If you're looking for a very broad commodity exposure that includes energy, precious metals, industrial metals, agriculture, and livestock, take a look at the DJP. Read through the prospectus carefully to see what kind of commodities the index tracks, because the mix often changes.

United States Oil

If you're looking for exposure to the oil markets without going through futures contracts, the United States Oil Fund (NYSE: USO) is an alternative. USO seeks to track the price changes of the front-month contract of light, sweet crude WTI contract traded on the NYMEX section of the Chicago Mercantile Exchange (CME). Check the prospectus for fees associated with rolling the contracts and operating the ETF.

United States Natural Gas

Like its crude oil counterpart, the United States Natural Gas ETF (NYSE: UNG) aims to give investors the ability to track the performance of natural gas, one of the bulwarks in the energy complex. The ETF mirrors the performance of the natural gas futures contract in the NYMEX section of the CME.

Natural gas can be a fairly volatile commodity, partly because it's highly responsive to changes in weather patterns, which are fairly unpredictable. Make sure that you carefully tread into the natural gas markets. For more information on natural gas, turn to Chapter 11.

SPDR Gold Shares

The SPDR Gold Shares ETF (NYSE: GLD) is one of the most popular ETFs ever created, not just as a commodity product, but also as an ETF product in general. Designed to track the spot price of bullion, GLD actually owns physical gold, which it stores in vaults protected by armed guards, high-tech security, and full-scale insurance coverage. With almost $60 billion in total assets (2011 figures), its popularity among investors has been so great that many analysts have to factor it in when examining daily and monthly price fluctuations of spot gold prices.

iShares Silver Trust

With more than $20 billion in assets, the iShares Silver Trust (NYSE: SLV) is an extremely popular ETF product with investors. It tracks the spot price of the silver contract in the NYMEX division of the CME. Before this ETF product arrived, novice investors without experience in the futures markets had tremendous difficulty getting direct exposure to silver prices.

Silver has many peculiar characteristics, so be sure to do your due diligence before you pull the trigger on this ETF. For more information on silver and its market fundamentals, go through Chapter 15.

iPath DJ-UBS Aluminum TR Sub-Index

This ETF product, courtesy of Dow Jones and UBS (JJU), is a new addition to the ETF commodity family. It tracks the aluminum contract on the CME through the use of futures contracts and gives you exposure to this important base metal. Look to Chapter 16 for more on aluminum.

PowerShares DB Agriculture Long Index

Agriculture has traditionally been an extremely difficult commodity subasset class to get exposure to, reserved for investors who owned farms or expert agricultural futures traders on one of the exchanges. However, driven by more investor demand for this asset class, new products are emerging to provide exposure to this unique segment of the market. The PowerShares Deutsche Bank Agriculture Index (NYSE: DBA) is the first ETF product of its kind to give you this kind of exposure. It tracks the Deutsche Bank Liquid Commodity Index Diversified Agriculture Excess Return Index, opening trading opportunities in commodities such as coffee, sugar, live cattle, corn, soybeans, and cocoa.

iPath DJ-UBS Coffee TR Subindex

This ETF product is relatively unique because it's based on the Dow Jones–UBS Commodity Index Total Return. It isolates a section of this popular index — in this case, the coffee contract — and seeks to replicate its performance via an ETF vehicle (JO). With about $35 million in assets (2011 figures), it's still a relatively small product, but it gives you exposure to coffee markets without going through the futures markets. For more information on coffee and other soft commodities, be sure to read Chapter 19.

Market Vectors Global Alternative Energy

If you want to get involved in the alternative energy space, check out the Market Vectors Global Alternative Energy ETF (NYSE: GEX). This product offers direct exposure to the leading names in the renewable energy space, including solar companies, wind companies, biomass players, and more. I like this ETF because it invests across market caps and in different markets, giving you a positive geographic and market size mix. For more information on renewable and alternative energy, check out Chapters 12 and 13.

Chapter 25

Top Ten Investment Vehicles for Commodities

. . . .

In This Chapter

▶ Investing through the futures markets

▶ Getting exposure through equities

▶ Uncovering the benefits of fund investing

. . . .

*B*ecause the commodities markets are so wide and deep, you have a number of investment vehicles to access these markets. A common misconception among investors is that you can only trade commodities by opening a futures account. While the futures markets certainly provide an avenue into the commodities markets, you have other tools at your disposal. I list the ten most important investment vehicles in this chapter.

Futures Commission Merchant

Opening an account with a *Futures Commission Merchant* (FCM) is the most direct way for you to invest in commodities through the futures markets. An FCM is registered with the National Futures Association (NFA) and its activities are monitored by the Commodity Futures Trading Commission (CFTC). When you open an account with an FCM, you can actually trade futures contracts, options, and other derivative products directly through the main commodity exchanges. Your orders are sometimes routed electronically or are placed during the open outcry trading session. However, you should only open an account with an FCM if you have a solid grasp of trading futures and options. For more on futures contracts, check out Chapter 9; I discuss FCMs in depth in Chapter 7.

Commodity Trading Advisor

A *Commodity Trading Advisor* (CTA) is authorized by the CFTC and the NFA to trade on behalf of individual clients in the futures markets. The CTA is a registered investment professional who has a good grasp of the concepts in the futures markets. However, before you invest through a CTA, you should research their track record and investment philosophy. Find out what you should be looking for when shopping for a CTA in Chapter 7.

Commodity Pool Operator

The *Commodity Pool Operator* (CPO) is similar to the CTA in that she has the authority to invest on behalf of clients in the futures markets. The biggest difference is that CPOs are allowed to "pool" client accounts under one giant account and enter the markets en masse. The pooling of client funds offers two advantages: It increases the purchasing power of the fund, and it provides additional leverage. In addition, because a CPO is usually registered as a company, you can only lose your principal (in case things go wrong). In other words, you won't get any margin calls and owe the exchange money. Make sure to read Chapter 7 for more information on CPOs.

Integrated Commodity Companies

The equity markets offer a way for you to get exposure to commodities by investing in companies that process these natural resources. Some of these companies include large, integrated commodity-processing companies. In the energy space, these are companies like ExxonMobil (NYSE: XOM) and Total (NYSE: TOT) that have exposure to crude oil and natural gas in both the exploration and distribution phase of the supply chain. (I examine the integrated energy companies in Chapter 10.)

In the metals complex, companies like Rio Tinto (NYSE: TRP) and BHP Billiton (NYSE: BHP) mine minerals and metals as varied as palladium and nickel. These integrated mining companies have operations throughout the globe. I cover them in Chapter 18.

Specialized Commodity Companies

If you want to get exposure to a specific commodity through the equity markets, you can always invest in *specialized* commodity companies. These companies focus on either one commodity or on one aspect of the supply chain. For example, oil tanker operators focus on transporting crude oil from Point A to Point B — that's the extent of their activities, which I uncover in Chapter 14. Other such companies include Starbucks (NASDAQ: SBUX) (Chapter 19), which focuses strictly on selling and marketing coffee-related products. These are good companies to invest in if you want exposure to a specific commodity through the equity markets.

Master Limited Partnerships

Master Limited Partnerships (MLPs) are hybrid investment vehicles that invest in energy infrastructure. They are in fact private partnerships that trade on public exchanges, just like stocks. This unique combination provides several advantages.

- ✔ Because the MLP is a partnership, it has tremendous tax advantages because it doesn't pay taxes on the corporate level, only on the individual level. It's therefore not subject to the double taxation that many corporations are subject to.

- ✔ Its mandate is to distribute practically all its cash flow directly to shareholders. It's therefore not uncommon to have an MLP return $3 or $4 per unit owned.

Check out MLPs in Chapter 7.

Exchange Traded Funds

Since they first emerged on the scene a few years ago, the popularity of *Exchange Traded Funds* (ETFs) has soared. And for good reason. They're privately run funds that trade on a public exchange, just like stocks. This ease-of-use has directly contributed to their popularity among investors. A number of ETFs have been introduced in recent years, which track the performance of commodity-related assets, such as gold, silver, and crude oil. But it's not just individual commodities that are now tracked by ETFs.

Commodity indexes, such as the Deutsche Bank Liquid Commodity Index (AMEX: DBC), also has an ETF that tracks its performance. Turn to Chapter 5 for a complete listing of ETFs on the market.

Commodity Mutual Funds

Investors who are used to investing in mutual funds will enjoy knowing that a number of mutual funds invest directly in commodities. Two of the biggest such mutual funds are the PIMCO commodity fund and the Oppenheimer fund, both covered in Chapter 6.

Some funds seek to mirror the performance of various commodity benchmarks, while others invest in companies that process commodities.

Commodity Indexes

A commodity index acts a lot like a stock index: It tracks a group of securities for benchmarking and investing purposes. Commodity indexes are constructed and offered by different financial institutions, such as Goldman Sachs and Standard & Poor's, and they follow different construction methodologies. As such, the performance of the indexes — there are currently five — is different across the board. Most of these indexes can be tracked either through the futures markets or through ETFs. I devote Chapter 6 to these indexes.

Emerging Market Funds

Due to geographical happenstance, commodities are scattered across the globe. No single country dominates all commodities across the board. However, a few countries do dominate specific commodities. South Africa, for instance, has the largest reserves of gold in the world, Saudi Arabia has the largest oil reserves, and Russia has the biggest palladium reserves. As the demand for commodities increases, the economies of these emerging markets have been soaring. One way to play the commodities boom is by opening up your portfolio to emerging market funds, which I discuss in Chapter 7.

Glossary

aframax: The Aframax tanker, whose first four letters are an acronym for Average Freight Rate Assessment, is considered the "workhorse" in the off-shore oil tanker fleet. Because of its smaller size, it is ideally suited for short-haul voyages and has the ability to transport crude and products in most ports around the world.

alpha coefficient: In portfolio allocation, *alpha* measures the ability of an asset to generate returns independently of what the broader portfolio or market is doing.

anthracite: The most valuable type of coal. Anthracite contains high levels of carbon and releases the most energy on a per-unit basis.

arbitrage: A trading technique that seeks to exploit price discrepancies of a particular security that trades in different exchanges. Ideally, an arbitrageur buys a security at a lower price on an exchange and sells it for a profit at a higher price in another trading venue.

backwardation: A term used in the futures markets to refer to a situation in which spot prices are higher than forward futures prices. The exact opposite is contango, in which forward prices are higher than spot prices. See also *contango.*

base metals: Metals that have low resistance to corrosion, unlike precious metals. Base metals include most of the industrial metals, such as copper, iron, nickel, and zinc. See also *precious metals.*

basis: The price difference between the actual (spot) commodity and the futures price.

beta coefficient: In the capital asset pricing model (CAPM), *beta* measures the returns of an asset relative to the broader portfolio.

bituminous: The second most valuable type of coal. Bituminous coal is used for both generating electricity and manufacturing high-quality steel.

Bollinger bands: Three "bands" that seek to measure a security's standard deviation from a moving average, usually the *simple moving average* (which is one of the three bands). The upper and lower bands track the price of the security on a simple moving average basis and attempt to determine whether a security is overbought or oversold based on its proximity to the two bands. If the price trend is flirting with the lower band, the security is oversold — it's undervalued and is expected to increase. On the other hand, if the security is approaching the upper band, it's overbought and may be ready for a downward price correction.

Brent, North Sea: A premium grade of crude oil (shortened to Brent) that's used as a global benchmark for crude oil prices.

British thermal unit (BTU): The standard unit of measurement for energy. Every bit of energy released from crude oil, natural gas, coal, or solar power can be quantified using BTUs. One BTU refers to the amount of energy required to raise 1 pound of water by 1 degree Fahrenheit.

buy-in: A purchase that will offset a previous short sale. Covers or liquidates a short position.

call option: A contract in the futures markets that gives the holder (buyer) of the contract the right, but not the obligation, to *purchase* an underlying asset at a specific point in time at a specific price. A call option is the opposite of a *put option.*

candlestick: In technical analysis, a candlestick is a type of chart used to indicate crucial pieces of information regarding the performance of a security. Specifically, candlesticks indicate the security's opening price, closing price, daily high, and daily low.

capital asset pricing model (CAPM): In portfolio theory, CAPM helps calculate the amount of returns an investor can expect, based on the amount of risk she's taking. The CAPM formula is fairly complex, but it stipulates that investors should be compensated based on how long they hold an investment (time value of money) and the amount of risk they take on.

carrying charge: The cost to store and insure a physical commodity over a period of time.

Chicago Board of Trade (CBOT): Although the CBOT offers a broad products mix, this exchange dominates the grain markets, offering futures contracts for grains such as corn, wheat, soybeans, soybean oil, and soybean meal. The CBOT is now part of the Chicago Mercantile Exchange (CME).

Chicago Mercantile Exchange (CME): The largest exchange in the world, based on total volume of contracts traded. The CME also offers the broadest product selection, providing contracts for commodities as varied as interest rates and butter. It's also the destination for folks who want to trade livestock because it has contracts for live cattle, feeder cattle, lean hogs, and frozen pork bellies.

Commodities Exchange (COMEX): A division of the New York Mercantile Exchange (NYMEX) that offers futures contracts and options on metals. Some of the metals on the COMEX include gold, silver, aluminum, and copper. The COMEX is now part of the Chicago Mercantile Exchange (CME).

Commodity Futures Trading Commission (CFTC): The regulatory body of the futures markets. The CFTC is a federal agency that's responsible for the oversight of all the major commodity exchanges in the United States. In addition, it's responsible for monitoring the futures markets to protect the public from fraud or other unnatural market risks. It has the authority to investigate suspicious activity and prosecute cases.

commodity pool operator (CPO): Similar to a futures fund manager, in that he can manage client assets under one fund for the purpose of investing in the futures markets.

commodity trading advisor (CTA): A firm or individual licensed by the Commodity Futures Trading Commission (CFTC) that's allowed to invest on behalf of individual clients in the futures markets.

Consumer Price Index (CPI): A statistically weighted average of a basket of goods and services purchased by consumers around the country, compiled by the Bureau of Labor Statistics (BLS). It's the closest indicator of how much consumers are spending on key products, including energy and agricultural products.

contango: In the futures markets, a situation in which forward futures prices exceed spot prices, or distant futures prices exceed nearer-term futures prices. Essentially, contango means that prices are increasing across time in the futures markets. Contango is the opposite of backwardation. See also *backwardation.*

contract month: The month in which a futures contract may be satisfied by making or accepting delivery.

delivery: The tender and receipt of the actual commodity or the warehouse receipt in settlement of the future contract.

delivery notice: A notice of a clearing member's intentions to deliver a stated quantity of a commodity in settlement of a futures contract.

derivative: A financial instrument that derives its value from an underlying security. Examples of derivatives include futures contracts, forward contracts, and options on futures. The underlying security can be anything from an interest rate to a metal such as palladium.

drill ship: A ship with a drilling platform that's easily deployed to remote offshore locations for oil and gas drilling.

drilling barge: A floating device usually towed by tugboat in still, shallow waters, such as rivers, lakes, and swamps. It's used for offshore oil and natural gas drilling.

Energy Information Administration (EIA): The statistical arm of the U.S. Department of Energy, which compiles information and statistics on all aspects of the global energy industry.

enhanced moving average (EMA): In technical analysis, the EMA is a moving average that emphasizes a security's most recent prices. This is the opposite of the simple moving average, which follows an equal-weight approach to all price closings. The EMA is also known as the exponential moving average. See also *simple moving average.*

exchange-traded fund (ETF): Fund that's traded on public exchanges, just like stocks. The benefit of investing in ETFs is that you can invest in a fund — which may be investing in everything from commodity indexes to crude oil — by simply buying its shares on an exchange. A number of ETFs cater specifically to the commodity trading community. ETFs are now available for crude oil, gold, silver, and commodity indexes such as the Deutsche Bank Liquid Commodity Index (DBLCI).

federal funds rate: Commonly referred to in the financial press simply as "short-term interest rates," the federal funds rate is established by the Federal Reserve's Federal Open Market Committee (FOMC). It is the rate at which one depository institution charges another depository institution for borrowing balances at the Federal Reserve overnight.

ferrous metals: Ferrous — derived from the Latin *ferrum,* which means "iron" — is one method of classifying metals. Ferrous metals are metals that contain iron, such as nickel, steel, and iron itself. Metals that don't contain iron are known as *nonferrous metals.* See also *nonferrous metals.*

Financial Services Authority (FSA): Britain's leading independent financial regulatory organization. The FSA is responsible for overseeing trading activity on U.K. stock and commodity exchanges. If you consider doing business in the U.K., make sure that you first consult the FSA.

forward contract: Similar to a futures contract, except that a forward contract is an agreement that two parties enter into beyond the scope of a regulated exchange. A futures contract is standardized and must meet specific requirements established by the futures exchange it's traded on. The forward contract agreement is crafted by two parties and falls outside the jurisdiction of a regulated exchange. See also *futures contract.*

futures commission merchant (FCM): A licensed provider of derivative products in the futures markets. An FCM is similar to a stockbroker and is allowed to act as a conduit between investors and the futures markets.

futures contract: A highly standardized financial instrument in which two parties agree to exchange an underlying security at a specific time in the future at a mutually agreed-upon price. Both parties are required to respect the contractual obligations of the agreement.

gross domestic product (GDP): A measure of all the goods and services produced in a country by private consumers, the government, and the business sector, as well as through trade (exports and imports).

Intercontinental Exchange (ICE): One of the only exchanges that doesn't have physical trading floors with open outcry pits. All of its trading is done electronically via computer terminals. The ICE offers the North Sea Brent crude oil contract and recently added the WTI crude oil contract.

International Energy Agency (IEA): An intergovernmental organization headquartered in Paris that's affiliated with the Organization for Economic Cooperation and Development (OECD). Besides compiling statistical information about global energy consumption and production, the IEA acts as an energy advisor to member states.

introducing broker (IB): A firm or individual that solicits and accepts orders from customers but doesn't accept money, securities, or property from customers. An IB must be registered with the Commodity Futures Trading Commission and must carry all of its accounts through a futures commission merchant on a fully disclosed basis. See also *futures commission merchant.*

jack-up rig: A hybrid vessel that's part floating barge, part drilling platform used for offshore drilling purposes.

last trading day: The final day in which trading may occur for a particular delivery month. After the last trading day, any remaining commitment must be settled by delivery.

lignite: The least valuable type of coal, because of its low energy value. Lignite coal is sometimes known as brown coal.

London Metal Exchange (LME): One of the oldest exchanges in the world, specializing in nonferrous metal trading. The LME includes contracts for aluminum, copper, nickel, lead, and zinc.

master limited partnership (MLP): MLPs are hybrid investment vehicles because they're private partnerships that trade on public exchanges. This unique structure is advantageous to investors because the MLP has the tax advantages associated with partnerships yet offers the benefit of trading publicly like a corporation. For an entity to qualify as an MLP, it must generate more than 90 percent of its revenues from activities in the commodities industry, such as operating gas storage facilities or crude oil pipelines.

Modern Portfolio Theory (MPT): The brainchild of economist Harry Markowitz, MPT stipulates that investors stand to benefit through diversification. MPT emphasizes the importance of the portfolio (the whole) over individual assets (the parts).

molybdenum: (Pronounced mah-*leb*-dah-num) A transition metal, primarily used as an alloying metal. Molybdenum's resistance to corrosion and high melting point make it ideal as a coating for metals such as steel and cast iron.

National Association of Securities Dealers (NASD): A private regulator of the securities industry in the United States. The NASD monitors virtually every security traded on American exchanges, from stocks and bonds to commodity futures and options. An individual who seeks to represent clients in the securities markets must pass rigorous qualification examinations administered by the NASD.

National Futures Association (NFA): The future's industry self-regulatory body. Any individual or firm that seeks to transact in the futures markets on behalf of the public must be registered with the NFA. The NFA maintains a database on all its members.

New York Board of Trade (NYBOT): A commodity exchange that focuses primarily on soft commodities, such as coffee, cocoa, sugar, and orange juice. The NYBOT is now part of the Intercontinental Exchange (ICE).

New York Mercantile Exchange (NYMEX): One of the major commodities exchanges in the United States. It's headquartered in New York and offers a wide range of products to investors, from its marquee West Texas Intermediate (WTI) crude oil contract to palladium futures. Its Commodity Exchange (COMEX) division specializes in metals contracts. The NYMEX is now part of the Chicago Mercantile Exchange (CME).

nonfarm payrolls: Compiled by the Bureau of Labor Statistics (BLS), this measures the increase or decrease of the number of jobs added by the business sector during a given month. It's a useful measure of unemployment.

nonferrous metals: Metals that don't contain iron. These metals include gold, silver, platinum, aluminum, copper, and zinc. Metals that contain iron are known as ferrous metals. See also *ferrous metals.*

North Sea Brent: See *Brent, North Sea.*

open interest: In the futures markets, open interest represents the number of outstanding contracts held by market participants at the end of the trading day. Whereas volume measures the amount of trading activity, open interest provides a measure of the amount of capital moving in and out of a specific security or market. See also *volume.*

option: Similar to a futures contract, an option is another type of derivative instrument traded in the futures markets. Options on futures are an agreement between a buyer and a seller. The buyer of the option, known as the holder, has the right but not the obligation to exercise the contract. On the other hand, the seller of the option, known as the underwriter, has both the right and the obligation to fulfill the contract's terms if the holder exercises her rights. See also *futures contract.*

Organization of Petroleum Exporting Countries (OPEC): An organization that includes 11 of the world's top oil-exporting countries. As an organization, OPEC is responsible for making sure that member states adhere to specific production and export quotas. Because OPEC members collectively hold 60 percent of the world's total crude reserves, the organization has significant influence in the oil markets.

over-the-counter (OTC): Transactions outside the purview of regulated commodity exchanges. Most transactions involving commodity futures contracts, options, and other derivatives take place in the OTC market. One of the benefits of OTC deals is that the parties that enter into these agreements can create specific deals to suit specific needs (which regulated exchanges might not be able to offer). The drawback is that the regulated exchanges offer regulatory oversight to all market participants. Despite this lack of oversight, or because of it, the OTC market is huge. The regulated exchanges conduct trillions of dollars of transactions, yet that accounts for only 20 percent of total activity. The other 80 percent of trading happens in the OTC markets.

Panamax: Oil tanker that gets its name from its ability to transit through the Panama Canal. This vessel is sometimes used for short-haul voyages between ports in the Caribbean, Europe, and the United States.

photovoltaic: In solar energy, the process by which solar power is captured and converted into electricity.

precious metals: One method of categorizing metals is based on their resistance to corrosion. Metals that are highly resistant to corrosion — and, therefore, don't rust easily — are known as precious metals. These metals include gold, silver, and the platinum group metals such as platinum and palladium. Metals that easily corrode are known as base metals. See also *base metals.*

Purchasing Managers Index (PMI): A composite index released by the Institute of Supply Management (ISM) that's a good indicator of total manufacturing activity — which, in turn, is an important barometer of overall economic activity.

put option: In the futures markets, a put option gives the holder the right but not the obligation to sell a security at a predetermined price at a specific point in the future. A put option is the opposite of a call option. See also *call option.*

refinery production: Actual production of crude oil products in a refinery, such as gasoline and heating oil.

refinery throughput: The capacity for refining crude oil over a given period of time, usually expressed in barrels.

refinery utilization: The difference between production capacity, the throughput, and what's actually produced.

Relative Strength Index (RSI): A metric used in technical analysis that helps measure the price velocity and momentum of a security. In other words, it quantifies the momentum at which a security is increasing or decreasing, and offers insight into how long an investor can expect that security to keep going on its price trajectory.

resistance: In technical analysis, the point at which the number of sellers of a security is so large that price cannot move beyond a certain level. The number of sellers causes resistance to the security's upside. See also *support.*

Securities and Exchange Commission (SEC): The main regulatory organization of U.S. capital markets. The SEC has oversight over all aspects of the capital markets, and its primary mandate is to monitor and regulate all the transactions that take place in the securities industry.

semisubmersible rig: Structure that has the capacity to drill in deep waters for energy under harsh and unforgiving conditions. Sometimes referred to as a "semi."

simple moving average (SMA): In technical analysis, the SMA is a moving average that follows an equal-weighted approach to all trading days, which the average tracks for a particular security. For example, a 50-day SMA places the same emphasis on the price of the security on Day 15 as it does on Day 48. See also *enhanced moving average.*

sub-bituminous: Type of coal that's the second least valuable in the coal family. Sub-bituminous coal is used primarily for electricity generation.

submersible rig: Similar to a jack-up rig, in that it's primarily used for shallow-water drilling activity. A submersible rig is secured to the seabed.

Suezmax: Vessel named because its design and size allow it to transit through the Suez Canal in Egypt. The Suezmax, ideally suited for medium-haul voyages, is used to transport oil from the Persian Gulf to Europe, as well as to other destinations.

support: In technical analysis, the point at which demand for a security is strong enough that prices for that security remain at or above a certain level. Thus, buying activity supports the price. See also *resistance.*

troy ounce: Unit of measurement for gold, silver, and other metals. One troy ounce is the equivalent of 31.10 grams.

Ultra Large Crude Carrier (ULCC): Type of vessel used to carry large amounts of oil across long distances.

Very Large Crude Carrier (VLCC): Vessel that's ideally suited for intercontinental maritime transportation of crude oil.

volume: In finance, the total number of shares, units, or contracts traded in a security or market during a specific period of time. See also *open interest.*

West Texas Intermediate (WTI): A premium type of crude oil that's used as a benchmark for global oil prices. As its name implies, WTI is extracted from a region in West Texas that produces high-grade, low-sulfur crude. The NYMEX crude oil futures contract, widely quoted in the financial press as a standard for crude oil prices around the world, tracks the price of WTI crude.

Index

Notes

Notes

Notes

Notes

Apple & Macs

iPad For Dummies
978-0-470-58027-1

iPhone For Dummies,
4th Edition
978-0-470-87870-5

MacBook For Dummies, 3rd
Edition
978-0-470-76918-8

Mac OS X Snow Leopard For
Dummies
978-0-470-43543-4

Business

Bookkeeping For Dummies
978-0-7645-9848-7

Job Interviews
For Dummies,
3rd Edition
978-0-470-17748-8

Resumes For Dummies,
5th Edition
978-0-470-08037-5

Starting an
Online Business
For Dummies,
6th Edition
978-0-470-60210-2

Stock Investing
For Dummies,
3rd Edition
978-0-470-40114-9

Successful
Time Management
For Dummies
978-0-470-29034-7

Computer Hardware

BlackBerry
For Dummies,
4th Edition
978-0-470-60700-8

Computers For Seniors
For Dummies,
2nd Edition
978-0-470-53483-0

PCs For Dummies,
Windows
7 Edition
978-0-470-46542-4

Laptops For Dummies,
4th Edition
978-0-470-57829-2

Cooking & Entertaining

Cooking Basics
For Dummies,
3rd Edition
978-0-7645-7206-7

Wine For Dummies,
4th Edition
978-0-470-04579-4

Diet & Nutrition

Dieting For Dummies,
2nd Edition
978-0-7645-4149-0

Nutrition For Dummies,
4th Edition
978-0-471-79868-2

Weight Training
For Dummies,
3rd Edition
978-0-471-76845-6

Digital Photography

Digital SLR Cameras &
Photography For Dummies,
3rd Edition
978-0-470-46606-3

Photoshop Elements 8
For Dummies
978-0-470-52967-6

Gardening

Gardening Basics
For Dummies
978-0-470-03749-2

Organic Gardening
For Dummies,
2nd Edition
978-0-470-43067-5

Green/Sustainable

Raising Chickens
For Dummies
978-0-470-46544-8

Green Cleaning
For Dummies
978-0-470-39106-8

Health

Diabetes For Dummies,
3rd Edition
978-0-470-27086-8

Food Allergies
For Dummies
978-0-470-09584-3

Living Gluten-Free
For Dummies,
2nd Edition
978-0-470-58589-4

Hobbies/General

Chess For Dummies,
2nd Edition
978-0-7645-8404-6

Drawing
Cartoons & Comics
For Dummies
978-0-470-42683-8

Knitting For Dummies,
2nd Edition
978-0-470-28747-7

Organizing
For Dummies
978-0-7645-5300-4

Su Doku For Dummies
978-0-470-01892-7

Home Improvement

Home Maintenance
For Dummies,
2nd Edition
978-0-470-43063-7

Home Theater
For Dummies,
3rd Edition
978-0-470-41189-6

Living the
Country Lifestyle
All-in-One
For Dummies
978-0-470-43061-3

Solar Power Your Home
For Dummies,
2nd Edition
978-0-470-59678-4

Available wherever books are sold. For more information or to order direct: U.S. customers visit www.dummies.com or call 1-877-762-2974. U.K. customers visit www.wileyeurope.com or call (0) 1243 843291. Canadian customers visit www.wiley.ca or call 1-800-567-4797.

Internet

Blogging For Dummies,
3rd Edition
978-0-470-61996-4

eBay For Dummies,
6th Edition
978-0-470-49741-8

Facebook For Dummies,
3rd Edition
978-0-470-87804-0

Web Marketing
For Dummies,
2nd Edition
978-0-470-37181-7

WordPress
For Dummies,
3rd Edition
978-0-470-59274-8

Language & Foreign Language

French For Dummies
978-0-7645-5193-2

Italian Phrases
For Dummies
978-0-7645-7203-6

Spanish For Dummies,
2nd Edition
978-0-470-87855-2

Spanish
For Dummies,
Audio Set
978-0-470-09585-0

Math & Science

Algebra I
For Dummies,
2nd Edition
978-0-470-55964-2

Biology For Dummies,
2nd Edition
978-0-470-59875-7

Calculus For Dummies
978-0-7645-2498-1

Chemistry For Dummies
978-0-7645-5430-8

Microsoft Office

Excel 2010 For Dummies
978-0-470-48953-6

Office 2010 All-in-One
For Dummies
978-0-470-49748-7

Office 2010 For Dummies,
Book + DVD Bundle
978-0-470-62698-6

Word 2010 For Dummies
978-0-470-48772-3

Music

Guitar For Dummies,
2nd Edition
978-0-7645-9904-0

iPod & iTunes For
Dummies, 8th Edition
978-0-470-87871-2

Piano Exercises
For Dummies
978-0-470-38765-8

Parenting & Education

Parenting For Dummies,
2nd Edition
978-0-7645-5418-6

Type 1 Diabetes
For Dummies
978-0-470-17811-9

Pets

Cats For Dummies,
2nd Edition
978-0-7645-5275-5

Dog Training For Dummies,
3rd Edition
978-0-470-60029-0

Puppies For Dummies,
2nd Edition
978-0-470-03717-1

Religion & Inspiration

The Bible For Dummies
978-0-7645-5296-0

Catholicism For Dummies
978-0-7645-5391-2

Women in the Bible
For Dummies
978-0-7645-8475-6

Self-Help & Relationship

Anger Management
For Dummies
978-0-470-03715-7

Overcoming Anxiety
For Dummies,
2nd Edition
978-0-470-57441-6

Sports

Baseball
For Dummies,
3rd Edition
978-0-7645-7537-2

Basketball
For Dummies,
2nd Edition
978-0-7645-5248-9

Golf For Dummies,
3rd Edition
978-0-471-76871-5

Web Development

Web Design
All-in-One
For Dummies
978-0-470-41796-6

Web Sites
Do-It-Yourself
For Dummies,
2nd Edition
978-0-470-56520-9

Windows 7

Windows 7
For Dummies
978-0-470-49743-2

Windows 7
For Dummies,
Book + DVD Bundle
978-0-470-52398-8

Windows 7 All-in-One
For Dummies
978-0-470-48763-1

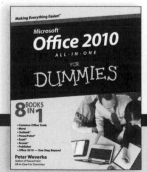

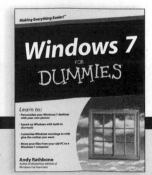

Available wherever books are sold. For more information or to order direct: U.S. customers visit www.dummies.com or call 1-877-762-2974.
U.K. customers visit www.wileyeurope.com or call (0) 1243 843291. Canadian customers visit www.wiley.ca or call 1-800-567-4797.

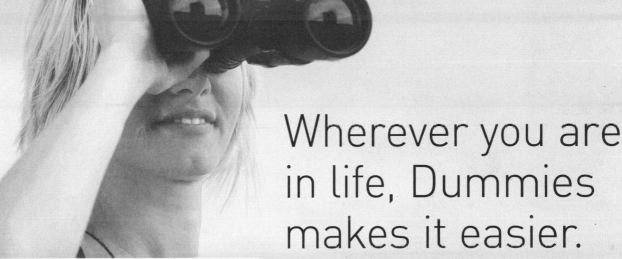

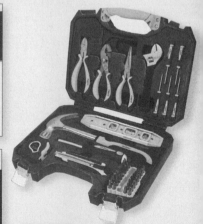